REPAST

Dining Out at the Dawn of the New American Century, 1900–1910

MICHAEL LESY AND LISA STOFFER

REPAST

Dining Out at the Dawn of the New American Century, 1900–1910

W. W. NORTON & COMPANY

New York   London

For Newbury and Harriet Meader
and for Sadie Garfield

REPAST: DINING OUT AT THE DAWN OF
THE NEW AMERICAN CENTURY, 1900–1910
Michael Lesy and Lisa Stoffer

Copyright © 2013 Michael Lesy and Lisa Stoffer

Printed in China

First Norton edition 2013

Book design and composition by Laura Lindgren

The text of this book is composed in Perpetua.

Manufacturing by South China Printing Co., Ltd

FRONTISPIECE: Hotel Belmont, 1906, Byron Company

Photography Credits: Chicago History Museum: p. 77; Keystone-Mast Collection, UCR/
California Museum of Photography, University of California, Riverside: pp. 41, 44, 52,
53, 54, 227; Library of Congress Prints and Photographs Division: jacket front and back
and pp. 98, 167, 189; Museum of the City of New York: frontispiece and pp. 2, 85, 90,
117, 119, 123, 124, 145, 146, 157, 172, 177, 180, 181, 195, 196, 197, 198, 203; New York
Public Library, Robert F. Byrnes Collection of Automat Memorabilia: p. 62

All menus and bills of fare reproduced in *Repast* are from the Buttolph collection of menus,
Rare Books Division, The New York Public Library, Astor, Lenox and Tilden Foundations.

Library of Congress Cataloging-in-Publication Data
Lesy, Michael, 1945–
 Repast : dining out at the dawn of the new American century, 1900–1910 / Michael Lesy
and Lisa Stoffer. — First edition.
     pages cm
 Includes index.
 ISBN 978-0-393-07067-5 (hardcover)
 1. Dinners and dining — United States — History — 20th century. 2. Restaurants —
United States — History — 20th century. 3. Gastronomy — History — 20th century.
 4. United States — History — 1901–1909. I. Stoffer, Lisa. II. Title.
 TX633.L533 2013
 394.1'25309730904—dc23   2013009410
W. W. Norton & Company, Inc.

500 Fifth Avenue
New York, N.Y. 10110
www.wwnorton.com

W. W. Norton & Company, Ltd.
Castle House, 75/76 Wells Street
London WIT 3QT

1 2 3 4 5 6 7 8 9 0

CONTENTS

Menu

BLUEPOINTS — Cocktails

CONSOMME WALDORF

CELERY — OLIVES

BLACK BASS A LA JOINVILLE — Cardener

POTATOES CHATEAU — CUCUMBERS

FILETS OF BEEF A LA PORTUGAISE — Montferrand

BREAST OF CHICKEN AU SUPREME

SORBETS AU KIRSCH

ROAST SQUABS — Champagne

LETTUCE AND TOMATOES

ICE CREAM — PETITS FOUR

ROQUEFORT

CAFE — Cognac
Cigars

Informal Dinner
of Representatives of the
Home Insurance Co. of New York
Grand Pacific Hotel
Chicago, September 26, 1900

INTRODUCTION

Just before the New York Public Library launched its website,[1] administrators convened a small group of teachers, academics, curators, and IT specialists who, after a few face-to-face meetings in an oak-paneled conference room, were asked to go home and test the site for themselves. Which is why, one evening, I sat at my writing desk and, for no good reason, clicked on a collection called "The Buttolph Menu Collection." Archival photo collections, map collections, collections of flora and fauna, artifacts and implements, rare books and personal papers—all these I'd heard of, but a collection of menus?

I clicked and followed the prompts. Curators had grouped menus according to the year they'd been printed. I clicked on "1908." The beauty of the first set of menu covers that came into view, twenty to a page, dazzled me. They were as opulently colored, as elegantly designed, and as precisely rendered as postage stamps. I scrolled through page after page of them, hundreds and hundreds of them, lithographed or engraved, stenciled, hand-colored, or embossed. Some were as fanciful as cartoons, some were as stark and graphic as family crests.

Garlands and beautiful girls, Father Time and Mother Goose, banners and flags, racing sloops and locomotives, animals and automobiles decorated them, one after another.

I looked and looked and looked, hoarding the images in my mind as if they were pieces of candy, or toys, or prizes. Then I remembered something: the menu covers were like the covers of books. Instead of a table of contents, they opened onto bills of fare.

The covers and the bills of fare could be read but they could also be experienced as sensory documents. In the same way that a photograph of a man dozing in the sun on a park bench in 1905 could transmit, at the moment someone saw it in the present, the sight of something long past, so those menus could conjure up the taste, smell, and sight of food (as perishable as that moment in the park) that had been prepared, served, and eaten more than one hundred years ago.

Menu, informal dinner for Home Insurance Co. of New York representatives, Grand Pacific Hotel, Chicago, September 26, 1900

Hotel Union Square, Union Square East and 15th Street, New York, 1905, Byron Company

As I clicked and scrolled from year to year, many of the bills of fare I saw were American banquet menus, souvenirs of gatherings of men; some were daily breakfast, lunch, and dinner (or after-theater supper) menus from high-end, big-city restaurants and hotels; and some were menus from modest restaurants — nice places with no pretensions and reasonable prices that served breakfast, lunch, and dinner to businessmen and travelers in one room and women in another. Now and then, I saw menus from restaurants that served German, French, Italian, or Chinese food to people who could speak only English.

There were dishes on the bills of fare that were as strange as the custom of serving the genders separately. Breakfast choices, for example, of "Graham bread" or crackers and milk or lamb kidneys; lunch choices of oxtail ragout, hasenpfeffer (rabbit stew), or cod cakes with fried salsify (oyster plant); desserts that in different price ranges included "wine jelly," Nesselrode pudding, Charlotte russe, apple tapioca, or something called "snowballs" (a boiled, sweet dumpling made of flavored egg whites). Some of the food on these menus wasn't strange: buckwheat cakes or bacon and eggs for breakfast, a dish of baked beans with a slice of brown bread or a ham and cheese sandwich for lunch, turkey with cranberry sauce and gravy or braised beef with cabbage (or mashed turnips) served for dinner. Some of the banquet menus had ten or twelve courses; some of the fanciest dinner menus listed one hundred different entrées, from fish to fowl, from roasts to wild game; and some of the simplest lunch menus were written and illustrated by the hand of the proprietor.

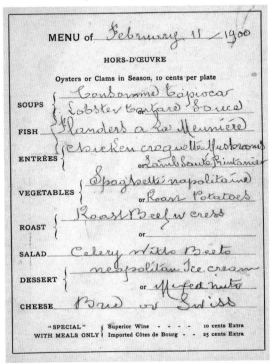

Table d'hôte, Au Chat Noir Hotel and Restaurant, New York, 1900

But just as the menu covers led to the food so, in my mind, the food led to the people who had prepared it, served it, and eaten it. Not just to the people themselves, but to the places they had sat and stood, worked and were nourished, and then beyond those places — the banquet halls and modest hotels and plain little lunchrooms — to the cities where those places did business. And then beyond them to the country itself and the stretch of time it inhabited, the era of Teddy Roosevelt, trusts, muckrakers, the Great White Fleet, W.E.B. DuBois, and the Wright brothers.

What happened next became the book that you're reading.

This book is as much a result of the beauty of the menus that seduced me that first night as the way the woman who collected them understood what she was doing.

The woman who signed her name "Miss Frank Buttolph" had begun life as Frances Buttles. She'd been born in 1844 in a little town in northern Pennsylvania, the daughter of a local eccentric — an inventor, grave digger, and carriage builder — whom people addressed as "Doctor."[2] As a young woman, she'd done something unusual: she'd graduated from the local high school (called a "normal school" — equivalent to a private secondary school). After that, she'd spent years traveling and teaching in the United States and Europe.

FLAT IRON RESTAURANT & CAFÉ

BROADWAY, FIFTH AVE. & 23ᴿᴰ ST., NEW YORK.

BANQUETS A SPECIALTY,

COSMOPOLITAN KITCHEN.

NOT RESPONSIBLE FOR PERSONAL PROPERTY UNLESS CHECKED AT THE COAT ROOM.

Menu, Flatiron Restaurant and Cafe, New York, 1906

BROADWAY & FIFTH AVE
22ND & 23RD STS.
NEW YORK.

Flat Iron Restaurant and Cafe'

Broadway, Fifth Avenue, 22d & 23d Streets

Lunch Ready

From 11 to 3 P. M.

MONDAY, JANUARY 28, 1907

Blue Points 20 cocktail 25   Rockaways 25 cocktail 30
Little Necks 20 cocktail 25   Fried oysters 35   Oyster stew 30

Malossol caviar [our own importation] 1 25

Table celery 25   Radishes 15   Chutney 15
Stuffed spiced cucumbers or green peppers 15   25
Stuffed sweet mangoes 15   25

Purée of green peas 15   Consommé leeks and rice 15

Cup consommé 15

Lobster cutlets (2), Aurore 50   Halibut steak, tomato sauce 50
Broiled shad au beurre 50   Crab flake meat au gratin 60
Fried scallops, tartare 50   Cold salmon in jelly 60

Rinderbrust, horseradish sauce, bouillon potatoes 40
Sauerbraten, potato balls 50
Knackwurst, saueren linsen 40

Boiled Philadelphia capon, salt pork 65
Prime beef croquettes, Jardinière 50
Veal goulash with spaetzle 45   Turkey hash with risotto 65

Deviled and grilled prime beef, baked sweet potatoes 50
Calf's head, vinaigrette 40
Fancy squab en casserole. Flat Iron 75
Hamburger rauchfleisch, purée of peas 50

Smoked brisket of beef, puree of peas 50
Omelette with Virginia ham, Jefferson 45
Breast of veal breaded, Westmoreland 45
Roast Maryland lamb, mashed turnips 50
Roast prime beef au jus 40   with rib bone 60   extra cut 75

SPECIAL TO ORDER
Mallard duck 2 00

COLD—Hamburger rauchfleisch, potato salad 50
Maryland lamb, bean salad 50   Half plain lobster 50
Prime beef, pickled beets 45   Spiced lamb's tongue 40   Suelze 40
Chicken salad 65   Pig's knuckle in jelly 45   Virginia ham 60

Rissotto 15   Purée of peas 15
String beans 15   Spinach 15   Knob celery salad 25
German asparagus 60   Red cabbage 15   Field salad 25
Brussels sprouts 20 Green peas 15 Sauerkraut 10 Chicory salad 30
Senfgurken 15   Lettuce 30   Tomatoes 35   Cucumbers 35
Potato salad 10 Mixed salad 15 Celery salad 15 New dill pickle 10
French artichokes, Hollandaise or vinaigrette 40
Broiled fresh mushrooms 75

Home-Made Pastry

Apple cake 10   Cheese cake 10   Coffee cake 10   Apple pie 15
Flat Iron éclair 10   Butter bretzels 10   Straussel cake 10
Assorted éclairs 10   Cold rice pudding 15   Grapes 15
Cinnamon cake 10   Pineapple pie 15   Pumpkin pie 15
Mocha torte 20   Nut pudding, orange sauce 15
Napoleons 15   Cream puffs 10
Jelly au Kümmel 15   Corn jelly meringue tarts 15
English plum pudding, hard and brandy sauce 25
Nesselrode pudding 30   Deutsche apfel torte mit schlagsahne 25
Biscuit Tortoni 25   Vanilla, strawberry or chocolate ice cream 25

Grape fruit (half) 15

Camembert 10   Edam 10   Roquefort 15   Swiss 10

Coffee 10

Patrons will confer a favor by Reporting to the Management
any incivility of the Waiters or inattention in the Service

For A la Carte orders, see order Bill of Fare

SEE WINE SPECIALTIES ON OTHER SIDE

Lunch menu, Flatiron Restaurant and Cafe, New York, 1907

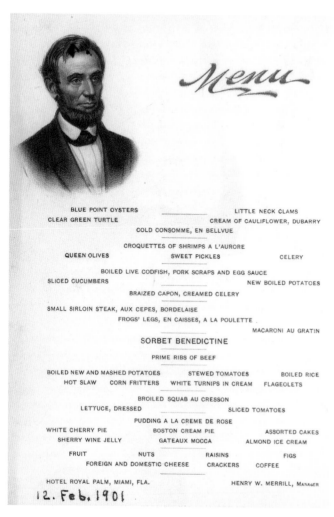

Menu

BLUE POINT OYSTERS LITTLE NECK CLAMS
CLEAR GREEN TURTLE CREAM OF CAULIFLOWER, DUBARRY
COLD CONSOMME, EN BELLVUE

CROQUETTES OF SHRIMPS A L'AURORE
QUEEN OLIVES SWEET PICKLES CELERY

BOILED LIVE CODFISH, PORK SCRAPS AND EGG SAUCE
SLICED CUCUMBERS NEW BOILED POTATOES
BRAIZED CAPON, CREAMED CELERY

SMALL SIRLOIN STEAK, AUX CEPES, BORDELAISE
FROGS' LEGS, EN CAISSES, A LA POULETTE
MACARONI AU GRATIN

SORBET BENEDICTINE

PRIME RIBS OF BEEF

BOILED NEW AND MASHED POTATOES STEWED TOMATOES BOILED RICE
HOT SLAW CORN FRITTERS WHITE TURNIPS IN CREAM FLAGEOLETS

BROILED SQUAB AU CRESSON
LETTUCE, DRESSED SLICED TOMATOES

PUDDING A LA CREME DE ROSE
WHITE CHERRY PIE BOSTON CREAM PIE ASSORTED CAKES
SHERRY WINE JELLY GATEAUX MOCCA ALMOND ICE CREAM

FRUIT NUTS RAISINS FIGS
FOREIGN AND DOMESTIC CHEESE CRACKERS COFFEE

HOTEL ROYAL PALM, MIAMI, FLA. HENRY W. MERRILL, MANAGER

12. Feb. 1901

*Menu, Royal Palm Hotel,
Miami, 1901*

She'd teach English in Germany, then return to the States and teach school here, then leave again. By the time she began collecting menus she'd become a little sparrow of a woman, with close-cropped, dark hair. By then, she lived alone in an apartment on Fifth Avenue, less than a block from what was then known as the Astor Library.

In 1899 she walked into the library and asked to speak to the director. She said she was prepared to offer the library her extraordinary collection — on the condition that she and her menus were inseparable. The director agreed. The director gave her a desk, an alcove, shelf space, and a mailing address. For the next thirty years Miss Buttolph added to her collection. She sent letters to hotel and hospitality trade journals; she walked into restaurants and hotels and asked for menus. Restaurant professionals sent her menus from all over the country — and all over the world. She'd stamp each menu with her acquisition stamp, make an index card for her catalog, then file the menu under one of eight categories (Complimentary Banquets; Military and Naval; Political; Greek Letter Fraternities; Medical Groups; School and Educational; Railroad Specials, Atlantic Steamships; and Daily Menus. She included menus from ethnic restaurants in her "Daily Menus" file).[3]

The *New York Times* took notice of her. In 1904, 1906, and 1909 *Times* reporters interviewed and wrote profiles about her.

What follows is an excerpt from the first article ("When Royalty Dines") the *Times* wrote about her.

Miss Buttolph seems to have made a practical improvement on the old idea that "the way to a man's heart is through his stomach." With her it is . . . [the] case that "the way to a man's history is through the dinners he has eaten." She does not care two pins for the food lists on her menus, but their historic interest is everything.[4]

To document "History in Food," not the "History of Food," seems to have been her purpose.

According to the Library's website, the bulk of her collection dates from 1890 to 1910, but as I clicked my way back and forth through it the years 1900 through 1910 appeared to have been her most active. These years were the beginning of what historians call "The New American Century." They were the best of times and the worst of times — a decade of glory, wealth, ambition, and degradation. Their outcomes — anticipated and unanticipated — shape our present, for better and worse.

Consider these facts:

Despite a short, savage depression in 1907, the gross domestic product of the United States (adjusted for inflation) grew by 26 percent during the decade.[5]

Cities metastasized: New York grew by 38 percent, Chicago by 23 percent, and the industrial "Iron Triangle" of Cleveland, Buffalo, and Detroit by 40 percent.[6]

People from everywhere on earth left their homes and came to America to work. Five hundred thousand people legally entered the United States in 1900; a million more entered in 1905. To the west, in California, the flow of Chinese immigrants that had begun in the 1840s, increased after the Civil War, and then been stanched by the Chinese Exclusion Act of 1882 had become a trickle, but in the Midwest and the East people from southern, central, and eastern Europe flooded the country.[7]

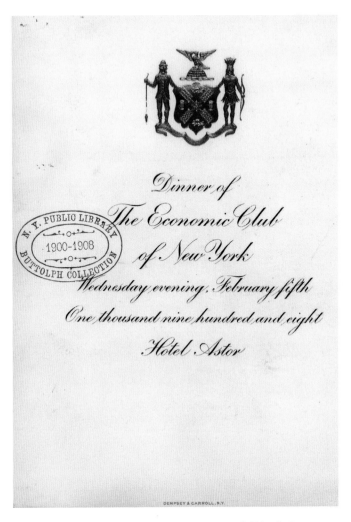

Dinner held by the Economic Club of New York, Hotel Astor, 1908

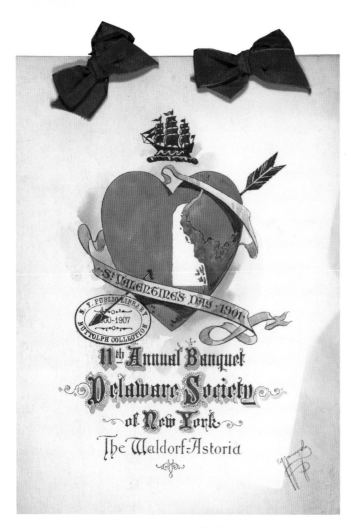

Eleventh annual banquet held by Delaware Society of New York, Waldorf-Astoria Hotel, New York, 1908

America's factories, mills, and mines, its railroads and docks, and the sparsely settled states of the north central and upper Midwest filled with the newcomers. In 1900 the U.S. population was 76 million; by 1910 it had grown to 92 million.

Iron, coal, copper, cotton, corn, sugar beets, winter wheat and timber, processed meat and tobacco, leather and steel — the production and consumption of every sort of commodity and finished product — grew faster than the population.[8] Whatever we didn't eat or use we sold abroad. Telegraphs and telephones, fast freight and passenger trains, high-speed presses and the first automobiles sped up the pace of life.

The rich grew richer. Fewer than a third of 1 percent of the population owned, controlled, and used for their personal or corporate benefit 75 percent of the nation's wealth.[9] At the same time, white- and blue collar workers had more money to spend. Wages for skilled and unskilled workers increased an average of 25 percent during the decade.[10] Corrected for inflation, the country's gross domestic product increased by nearly 26 percent from 1900 to 1910.[11]

The extra money changed ordinary people's eating habits.

Factory workers (a total of six million people) began the decade by bringing their food to work, but by the end of the decade more and more of them, day shift or night shift, bought their food — and their beer — from lunch carts and saloons just outside factory gates.

Forty percent of the U.S. population now lived in cities.[12] Three million of them — office workers and clerks, bankers, brokers, salesmen, and supervisors, a group that, as the decade progressed, included an increasing number of young women — often went out to eat their lunch. As more and more women searched for inoffensive and nourishing places to eat lunch (and sometimes dinner) near their offices, they pressed

Christmas Dinner

CARTE DU JOUR

Cape Cod, 25 Buzzard Bay, 25 Blue Points, 25 Lynnhaven, 25 Little Neck Clams, 25
Oyster Cocktail, 25 Clam Cocktail, 25

SOUPS

Consomme Argentine, 40 Creme of Cauliflower, Dubarry, 40 ; 25 Mock Turtle, Oloroso, 40
Petit Marmite, 60 Strained Chicken Okra, per Cup, 25 Consomme, per Cup, 25 Tomato, 30 Chicken Okra, 40
Mongol, 40 Julienne, 30 Clam Broth a la Pabst, per Cup, 25 Green Turtle, to order, 75

RELISHES

Baked Oysters a la Pabst, 1900, 75 Umbrella d'Ostende, 75 Cassolette of Fresh Mushrooms, 75
Timbale de foie gras a la Geiee, 75 Quenelles de Volaille Richelieu, 75 Escargots a la Bourguignonne, 75
Andouillette Grille a la Colbert, 50 Lyon Sausages, 60 Celery a la Pabst, 60 Celery, 40 Radishes, 25
Stuffed Olives, 25 Canape de Caviar, 50 Anchovy Salade, 50 Feuille a la Russe, 40
Salted Almonds, 25 Salted Nuts, 25 Fonds d'Artichokes Farcis au Anchovies, 75

FISH

Planked Striped Bass, Parmentier, 90 ; 50
Boiled Salmon, Mousseline, 90 ; 50 Kingfish, Saute, Meuniere, 90 ; 50 Paupiette of Pompano, Bercy, 90 ; 50
Halibut Steak, Bearnaise, 75 ; 40 Filet of Sole, Marguerite, 75 ; 40 Eperlans a la Melba, 60
Weakfish en Papillote, 60 Oyster Crabs a la Gourmet, 1.00 Frog Legs, Saute, Provencale, 80 Scallops and Bacon, 60 ; 35
Fresh Mackerel au four Balois, 75 Matelote de Poisson Marsellaise, 75 Fried Whitebait en Croustade, 75; 40
Fried Perches, Barnova, 60

RELEVES

Chartreuse de Perdreau a l'Americaine, 2.50 Boiled Capon, Oyster Sauce, 1.00 ; 60

ENTREES

Filet Mignon Armentier, 90 ; 50 Lamb Chops, Florentine, 40 Sweetbreads, larded, Henry IV, 90 ; 50
Chicken, Saute, Lavaliere. 1.50 ; 80 Kernel of Veal, Monecasque, 75 ; 40 Squabs, Braise, Montmorency, 75
Croquette of Red-Head Duck, St. Hubert, 1.50 ; 80 Calf's Head, en tortue, 60
Cromesquis a la Russe, 60 Pilaf a la Turque, 75 ; 40 Chaud-froid de Grouse, Lancastre, 1.00 Rice a l'Imperatrice, 40

Broiled Fresh Mushrooms on Toast, 1.00 Sous Cloche a la Creme, 1.25 Bouchee de Capucins, 1.00

TERRAPIN a la Maryland, 2.00 a la Baltimore, 2.00 a la Pabst, 2.25

READY ROAST

Ribs of Prime Beef, Yorkshire Pudding, 75 ; 40 Stuffed Gosling, Apple Sauce, 1.00 ; 60 Spring Lamb, Mint Sauce, 1.00
Spring Chicken, Giblet Sauce, 1.50 ; 80 Stuffed Turkey with Chestnuts and Truffles, 80 ; 50 Cold Game Pie, 75

GAME AND POULTRY TO ORDER

Spring Chicken, Roast or Broiled, 1 50 ; 75 Philadelphia Squabs on Toast, 75
Partridge, whole, 2.00 half, 1.00 Grouse, whole, 2.00 half, 1.00 Quail, 75 Canvas-Back Duck, 4.00
Red-Head Duck, 2 50 Mallard, 1.50 Teal, 1.00 Ruddy Duck, 1.50 Plover, 75
Reed Birds en Brochette, 75 Broiled Spring Turkey, whole, 2.50 half, 1.25

VEGETABLES

Pommes, Hollandaise, 30 Pommes Brabant, 30 Mashed Potatoes, 20 Boiled Potatoes, 15 Stewed Potatoes, 20
French Fried, 15 German Fried, 15 Hashed in Cream, 25 Au Gratin, 25 Saratoga, 25 Hashed Brown, 15
Lyonnaise, 15 Croquette, 25 Julienne, 20 Boiled or Baked Sweet Potatoes, 20 Fried, 25 Grilled, 25
Brussels Sprouts, 30 Celery Knobs, Poulette, 30 Celery, Braise, with Marrons, 35 Spinach, 25
Cauliflower, 40 Succotash, 25 String Beans, 20 Stewed Tomatoes, 20 Lima Beans, 20 Stewed Corn, 20
New Peas, 25 French Peas, 30 Boiled Onions. 25 Boiled Rice, 20 Long Island Asparagus, 40
German Asparagus, 75 French Asparagus, 75 French Artichokes, 75 Egg Plant, 25 Beets, 25
Stewed Mushrooms, 40 Spaghetti a l'Italienne, 25 Macaroni, 25 au Gratin, 25 Napolitaine, 30
Oyster Plant, Fried or Stewed in Cream, 25 Parsnips, Fried or Stewed in Cream, 25
Stuffed Tomatoes, 60 Stuffed Green Peppers, 60

SALADS

Anchovy, 40 Escarole, 40 Romain, 40 Lettuce, 40 Lettuce and Tomatoes, 50 Celery, 40 a la Pabst, 60
Chicken, 75 Lobster, 75 Shrimps, 75 Combination, 40

CHEESE

Camembert, 25 Philadelphia Cream, 20 Swiss, 25 Roquefort, 25 Brie, 25 Edam, 25 American, 20 Gorgonzola, 25

FRUITS

Oranges, 30 Grape Fruit, 40 Apples, 15 Pears, 25 Bananas, 15 Pineapples, 25 Niagara Grapes, 25

DESSERT

Cream Puffs a la Vanille, 30 Gateau de Mokka, 30
Plum Pudding, Hard and Rum Sauce, 40 Mince Pie, hot, 25 Pumpkin Pie, 20 Apple Pie, 20 Peach Pie, 20
Omelette, Souffle, 75 au Kirsch, 40 au Rhum, 40 aux Confiture, 40 Omelette, Celestine, 50
French Pancakes, 40 Assorted Eclairs, 25 Chocolate Ice Cream, 25 Vanilla Ice Cream, 25 Strawberry Ice Cream, 25
Bisquit Tortoni, 30 Lemon Water Ice, 25 Woodmansten Inn Sherbet, 30 Lalla Rookh, 30 Romain Punch, 30
Nesselrode Pudding, 40 Macedoine de Fruit, 50
Turkish Coffee, special, service for two, 50 French Coffee, special, service for two, 50
Demi Tasse, 10

Half Portions Served to One Person Only Special Arrangements Made for Theatre Parties

HOTEL PABST
NEW YORK
JAMES B. REGAN, Prop.

DECEMBER 25th, 1900

Christmas dinner, Hotel Pabst, New York, 1900

Dinner held by Le Club Fellowship, Cafe Kinsley, Chicago, 1900

against and then breached the custom of "separate but equal" accommodations. (The story of how this happened—how male, single-sex eating places changed and how new, female-friendly or mixed-gender eating places opened—is told in the "Her Food" and "Quick Food" chapters of this book.)

The result of all this—of prosperity, the growth of cities, changes in the workforce and in the pace of living and working—was a 78 percent increase in the number of restaurants.[13]

Miss Buttolph didn't just love beautiful menus, she collected them as documents of the social, economic, demographic, and cultural tumult she saw around her. This book travels the path she marked.

Since I knew more about the history of this country than its food, I asked Lisa Stoffer to collaborate with me. One reason I asked her was because of her family history. Her grandfather and great-grandfather had been chefs. Her great-grandfather had worked in resort hotels in Florida and Bermuda. Her grandfather had been a chef on a yacht, and then, for thirty years, ran the kitchens at Amherst College. After he died, one of the things Lisa inherited from him was his red leather-bound copy of *The Chef's Reminder*, a vest pocket reference book of menus, recipes, and techniques that professionals kept with them at work. Its index began with "Banquet Luncheon Menus" and ended with "Yorkshire Buck, chafing dish."[14] Lisa's copy of the *Reminder* was a tenth edition, published in 1904 by the Hotel Monthly Press of Chicago—the same company whose *Hotel Monthly* magazine published letters from the Astor Library's Miss Frank Buttolph soliciting menus (in spotless condition only!) from the magazine's readers.[15]

I knew all this about Lisa because she and I are married. The moment I'd shown her Miss Buttolph's menus her eyes had lit up. Lisa read cookbooks the way other people read novels. At dinner she'd talk about the things that people usually do—work, family, the fate of the human race—but, invariably, she'd also talk about food, and not just the food we were eating. One ingredient would lead to another; one way of cooking would lead to the next. She had a palate as sensitive as the ear of a professional musician. Compared with her "perfect pitch," I was tone deaf. Best of all, she knew, and could tell, "chef stories." One of her favorites was about a chef named Jeremiah Tower, who'd worked at Alice Waters's Chez Panisse in Berkeley in its seminal, early days. The story came from Tower's own memoir, *California Dish*. It was a story about menus. Lisa told Tower's story wonderfully, but Tower tells his own story even better.

"To me," Tower wrote, "menus are a language unto themselves . . . I have been collecting them and acting them out since I was a teenager. They spoke to me as clearly as any childhood fantasy novel. Reading an old menu slowly forms in my mind's eye its era, the sensibility of the restaurateur or the chef, even the physical details of the dining room. I can picture the guests, even when I don't know who they were. Sometimes I can conjure up an entire evening, a three act play, orchestrated around food . . . I have used the language of menus as the basis of dialogues with mentors, colleagues, and friends . . . I [have] always assumed that this language is universal."[16]

Lisa knew how to speak and understand that language fluently.

Together we set off to investigate the food Americans ate, where they ate it, and why they ate it at the beginning of the twentieth century.

The chapters "Pure Food" and "Splendid Food" serve as counterpoints, one to the other.

"Pure Food" is about the canned meat American corporations sold to ordinary people in this country and in Europe. The revelation (spread far and wide by the publisher of the 1906 novel *The Jungle*—the same publisher who'd released in 1905 the astonishingly racist best seller *The Clansman*) that the "meat" in those cans was either adulterated, ersatz, or toxic sounds all too familiar today.

Upton Sinclair, the author of *The Jungle*, had intended his book to serve as an *Uncle Tom's Cabin* for wage-slave, immigrant workers. Instead, as Sinclair said, "I aimed at the public's heart . . . but hit its stomach." The self-protective, self-serving reaction of the American middle class, then (in the shape of whole-grain diets and "pure food" restaurants) and now (in the shape of Whole Foods supermarkets, shares in community-supported agriculture, farmers' markets, and locavore restaurants), was to think of itself before it thought of the people who'd been used as tools to feed it. In the United States, the political outcome of the "poison meat" scandal was the Pure Food and Drug Act of 1906. In Europe, the scandal led to government bans, public boycotts, and the near total collapse of American processed meat exports to Europe.

"Splendid Food" describes the ceremonies of conspicuous consumption indulged in by the very rich (and not so very rich) at their banquets.

Today, the staggeringly complicated recipes developed and published by the great chef Charles Ranhofer, in his highly influential cookbook *The Epicurean*, can be seen as precursors to the complex and arcane procedures practiced and promulgated by Ferran Adrià in his "molecular gastronomy."

Lengthy courses, sumptuously caloric dishes, food-based but inedible table decorations, exotic ingredients obtained from afar, domestic ingredients obtained out-of-season, wild game hunted to extinction to serve as appetizers or entrées, balls and entertainments that were willful displays of "wealth and taste"—all these potlatch ingredients were used to (1) confirm the ruling class's supremacy to itself, (2) advertise its aristocratic way of life—copied from eighteenth-century European courts—to an audience of newspaper readers, and (3) attract less wealthy aspirants and imitators to the dining rooms and palm courts of luxury hotels, places that pandered to people who wanted to be seen as richer and more prominent than they were.

These two counterpoint chapters serve as bookends for *Repast*'s central chapters.

The first of these chapters, "Quick Food," describes "the problem of lunch" and the innovative solutions that, though developed more than one hundred years ago, are part of our lives today.

Early solutions to the tyranny of the lunch hour were places called "quick lunches." They were crowded, poorly lit, and improperly ventilated places, often with plate-glass windows at sidewalk level. Men—clerks and office workers—were served at counters where they sat, jammed shoulder to shoulder, wolfing their food. In some places, the men served themselves, grabbing sandwiches and wedges of pie stacked on countertops. With their food in hand, they'd push past others, looking for unoccupied chairs. Those chairs had single, broad arms where the men could set their food and eat, hunched down, while other men, as hungry and impatient as they were, milled around. The result was dyspepsia, a nationwide, gastrointestinal epidemic, a disease characterized by indigestion and constipation, aggravated by anxiety and anger, that doctors — and newspaper editors — believed was caused by modern city life.

Two evolutionary/revolutionary restaurant chains owed their success to solving "the lunch problem." One, a national chain, begun in New York City by two brothers who'd grown up on a well-run New Jersey dairy farm, was called Childs. To a public that was upset by indigestion and still anxious about impure foods, Childs offered scrupulously clean, spacious, well-lit, and well-ventilated restaurants that consistently served simple, wholesome food in cities all across the country. Big windows, marble and white tile floors and walls, and waitresses whose uniforms fused the dress codes of maids with those of nurses, sent reassuring messages to hungry office workers, male *and* female.

The other restaurant chain, based on the east coast and founded in Philadelphia by two partners — one a hardworking, quick-lunch cook named Hardart, the other the son of a prosperous family of surgical-instrument makers named Horn — was a self-service operation that replaced waiters and waitresses with Automats, big Swiss-German machines that dispensed cold or hot food from little window boxes (much like glass-fronted U.S. Post Office boxes) that customers could open with coins (cashiers made change for customers as they entered the restaurant).

The origin and long-term success of Horn and Hardart was its potent, always fresh, and flavorful coffee, brewed (rather than the usual quick-lunch coffee that was boiled, strained, and then kept hot indefinitely) using the method that Hardart had learned while working in a low-end quick lunch in New Orleans.

Predating Starbucks and McDonald's, both Childs and Horn and Hardart were real estate operations that understood that "location-location-location" was as important as carefully controlled, scrupulously regulated, taste-tested, formulaically consistent, centrally warehoused and distributed food products and food supplies. Though Horn and Hardart never managed to spread much beyond Philadelphia and

Daily menu, Lippe's Restaurant, St. Louis, 1907

MENU

1880—1905

Clams

Clear Green Turtle

Filet Bass aux vin Blanc

Chablis

Filet Beef, Mushrooms

Peas

Sorbet aux Rum

**Moet & Chandon
White Seal**

Roast Squab Chicken

Salad Romaine

Bisque Tortoni

Cheese   Coffee

Liqueurs   Segars

Larchmont Yacht Club
Monday, June 26, 1905

Twenty-fifth anniversary of founding of Larchmont Yacht Club, New York, 1905

New York City, Childs restaurants were prominently located in the business and shopping districts of cities across the United States and eastern Canada. Though some items on the Childs menus were regional specialties, a traveler in 1907 (much like a Starbucks or McDonald's customer now) could expect that whatever he or she usually ordered for breakfast at a Childs in Boston would taste and look like the breakfast he or she ordered in Cleveland when he or she was there for business or pleasure. Much of what chain restaurants do now, whether visible to the customers in the "front of the house" or hidden from them in the "back of the house," was either invented or perfected and practiced more than a century ago by Childs and Horn and Hardart.

"Her Food," the companion chapter to "Quick Food," describes the problem of finding work, and then finding places to eat, that confronted women as they entered the workforce in greater and greater numbers during the first decade of the twentieth century.

All too many of the youngest and most inexperienced women — whether they (like Theodore Dreiser's heroine Carrie) were from American small towns and farms or from villages in central, southern, and eastern Europe — had to choose between chronic malnutrition and sex work (the phrase "white slavery" was the way the era's newspapers and magazines described such work) when they came to the city looking for a job. Even when they found work, starvation wages, predatory male coworkers, and bosses "looking for company" trapped them in situations whose walls continually closed in on them.

The fortunate roomed with relatives, sought help from aid associations, or developed friendships with older women who worked where they did. Those who could brought leftovers to work and ate them hurriedly.

Less improvised — or morally compromised — solutions developed over the course of the decade:

1. Candy stores sold sweets and "soft drinks" that were cheap, quick to eat, and easy to carry back to work. Sweet shops (Schrafft's, for example) began adding soda fountains and quick-lunch counters that catered to "working girls." Over time, some of these places evolved into table-service restaurants for women office workers and shoppers.
2. Women-only, cafeteria-style "lunch clubs," founded by women philanthropists or entrepreneurs, sold hot, inexpensive meals to office

carte B du jour

LUNCHEON

MONDAY, NOVEMBER 25, 1907

OYSTERS and CLAMS

California Oyster Cocktail	$0.35	Toke Points	$0.40
Toke Points Mignonette	.50	Blue Points	.40
Little Neck Clams	.40	California Oysters	.40

SOUP

Potage Gastronome	$0.20	Cream of Cauliflower	$0.25
Clam Broth	.25	Cup Consommé	.15

Clear Green Turtle .... .30

HORS D'OEUVRES

Crab Legs Mayonnaise	$0.40	Queen Olives	$0.20
Green or Ripe Olives	.15	Anchovies in Oil	.35
Dill Pickles	.15	Caviar on Toast	.50
Celery	.20	Canapé Bellevue	.30
Tomatoes en Suprise	.35	**Fresh Astrakhan Caviar**	**1.00**

FISH

Striped Bass Broiled, Maitre d'Hotel	$0.40	White Bait, Deviled	$0.35
English Sole au Gratin	.50	Shad	.35
Sand Dabs Meuniér	.40	Salmon Trout	.40

ENTREES

Lamb's Tongue, Mashed Turnips	$0.35	Broiled Pork Tenderloin, with Brussels	
Beef à la Mode	.35	Sprouts	$0.50
Chicken Croquette à la Nesle	.50	Stuffed Tomatoes	.35
Calf's Feet à la Poulette	.40	Spaghetti au Gratin	.25
Boiled Shoulder of Lamb, Caper Sauce	.35	Scotch Wood Cock	.40

Chicken Fricassée and Mushrooms ..... .75

ROAST, POULTRY and GAME

Ribs of Beef	$0.40	Teal Duck	$0.75
Spring Lamb, Mint Sauce	.40	Sprig	1.50
Squab	.75	Mallard	2.00
Squab Chicken	1.25	Canvas Back	2.50
Broiled Chicken, half 75c; whole	1.50	Saddle of Lamb	3.00

FROM GRILL, SEE GENERAL BILL OF FARE

VEGETABLES

Petit Pois, extra fine	$0.50	Fresh String Beans	$0.20
Cauliflower	.25	Potatoes—	
French Peas	.25	Fried, Julienne, or Stewed in Cream	.15
Brussels Sprouts	.20	Soufflé	.25
Egg Plant	.25	Au gratin	.25
Haricots Verts	.40	Baked or Fried Sweet Potatoes	.20
Asparagus	.50	Sweet Potatoes, Southern Style	.25
German Asparagus	1.25	Artichokes	.25
French Asparagus	.75	Spinach	.20

SALADS

Lettuce	$0.20	Chicken	$0.40
Romaine	.20	Shrimp	.40
Tomato	.25	Crab	.40
Cucumbers	.25	Lobster	.40
Douxette	.25	Combination	.40
Celery and Mayonnaise	.40	Chiffonade Salad	.40

Pimentos Marones .... .50

COLD MEATS

Ribs of Beef	$0.40	Tongue	.40
Lamb	.40	Goose Liver Paté	1.00
Turkey	.65	Terrine de Paté de Foie gras—One	.50
Ham	.30	Two	1.00
Kalter Aufschnitt	.60	Galantine	.50
Pommerische Gausebrust	.60	Westphalia Ham	.50

German Mettwurst .... .40

DESSERTS AND ICES

Café Parfait	$0.35	Orange Water Ice	$0.25
French Pastry or Fruit Tarts, each	.10	Lallah Rook	.30
Apple Pie	.15	Smyrna Dates	.35
Apple or Grape Square	.15	Grape Fruit and Sherry or Maraschino	.35
Baked Apples	.20	Raspberries, 25c; with Ice Cream	.35
Vanilla or Café Ice Cream	.25	Omelette au Rhum or Kirsch	.40
Strawberries and Cream	.25	Peach Flambé	.50
Sliced Bananas and Cream	.25	Plum Pudding	.50

Roman or Russian Punch .... .25

FRUITS in season, 25c.

CHEESE

Brie, Swiss, Roquefort, Oregon Cream, or		New Chatel	$0.25
Cream	$0.15	Individual Imported Camembert	.25
Confitures de Bar-le-duc	.50	Guava Jelly	.50

CAFE

Demi Tasse	$0.10	Turc	$0.20	Special	$0.25
Pabst Selected Brew	$0.10		Pilsner or Hofbrau		$0.15

Daily luncheon menu, Blanco's, San Francisco, 1907

workers. The clubs' low prices were the result of their self-service dining and their low-rent, second-floor locations.

3. Enlightened employers with mostly female office or factory workforces—Sears' home offices in Chicago; the National Cash Register Company in Dayton—built in-house cafeterias and dining rooms. Such employers believed it was in their best interest to keep their workers healthy—and close to their work.

4. Big-city department stores—Marshall Field's in Chicago, Wanamaker's in Philadelphia, Siegel-Cooper in New York City—opened tearooms, often on their upper floors, that served soups, sandwiches, salads, entrées, and desserts to genteel women shoppers and their children and sometimes to women workers from nearby offices.

5. Smaller, owner-operated tearooms—modest, cozy places, sometimes located at street level, sometimes one flight down—served refreshments and offered respite to single women and small groups of female friends. Sometimes, after graduation, college girls opened tearooms as first-time, pioneering business ventures near their alma mater.

6. At the top of the tearoom hierarchy were grand and glittering palm courts, adjacent to the lobbies of big-city luxury hotels. Palm courts served decorative food to well-to-do, fashionable ladies who went there with their friends (and sometimes their lapdogs) in order to see and be seen. On request, for special guests, palm courts provided cocktails demurely hidden in teapots.

Finally, as women took jobs in offices and stores—retail, clerical, managerial, and professional jobs men had long done—they pressed against the conventions of "separate but equal" restaurant and hotel dining rooms. During the day, the quality of the food, service, location, and convenience of the "women only" dining rooms rarely matched the quality of the men's. Worse yet, in the evening, single women or groups of women who came to a hotel for dinner were routinely turned away. Even women hotel guests were expected to have the good sense to dine in private dining rooms, hidden from public view. Unless, of course, they were escorted by men. A woman in the company of a man was, by definition, "a lady." A woman alone had no polite definition.

Confrontations followed by lawsuits erupted throughout the decade. Customs changed when high-end proprietors discovered that they had

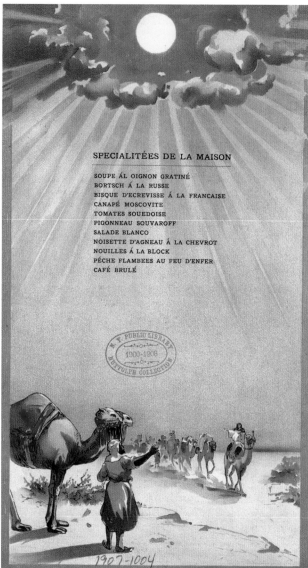

SPECIALITÉES DE LA MAISON

SOUPE ÁL OIGNON GRATINÉ
BORTSCH Á LA RUSSE
BISQUE D'ECREVISSE Á LA FRANCAISE
CANAPÉ MOSCOVITE
TOMATES SOUEDOISE
PIGONNEAU SOUVAROFF
SALADE BLANCO
NOISETTE D'AGNEAU Á LA CHEVROT
NOUILLES Á LA BLOCK
PÉCHE FLAMBEES AU FEU D'ENFER
CAFÉ BRULÉ

Daily luncheon menu, Blanco's, San Francisco, 1907

more tables, more waiters, more cooks, more kitchen capacity — and more bills — than they had revenue. Women, dining alone or in groups, were known not to tip as well as men, but by the end of the decade proprietors understood that their dining rooms would remain half empty without them. Money, not manners — the power of the purse, not enlightened thinking and lawsuits — brought an end to gender-segregated dining.

Finally: "Other People's Food" offers a counternarrative to the historical cliché that early-twentieth-century Americans were as xenophobic and anti-immigrant as some of their descendants are now. Though xenophobic anger and fear were historical facts, this chapter documents the way many Americans living in cities across the country frequented immigrant restaurants and beer gardens for emotional and psychological reasons — reasons as important to them as the cost and the taste of the food, wine, and beer they enjoyed. In addition, "Other People's Food" provides a new explanation for why Chinese restaurants — restaurants that some of our more unconventional ancestors valued as edgy, intriguing, and unpredictable places — spread and then, seemingly overnight, proliferated outside the ghettos of the nation's Chinatowns.

In conclusion: *Repast* tells new stories, uncovers new facts, and provides insights into what and why our ancestors ate what they ate. *Repast* reveals how *our* eating habits, food fears, food fads, and diets bear a striking resemblance to *theirs*. Although much of what we think and do appears to have changed — and, in truth, has changed — a great deal remains the same.

By combining newly available, online databases, newspapers, and magazines with cookbooks, recipe guides, diaries, and memoirs from an era that was as food-obsessed as our own, *Repast* answers the challenge made two hundred years ago by the French philosopher and epicure Brillat-Savarin: *Tell me what you eat, and I will tell you what you are.*

— ML

Swift's Premium Hams and Bacon

Confidence

There is no need of going to the market yourself to select Premium Ham or Premium Bacon— they are always the same and of the finest quality. Send one of the children. Tell him to look for the brand, "Swift's Premium." He will bring back a tender, delicate piece of smoked meat, delicious in flavor.

You may feel the same confidence if you are sending for a pail of Silver Leaf Lard. It has become America's standard on account of its invariable purity.

Swift & Company
Chicago

Before your dealer slices your order ask to see the brand "Swift's Premium"

PURE FOOD

The Spanish-American War began in April and ended in August 1898. In those four months, ten times more enlisted men and officers died from disease and malnutrition than from combat. "A splendid little war" was the way patricians such as John Hay, high and dry and well fed in his American ambassador's residence in London, chose to think about what happened. In the huge, filthy army camps in Virginia and Tennessee where most of the 200,000 men who'd volunteered spent the war, and in the tall grass, heat, and mud outside Santiago, Cuba, inadequate hygiene, inedible food, and inept medical care came close to producing a catastrophe.

Typhoid fever swept through the volunteers held in reserve in the United States. One month after 15,000 American troops took San Juan Hill, malaria had disabled 75 percent of them. Rancid food, unpalatable and indigestible, worsened their suffering.

On the first of August, 1898, ten generals and colonels, all line officers in Cuba, sent an alarming letter to their commander: "We, the undersigned . . . are of the unanimous opinion that this army must at once be taken out of the island of Cuba and be sent to some point on the northern sea coast of the United States . . . the army is disabled by malarial fever to such an extent that its efficiency is destroyed . . . it is in the position to be practically entirely destroyed by the epidemic of yellow fever sure to come in the future . . . this army must be moved now or it will perish."

On August 4, copies or paraphrases of the officers' letter appeared in the morning editions of nearly every major newspaper in America. Teddy

Harper's Magazine, 1901

Roosevelt had been one of the colonels who'd signed the original. As shouts of alarm and accusation spread across the country and crashed into the White House, Roosevelt offered a few additional comments of his own. "The whole command," he said, "is so weakened and shattered as to be ripe for dying like rotten sheep."

President McKinley's White House found itself in an awkward position. Peace negotiations with Spain were well under way. Spain's naval forces had been destroyed, but an American withdrawal from Cuba might make Spain less willing to surrender. Worse yet, American midterm elections were in the offing. A panic-stricken evacuation of men—some of whom might be carrying yellow fever home with them—wouldn't help the Republican Party.

Fortunately, Spain capitulated within weeks of the issuing of the letter. Just as fortunately, so the story goes, McKinley received a letter from the mother of a soldier. "We are living under a generous government," wrote the lady, "with a good, kind man at its head, willing to give the Army the best possible, and yet thieving corporations will give the boys the worst."[1] By "the worst" the lady meant the so-called food her boy had been given to eat.

The president did what any good, kind man would have done: he appointed a special commission to investigate the way the War Department had fed and cared for every mother's son who had fought to avenge the *Maine*.

The White House had a difficult time finding an army general willing to conduct a dog and pony show for the Republican Party. Eventually, McKinley found a retired general named Dodge who was not only a Republican and a millionaire but a friend of the secretary of war. Neither the White House nor its General Dodge anticipated the "embalmed beef" scandal that was about to break.

The man who hauled into public all the stinking meat that the army had fed its soldiers was none other than the army's own commanding general, Nelson Miles. Miles was a Medal of Honor winner and Civil War officer who'd gone west to fight Indians. In 1894 the government had sent 12,000 men under his command to break the Pullman strike in Chicago.

Miles disliked army bureaucrats and staff officers a little less than he disliked Indians. As to beef, as long as it came fresh on the hoof he was glad to eat it.

Miles had begun to hear reports about bad beef in June 1898, when he'd inspected troops waiting in Tampa and Jacksonville to be sent to

Cuba and Puerto Rico. The refrigerated beef—killed and quartered in Chicago by Swift & Company, then sent to Tampa in iced refrigerator cars (ammonia refrigeration didn't come into use until two years later)—smelled as if it had been injected with chemicals to keep it from spoiling. The general and one of his medical officers thought the stuff smelled as if it had been embalmed. Embalmed or not, some of the meat still went bad and had to be tossed into the ocean. As to the canned "roast beef": it ranged from the lowest-quality scrap and gristle to the lowest-quality stew meat. Millions of cans of it had been sold to the army by the Chicago packinghouse Libby, McNeill & Libby.

In July, Miles himself directed the invasion of Puerto Rico. Even though there was plenty of cattle on the island and plenty of fresh beef for sale (at half the price American cattle growers charged the army) Miles's men were forced to eat the rank, refrigerated beef they'd brought with them or the gray, gristly stuff in cans. Miles began to believe that "the chemicals used in treating the beef were responsible for the great sickness in the American army."

In September, Miles ordered every regimental commander who'd served in Cuba or Puerto Rico to write evaluations of the canned beef rations they and their men had been issued. He directed his officers to submit their evaluations to the War Department. The officers described opening cans of beef with pieces of rope and dead maggots in them. They described cans that, once opened, gave off odors so foul that, according to the *Chicago Tribune*, their men "had to retire to a distance to prevent being overcome."

The poet Carl Sandburg was a young army enlisted man back then; years later, at the age of seventy-two, he still remembered what happened when he and his buddies opened one of those cans on board a troopship headed to Puerto Rico. He wrote: "A tin of 'Red Horse' would be handed to one man who opened it. He put it to his nose, took a spit, then the tin of 'Red Horse' was thrown overboard . . . We buried it at sea because it was so duly embalmed with all the flavor of life and every suck of nourishment gone from it though having, nonetheless, a putridity of odor more pungent than ever reaches the nostrils of a properly embalmed cadaver."[2]

A few days before Christmas 1898, McKinley's Dodge commission made the mistake of asking General Miles to testify about the rations issued to his men. For the first time, Miles used the term "embalmed beef" in public. Every big-city newspaper in the country reported

his remarks. Papers began to use the term "embalmed beef" whether they were writing about the refrigerated sides of beef that Swift had supplied or the cans (seven million to be exact) that Libby had sold as travel and field rations.

The army general who headed the War Department's Commissary Department was so outraged by Miles's remarks that he called Miles a liar in public. In testimony before the Dodge commission the general went even further. "I wish to force the lie back into his throat," said the general, "coated with the contents of a camp latrine . . . unless he can prove his statement, he should be denounced by every honest man, barred from the clubs, barred from society of decent people, and so ostracized that even the street bootblacks would not condescend to speak to him."

The army court-martialed the man — not because of the "embalmed beef" he'd bought as rations but because of the intemperate remarks he'd made about a superior officer.

The packers denied any wrongdoing.

A spokesman for Swift said, "The beef we sent the army was just the same as we sell to our trade throughout the country . . . I will state unequivocally that no chemicals of any kind were used in the dressed beef sent to the army."

A spokesman for Libby said, "We have been in the business for more than twenty-five years. Our employees fully understand their business . . . We sold millions of pounds of canned meats to the government for use on the war and no cans have ever been returned to us as bad . . . All meats require pepper and salt and as the soldiers did not have any seasoning, it is likely the canned meat tasted flat to them. That may have had same effect on the meat. The climate certainly could have some . . ."

Early in February 1899 the *New York Times* reported that a U.S. Army general in Havana had discovered "among the army rations issued to the destitute in Havana, hundreds of cases of spoiled beef. It is said these

canned roast and boiled goods were put up by the 'embalming process.' The marks on the cases show 'Chicago, July, 1898' . . . yesterday some of the cans were given to the destitute who refused to open the contents . . . several cases were then broken open . . . the [smell of the] air at La Punta Park, one of the distributing stations, leaves no doubt as to the presence of the offensive supplies."

Midterm elections weren't kind to the Republicans. The GOP lost thirty seats in the House and the Senate. The Dodge commission's final report exonerated the War Department, the army, and the beef it fed its men. No one believed any of it. Some papers began to compare the beef scandal to the Dreyfus affair in France.

Early in 1899 McKinley appointed a new commission — this time a formal military court of inquiry presided over by a major general — to conduct its own investigation. The papers called this new commission "the Beef Court."

The Beef Court ordered samples of refrigerated beef, held in cold storage lockers in army camps in Tennessee and Florida, to be sent north, packed in ice, so they could be analyzed by Department of Agriculture chemists. The Beef Court also ordered the army to send cans of roast beef/cooked beef rations to those same chemists for analysis.

While the chemists did their work, the Beef Court called witnesses. Captains and lieutenants, colonels and brigadier generals came and went, often accompanied by their own lawyers. The newspapers reported their testimony in articles headlined BEEF MADE TROOPS ILL and SAD REPORTS OF SUFFERING.

On February 26 the Beef Court called former colonel Teddy Roosevelt — now governor of New York — to testify.

"What kind of meat was supplied to you on the journey from Tampa to Cuba?" the court asked the governor.

"The so-called canned roast beef," Roosevelt answered.

"What was furnished to you after you landed in Cuba?"

"We had pork but sometimes canned roast beef . . . I tried the canned roast beef but could not eat it."

"Describe to the court the condition of the cans."

"When the cans were opened, the top was nothing more than a layer of slime . . . The beef was stringy and coarse and seemed to be nothing more than a bundle of fiber. All the men complained about it. Sometimes we stewed it with potatoes and onions, but I could have eaten my hat stewed with potatoes and onions rather than the beef. Then we tried to improve it by stewing it with mangoes. This did not improve it . . . Nearly all the men were sickened after eating it . . . The majority of the men, if put on it, would get sick in one or two days."

"What was the health of your troops," asked the court.

"Like all the others," Roosevelt said. "Sick. Toward the end of the campaign, I did not regard twenty percent of my men as fit for service. At the end of the campaign, only two percent of my men were as fit as when they left home."

The court then asked, "Governor, can you recall the names of the brands on the labels of the canned beef?"

"No," said Roosevelt. "Some were Armour's; some were Swift's."

The court continued.

"With your experience with the First Volunteer Cavalry [the Rough Riders] will you tell the court whether or not you consider the caned beef wholesome?"

Roosevelt answered plainly. "I regard it as an utterly unfit and unwholesome ration. The canned roast beef that we received at Santiago was wholly unfit to eat . . . unpalatable, inedible, and unwholesome . . . to the majority of the men under me . . . it did not appease their hunger, but it made them sick."

After his testimony Roosevelt headed for the elevators accompanied by his private secretary and a few reporters.

As Roosevelt stepped into an elevator, he turned to a friend. "It was a disgrace to our country," he said.[3]

A few weeks after Roosevelt testified, the Department of Agriculture's chemists reported their findings to the court.

The refrigerated beef they'd analyzed had no chemicals in it. Poor refrigeration, poor handling, and poor sanitation had degraded it. As to the canned beef, it was no better and no worse than the canned beef sold to the public. The only thing the chemists found in the cans, other than the meat itself, was salt.

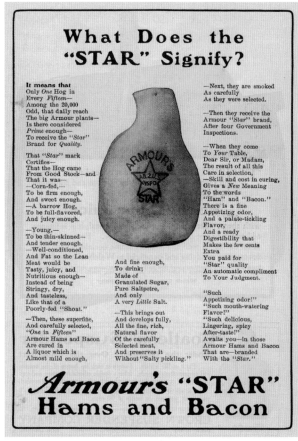

Munsey's Magazine, 1906

Based on these findings the court exonerated the army of feeding refrigerated "embalmed beef" to its troops.

The court was less forgiving about the army's canned beef. It called the army's purchase and distribution of those rations "a colossal error for which there is no palliation."[4]

✧

Munsey's Magazine, *1900*

The man who directed the Department of Agriculture's analysis of the army's beef was a Harvard-educated chemist named Harvey Wiley. Despite Wiley's report to the court, he was no apologist for the packers.

For the next seven years, from the day the Beef Court passed judgment on the army until the day seven years later President Roosevelt signed the Pure Food and Drug Act into law, Wiley stood at the center of every public investigation and debate about "pure food." Today, Wiley would be described as a consumer advocate. He might even be called an activist.

Wiley had taught at Purdue for years. The Department of Agriculture hired him as its chief chemist because of his research specialty: the corn-derived "starch sugar" known as glucose, now called corn syrup.

Glucose was a late-eighteenth-century wartime invention, developed in response to Napoleon's embargo of British cane sugar. After Napoleon's defeat, German and French scientists and manufacturers perfected the use of potatoes as a sugar starch source. In America, food manufacturers relied on maize.

By the 1880s there were dozens of American factories making glucose from corn. Cheap, corn-based glucose began to be used in everything from candy to table syrup to commercial baked goods. As Wiley himself wrote in 1881 in *Popular Science Monthly*, "Corn, the new American king, now supplies us with bread, meat, and sugar, which we need, as well as whisky, which we could do without." American cane sugar manufacturers protested. If any food products used glucose instead of "real sugar," manufacturers should have to list the glucose on their labels. Wiley agreed. It was wrong to charge high sugar prices for a cheap sweetener.

About the time the Beef Court began calling witnesses, a Senate committee—the Committee on Manufacturers—began its own investigation of the food Americans ate. The man who chaired the committee was a maverick Republican from Illinois named William Mason. Mason asked the Department of Agriculture to permit Wiley to serve as the committee's analyst and adviser.

Starting in the spring, and ending in the fall of 1899, Mason's Pure Food Investigation Committee called nearly two hundred witnesses and collected more than four hundred samples of adulterated food. Harvey Wiley not only analyzed those samples but testified about them. His testimony during public committee meetings held in Chicago in May of 1899 was nothing less than sensational.

Wiley began quietly and patriotically. He told the committee that he'd just been authorized to establish "a national kitchen" in the Department of Agriculture to test food for the army. "The necessity of work in this direction," said Wiley, as quoted in the *Chicago Tribune*, "after our unfortunate experience in the recent war is apparent . . . It is my purpose to establish a kitchen in my department . . . to determine what foods possess the greatest nutritive qualities and how they should be prepared and served to retain those qualities and make them as palatable as possible. The latter is a most important question as the results of the use of the canned roast beef ration demonstrated. Nothing that culinary skill can accomplish shall be wanting. I will have the services of a thoroughly competent chef."

After saluting the flag, Wiley began to recite a long list of adulterants—some harmless, some poisonous.

- Beer, Wiley said, was often 70 percent adulterated "by the use of hominy grits and glucose instead of pure malt."

Munsey's Magazine, *1900*

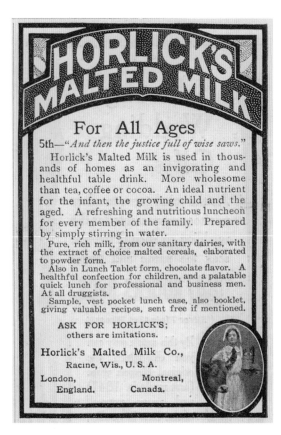

Munsey's Magazine,
January 1901

- Olive oil was often American cottonseed or sunflower oil that had been shipped abroad then shipped back to the United States labeled "Imported Pure Olive Oil."
- Cinnamon was "likely to contain ground peanut shells."
- Cayenne pepper was often "ground, red lead."
- Coffee beans, labeled and sold as whole beans imported from Yemen ("Mocha coffee") or from Java ("Java coffee"), were—at best—whole beans from Brazil. At worst, the beans weren't even beans but pellets, made from an amalgam of flour, sugar, molasses, and ground coffee.
- "Milk" was often watered-down or skimmed milk, colored with annatto (made from the seed-pod pulp of the achiote tree). Infants fed such milk became sick and malnourished and sometimes died.
- Butter was often adulterated with cottonseed oil or lard.
- "Maple sugar" was often a blend of brown sugar and hickory bark.
- "Pure honey" was usually made from glucose colored with caramel.
- Zinc and copper salts were routinely added to canned peas and beans to keep them green.
- Salicylic acid was routinely added to fruit preserves to keep them from spoiling.

The food chemists who testified after Wiley presented even more alarming evidence.

A product called Freezine, sold to farmers and routinely used by them to keep milk and butter fresh, was found to be a 6 percent solution of formaldehyde. (A representative of the company that made Freezine claimed not only that it was healthy and harmless but that its use could cut infant cholera deaths by 70 percent.)

Another product—a powder sold under the name Freezem—was used by butchers to keep meat scraps fresh so that they could be ground into hamburger, or it was mixed with hamburger meat to keep it from going bad. Freezem was found to be an antiseptic ("a sulphide of soda," according to the

Chicago Tribune) that was commonly used by public health officers to disinfect smallpox houses or by medical schools to preserve cadavers for anatomy classes.

The news headlines that reported this testimony began with such words as "startling" and "appalling." CHIEF CHEMIST WILEY SAYS 90% OF THIS COUNTRY'S FOODS AND DRINKS ARE FRAUDS, announced the *Tribune*. Wiley later disavowed the *Tribune* report: "I might go to a store today and buy 100 food articles at random and scarcely 5 percent would be adulterated" was what he said later that year. Spices and coffees, he said, were the items most likely to be adulterated. So were manufactured foods, especially foods made to be sold to the poor. Said Wiley: the poor were exposed to the most impure kinds of food.

After fifty-one days of hearings, Mason asked Wiley to help draft a pure food bill. The result? Mason's bill died without debate. Seven years later, as the bill that became the Pure Food and Drug Act made its way through Congress, newspaper reporters who'd written "pure food" articles for years added up the number of bills that had died like Mason's.

Over the course of sixteen years, fifty-six "pure food" bills had died before birth.[5]

Munsey's Magazine, *January 1901*

The only practical result of Mason's hearings and Wiley's testimony was a 1902 congressional appropriation of $5,000 (equivalent to $130,000 today) authorizing the Department of Agriculture to investigate the effect of preservatives on "digestion and health."

Wiley changed the mission of his "national kitchen" from testing food for the army to preparing and testing food for what he called his "hygiene table." Wiley recruited civilian volunteers for his experiments. All were young, healthy men; most were Department of Agriculture staffers; a few were medical students. When a reporter for the *Washington Post* found out about what Wiley was doing, he nicknamed Wiley's volunteers "the Poison Squad." For a year the *Post* published stories about Wiley and his human guinea pigs as if they were all part of a darkly funny, long-running

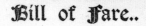

Bill of Fare..

53 VESEY STREET

17. May. 1905

Our New system—Full aroma coffee is pure and
wholesome.

Standard of excellence maintained at all times.

Served with pure cream.

⬛UDE ⬛ALK

All our food is pure and of the best quality obtainable

OUR MILK AND CREAM

Pure, Rich and Fresh Daily

Try our GOLDEN WAFFLES, made of material
and in a manner that makes them wholesome.
nutritious and healthful—served with butter, sap
maple syrup or sugar.

OUR COFFEE——

It is made by a new system, that eliminates all
the impurities and makes :—

GOLDEN IN COLOR
RICH IN AROMA
PURE AND WHOLESOME

Run in for a cup any time, quality the same at all hours.

PURE FILTERED WATER

Open Day and Night

NOT RESPONSIBLE FOR PERSONAL PROPERTY UNLESS CHECKED

_1905 – 396_

_Daily menu, Spencer Dining
Hall Co., New York, 1905_

college farce. Wiley resisted and then played along with the _Post_. He
knew he needed the publicity.

This was Wiley's research protocol: For ten days, a Department of
Agriculture cook (certified as an expert by the Civil Service) prepared
wholesome meals for Wiley's volunteers, using either the best-quality,
fresh ingredients or canned ingredients preserved without anything
but salt. The volunteers agreed not to eat or drink anything (including
alcohol) except what was served to them by Wiley's staff. Wiley enforced
this rule by insisting that the men live in a Department of Agriculture
boardinghouse. Before each meal each man's weight, temperature, and

pulse rate were recorded. During the workday, the men carried satchels so they could provide the Public Health Service with daily urine and stool samples. Once a week, the young men were given physicals by Public Health Service and Marine Corps doctors.

The volunteers' first ten-day, preservative-free existence provided baseline data for their next ten days, during which they were served increasing amounts of commonly used preservatives. Wiley began by feeding his men tiny amounts of borax. (U.S. packers routinely added borax to ham and bacon during this era. The German government considered borax to be so harmful to the kidneys that it had banned the import of all American pork products.)

Wiley began his experiments thinking that borax was no more dangerous than table salt. When his volunteers' intake of borax passed three grams per day (by then Wiley was administering the stuff in capsules), they began to lose their appetites, suffer from stomachaches and diarrhea, and complain of persistent, dull headaches. By the time their intake passed four grams per day they became so incapacited they couldn't work.

Wiley understood that an average American might consume, at most, a quarter gram of borax per day. He knew, though, that there were preservatives—in addition to borax—in much of what Americans ate. The cumulative effect of these preservatives began to worry him.

Wiley switched volunteers every time he switched preservatives. After borax came salicylic acid, after salicylic acid came sulfites, then benzoic acid, then formaldehyde. Wiley's tests went in six-month intervals for five years. Each course of testing produced clinical results that were more and more alarming. Wiley began to grant more interviews with more newspapers. He published his findings, year after year, in special bulletins issued by the Department of Agriculture.

In 1903, Wiley and his Poison Squad became the subjects of a popular song called "They'll Never Be the Same." Its chorus was: "Oh, they may get over it, but they'll never be the same / That kind of bill of fare would drive most men insane / Next week he'll give them mothballs, *a la* Newburgh or else plain / Oh, they may get over it but they'll never be the same."[6]

In February 1906 the House Committee on Interstate and Foreign Commerce called Wiley to testify. The *Washington Post* referred to him as "Old Borax." Wiley told the committee what five years of human testing had taught him. Preservatives had their uses, he said. Remote

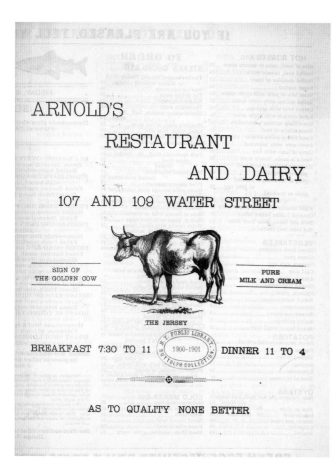

Menu, Arnold's Restaurant and Dairy, New York, 1901

expeditions and voyages, distant outposts in faraway places might need to rely on preserved food. But why was such food sold in grocery stores? he asked. Were the packers and manufacturers scared of poisoning their customers? Is that why they used the chemicals they used? Clean manufacturing plants, not chemicals, would keep their customers safe.[7] Ban the use of preservatives in all processed food was his recommendation. "I was converted by my own investigations," he said.[8]

None of this seemed to have any effect on the general public.

General Miles's outrage, Governor Roosevelt's disgust, the Beef Court's findings of "colossal error," Senator Mason's fifty-one days of hearings, Harvey Wiley and his five years of Poison Squads—nothing seemed to affect the public's opinion of the packers and the food they sold.

In fact, in September 1900 the *Chicago Tribune* published an article that reported "Most Visitors to Chicago Flock to See Cattle Killed / Average 500 a Day / Sometimes Number Reaches 30,000."

The article described the tours the packers conducted through their plants. Crowds of visitors on elevated walkways jammed balconies to watch the spectacle below: snorts and bellows and squeals came in at one end and, out the other, brightly labeled cans and neatly wrapped packages. Tour guides recited the plants' production figures: fifty varieties of canned meats, thirty varieties of smoked meats, twenty kinds of salted meats, 123 varieties of sausages, twelve varieties of pharmaceutical and commercial pepsins, eighty kinds of lubricating oils, 150 varieties of soap . . .

People from everywhere came to watch the packers work their magic. "Ordinarily," wrote a reporter for the *Tribune*, "an Englishman can not

EGGS

FRESH LONG-ISLAND EGGS—With Bread and Butter
Boiled, two 15   Fried, two 15
Shirred 20   Scrambled 20
Scrambled on toast 25
Scrambled on toast with asparagus tips 30
Poached, two...........20   Poached on toast, two 25
Plain omelet 25
Omelet with ham, parsley, asparagus tips or tomatoes 30
Oyster omelet.... 35
Each additional egg with above orders 5
Two boiled or fried eggs when served with any
    order, where bread and butter is served
    without extra of either 10
When poached, scrambled or shirred 15

TOASTS—ALL KINDS
WITH OR WITHOUT BUTTER
Cream or milk toast, white or Graham bread 15
    "   "   health or gluten   " --- 15
    "   "   Boston brown   " --- 15
    "   "   crackers or muffins..........15
Toasted corn or English muffins, dry or buttered ..10
Toasted rolls or crackers, dry or buttered 10
Dry or buttered toast, any kind 10
Dry toast with pitcher of milk.... 15
Dry or buttered toast in place of bread with orders 5

HOT GRIDDLE CAKES
WITH GOLDEN DRIPS, MAPLE SYRUP
OR NEW ORLEANS MOLASSES
Buckwheat, Rice, Wheat or Indian griddle cakes..15

FARINACEOUS FOOD

Oatmeal, hot or cold   } with pure maple syrup ..15
Boiled rice, hot or cold   with N. O. molasses ...15
Hot crushed wheat   with pitcher of milk ...15
Hominy, cold   with small jug of cream. 15
     with pitcher of cream ..25
     with ½ milk and ½ cream 20
     Additional plate oatmeal,
Plain 10   With butter 15   rice or wheat, etc.... 5
     Additional pitcher milk..10

CRACKERS, ROLLS ETC.

Milk crackers
Oatmeal crackers   plain 5
Boston crackers   toasted 10
Graham crackers   with butter 10
Pilot crackers   with pure maple syrup ..10
Uneeda biscuit   with N. O. molasses.....10
Shredded wheat   with pitcher of milk 15
Corn muffins   with pitcher of cream ...25
Zwieback   with ½ milk, ½ cream 20
Vienna rolls   Additional plate rolls,
Vienna bread   bread, crackers etc..... 5
Rye bread   Additional pitcher milk ..10
Graham bread
Boston brown bread
Health or gluten bread

BREAD, ROLLS ETC.

Vienna bread 5   with butter 10
Rye or Graham bread .. 5   with butter 10
Genuine Boston brown bread 5   with butter 10
Zwieback 5   with butter 10
Crackers, plate 5   with butter ... .10
English muffins, hot or cold, two 5   with butter....10
Corn muffins.. 5   with butter   10   with milk 15
Vienna rolls 5   with butter 10
Cheese, plate. 5
Maple syrup.... 5
Cream, small jug 5
Butter, plate..... 5

Rye, Graham, Vienna, Boston brown or health bread
  served with orders.

Crackers served in place of bread with orders, if
  desired.   Rolls, muffins and all other articles
  are extra.

*We strive to please our customers in every way,
and to make this Restaurant as* **home-like**
as possible.

We do not claim that our **Milk** *and*
Cream *come from our own dairy, but* **do**
claim them to be **unexcelled.** *Meats used
are the* **best** *obtainable, and while* **Philadelphia Poultry, Boston Ducks**
and **Long Island Eggs** *cost us more,
you will find nothing else on our tables.*

Everything *used is absolutely fresh and the best in the market, but special
mention is made of our* **Coffee.** *Try it!*

Fridays *a special* **Fish** *Bill of Fare.*

THOMAS H. BORDEN, 46 VESEY STREET, N. Y.

Menu, Arnold's Restaurant and Dairy, New York, 1901

be held away from the yards [even] with a cowboy's lariat. Chinese visitors are not infrequent. Japanese travelers go there in shoal . . . a few days ago, a guide in a big plant had a group of ten [visitors] in tow when it developed that there were an Australian, an Afrikaner, a Japanese, three Englishmen and a Scotchman among the larger groups of Western [ranchers] who wished to see where their corn-fed cattle went."

The facade of this grand industrial edifice — where animal chaos was changed into packaged convenience — held until 1902, when a teamsters' strike — a short, vicious, and violent strike — cracked the plaster of the packers' stage set. Two years later another strike — a long, difficult, and inconclusive butchers' strike — shook the packers' scenery once again.

The teamsters' strike succeeded; the butchers' strike appeared to accomplish nothing except that it brought Upton Sinclair to Chicago. Whatever the packers had been able to convince the public to believe, whatever the public itself had chosen to believe, Upton Sinclair's *The Jungle* changed everything.

Very briefly: the butchers' strike of 1904 lasted fifty-nine days, from July into September. It involved 40,000 men in nine cities, from Chicago to Omaha to New York. It failed not only because the teamsters didn't support it, but because most of the butchers union's 40,000 men were unskilled and easily replaced. The year 1904 was a recession year. The packers kept operating, in one city, then another, by hiring thousands of replacements. African Americans and brand-new immigrants (Italians, mostly) kept the kill lines running. The packers paid the new men even less than they'd paid the butchers.

"I never saw such a quiet strike where there are so many men involved in my twenty-eight years experience," said a police sergeant stationed outside the main entrance to the Chicago yards.

By "quiet" he meant that a mob of a thousand boys and girls ambushed a sixteen-year old named Josephine Rominsky when she was walking home after work "in the dried beef department of the Armour plant." The mob stoned her but didn't kill her. "My mother and father are dead and I have to work for a living," she was quoted as saying in the *Chicago Tribune.*

Another mob — two thousand union men — "treed" an African-American man who had just come to town from Kansas City. The mob treed the man by chasing him through the streets, then up onto the roof of a house. Stockyard police rescued him. The man said he wasn't a strikebreaker.

A larger mob—some five thousand this time—ambushed three trolley cars full of African Americans who'd been hired by the Hammond Company. The mob stoned the cars, but police stopped them before they could drag anyone away to be killed.

Because of all the strikes and upheavals in Chicago in the past, from the McCormick Harvesting Machine Company strike and Haymarket riot of 1886 to the Pullman strike of 1894 and the extraordinarily violent teamsters' strike of 1902, people everywhere in the United States watched and worried and thought about what might happen as the butchers' strike continued.

Many of the people who watched and worried about the butchers' strike read the same magazine: an illustrated monthly called *McClure's*, which was probably the best written, best edited, and most financially successful magazine of its time. In 1902 *McClure's* published, in a single issue, three articles (an article on Standard Oil by Ida Tarbell, an article about municipal corruption by Lincoln Steffens, and an article on labor unions by Ray Stannard Baker) by three of the greatest investigative reporters and writers in the history of American journalism. *McClure's* investigative and reformist agenda—what President Roosevelt later called "muckraking"—made it one of the most popular *and* most profitable magazines in the country.[9] Other publishers took note. They could do well by doing good. Magazines modeled on *McClure's* proliferated.

One of those magazines—a pulpy, scrappy, 250,000-circulation socialist broadside, based in Girard, Kansas, and run by a man whose admirers fancied him to be a reincarnation of Tom Paine—was a weekly called the *Appeal to Reason*.

In September 1904 Upton Sinclair sent the *Appeal* a long, unsolicited article about the glorious struggle of the butchers in Chicago. The butchers' strike had collapsed by then, but Sinclair and the editors of the *Appeal* loved proletarian martyrs. The *Appeal* published Sinclair's article.

The *Appeal*'s readers—hard-luck farmers, small-town druggists, one-room-school teachers, time-clock-driven factory workers—loved Sinclair's message: the plutocrats' days are numbered! Their fate is written on the wall! Lincoln freed the slaves. But now (asked Sinclair) who would free the wage slaves, the toilers, the workers of the world? Eugene Debs, answered Sinclair. Debs, the Socialist Party's candidate for president, is the workers' new Lincoln! The ballot box is the workers' hope! The future belongs to them!

Sinclair was a very boyish and ambitious twenty-six-year-old when he sent his version of "workers of the world unite" to the *Appeal*. For years, Sinclair had supported himself as a hack, writing fake autobiographical accounts of himself as a West Point cadet or an Annapolis midshipman.

At the age of twenty-two Sinclair had decided his destiny was to become a pure, literary artist. Between 1900 and 1904 he wrote three barely readable novels—one called *Springtime and Harvest*, about "a woman's soul, redeemed by love"; another, called *A Captain of Industry*, was about an American robber baron named Robbie van Rensselaer. In between writing about redemptive love and ruthless moneymaking, Sinclair produced something called the *Journal of Arthur Sterling*. The *Journal* was a fabricated document, said to have been left behind by a fabricated "poet and man of genius" who'd killed himself because he was too pure a soul to live in so crass and shallow a world.[10]

In 1902 Sinclair fell into the hands of a little group of caviar and champagne socialists who shamed him into reading Marx, Veblen, and Bellamy (the author of the utopian novel *Looking Backward*). Sinclair had been to college; he'd even gone to graduate school (at Columbia), but nothing by Marx or Veblen had appeared on his reading lists.

In 1903 Sinclair wrote and signed a manifesto/squawk of protest entitled "My Cause." It read as if it had been written by Sinclair's alter ego, the dead poet and man of genius Arthur Sterling.

One of Sinclair's new socialist friends, a middle-aged ex-minister and former college professor, married to a rich bluestocking, read "My Cause" and took it to heart. He asked Sinclair what he really wanted to do with his life. Sinclair told him he wanted to write a Civil War trilogy, an American *War and Peace*. How much would he need to get started? asked the man. Would $800 (equivalent to about $20,000 today) be enough for him to begin?

Sinclair took the money, packed up his wife and baby son, and moved to Princeton, New Jersey. He moved there because Princeton University's library contained Civil War documents. For a year, Sinclair sat and read and studied and wrote, surrounded by Princeton's gilded youth—the sons and grandsons of America's robber barons. Sinclair and his wife and child lived in a one-room cabin. The place was cold and damp and lonely. Sinclair's wife tried to kill herself.

Sinclair called the first volume of his trilogy *Manassas*, which was the name of the first bloody battle of the Civil War, a Union defeat that the North remembered as the Battle of Bull Run. He sent a manuscript copy of his book to George Brett, the publisher of Macmillan. The same people who read such magazines as *McClure's* had begun to buy such books as *The Red Badge of Courage* (1895) and *McTeague* (1899). In 1902 Brett had acquired and Macmillan had published Owen Wister's *The Virginian*; the next year Macmillan published Jack London's *Call of the Wild*. Brett had a reputation for spotting new talent and publishing books that became best sellers.

Brett not only read Sinclair's manuscript but offered him a contract with an advance of $500 (equivalent to $12,000 today). Sinclair thought his future had arrived.

As *Manassas* moved from manuscript to galleys Sinclair had time to sit and think. He read about the butchers' strike in Chicago; he read the investigations and revelations that *McClure's* kept publishing; he read and reread the books his socialist friends had given him.

He had an epiphany.

Everything he'd learned and believed while writing *Manassas* collided with everything he'd learned while reading Marx and Veblen and Bellamy: Lincoln and the Union dead had sacrificed their lives to free the slaves; the planter class had been swept away. A new class of masters now ruled a new class of slaves. The plutocrats — Rockefeller and Swift, Carnegie and Armour — were the new Simon Legrees. The men who toiled in their mills and factories and packing plants were the new slaves.

Manassas was published in the summer of 1904. Reviewers liked it but no one hailed its author as America's new Tolstoy. Worse yet, it sold under 2,000 copies. No fame; no fortune. George Brett thought it was all very promising. Sinclair was dismayed. His wife hadn't come close to killing herself for the sake of "promising." Stories about the present were what people wanted to read. The world was in turmoil. There were fires burning, visible on the horizon. It was the destiny of a literary artist to write about them.

Sinclair sent his article about the butchers' strike — along with a copy of *Manassas* — to the *Appeal*. The *Appeal*'s editors made him an offer: he would be paid $500 for a novel about the men who had just risen up against their masters in Chicago. The *Appeal* would publish what Sinclair wrote, in installments, as he wrote it.

Sinclair took the offer to Macmillan. Brett did the math: 250,000 potential readers were more promising than 2,000 in sales. He offered

Sinclair a new contract and he advanced him $500 for his new wage-slave book. The promise of a book about slaves had just won Sinclair the equivalent of $24,000.

On November 3, 1904, Sinclair checked into the Transit House hotel next to the Union Stock Yards. The Transit House was a place where cattlemen and cattle dealers, newspaper reporters and union strike committees met and drank and talked and took one another's measure. Sinclair walked in wearing the uniform of an East Coast aesthete — wide-brimmed hat, loose, floppy tie. Everyone looked at him, then looked away.

The first man who saw Sinclair for what he was — and talked to him — was an East Coast transplant to Chicago named Ernest Poole. Poole was a 1902 Princeton graduate who was nothing like the gilded youth who'd surrounded Sinclair while he wrote *Manassas*. Poole's first job had been in a New York City settlement house; his second job — which is why he was hanging out at the Transit House — was as an unpaid publicist for the butchers union. Unpaid or not, Poole had written news articles about the butchers' strike. One of them featured a fabricated interview with a fabricated stockyard worker named "Antanas Kaztauskis." Poole intended Kaztauskis to serve as an immigrant-worker everyman. Much of what Kaztauskis said happened to him would later happen to another imaginary stockyard worker, *The Jungle*'s Lithuanian hero, Jurgis Rudkus.

The story goes that the first thing Sinclair said to Poole when they met was that he'd come to Chicago to write the "*Uncle Tom's Cabin* of the labor movement."[11] Whether Sinclair actually said that or not, Poole began to introduce him to helpful people.

Poole began with a Bureau of Charities' welfare agent and Board of Health "volunteer inspector" named Algie Simons. In 1899 Simons had written a pamphlet called "Packing Town" that was full of hair-raising stories about the misfortunes immigrant workers and their families suffered. Just as the stories that "Antanas Kaztauskis" told Ernest Poole later ended up in *The Jungle*, so did many of the degradations, dismemberments, and catastrophes Algie Simons described in "Packing Town."

After Simons, Poole introduced Sinclair to two remarkable women: Mary McDowell, the director of the settlement house run by the University of Chicago next to the stockyards, and Jane Addams, the legendary director of Hull House. McDowell had served the stockyard

The sheep department—Armour's great packinghouse, Chicago, Illinois

workers and their families since 1894. During the butchers' strike she had done everything she could to help them. People called her the Angel of the Stockyards. She offered Sinclair a room. McDowell's settlement house became Sinclair's base of operations, as he came and went from the yards, disguised as a workman.

Jane Addams seemed to know everyone, rich or poor, distinguished or destitute, in the city. A man to whom she introduced Sinclair, a British public health investigator and writer named Adolph Smith, became Sinclair's medical expert, adviser, and guide. Smith had studied commercial slaughterhouse operations in England and Germany. In particular, he had studied slaughterhouse hygiene and worker health and safety. The conditions he observed in Chicago — conditions he showed and explained to Sinclair during undercover visits to the Armour plant — were not just filthy, and not just cruel to the animals, but they were dangerous and degrading to the men and women whom Armour employed. A few months later, as Sinclair sat in New Jersey beginning work on *The Jungle*, the British medical journal the *Lancet* published a series of articles by Smith that described and analyzed all that he'd witnessed in Chicago.[12]

After seven weeks of sneaking into and out of the stockyards, and talking to anyone with a story to tell — from workers and saloon keepers to priests and undertakers — Sinclair returned to New Jersey. He moved his family into an old farmhouse with a scrollwork porch and three chimneys. On Christmas day he began work on *The Jungle*.

For three months, Sinclair wrote without pause. In February 1905 his son nearly died of pneumonia. Sinclair wept as he wrote. At the end of the month, the *Appeal* published *The Jungle*'s first chapter. For eight months, as Sinclair sent installments to the *Appeal*, he sent copies to George Brett. The more Brett read, the more uneasy he became.

The end of chapter nine alarmed him.

Jurgis, the book's hero, had just begun to learn English. And he began to understand the stories other people told him.

> Jurgis heard these things, little by little . . . There was, for instance, a Lithuanian who was a cattle butcher for a plant . . . which killed meat for canning only . . . to hear this man describe the animals which came to his killing floor would have been worthwhile for Dante or a Zola . . . On the prairies nearby . . . were hundreds of farms which supplied the city with milk, and all the cows that . . . fell sick or died of old age — they kept them till they had a carload, then shipped them to this place to be canned. Here came also cattle which had been fed on . . . the refuse of the breweries and had become covered with boils . . . It was a nasty job killing these, for when you plunged your knife into them, they would burst and splash foul smelly stuff into your face . . . it was enough to make anybody sick to think that people had to eat such meat as this; but they must be eating it — for the canners were going on preparing it, year after year! . . . No doubt

it was stuff such as this that made the "embalmed beef" that killed
several times as many United States soldiers as all the bullets of the
Spaniards; only the army beef besides, was not fresh canned, it was
old stuff that had been lying around for years in the cellars.

The chapter continued. Brett kept reading:

Then, one Sunday evening, Jurgis sat, puffing his pipe . . . and talking
with an old fellow . . . who worked in the cannery room at Anderson
["Anderson" was the name Sinclair had given to Armour] . . . They
were regular alchemists to Anderson . . . they advertised "potted
chicken" and it was like the boarding house soup of the comic papers
through which a chicken had walked with rubbers on. Perhaps they
had a secret process for making chickens chemically . . . the things that
went into the mixture were tripe and the fat of pork and beef suet
and hearts of beef and finally the waste ends of veal, when they had
any . . . and then there was the "potted ham" and the "deviled ham" . . .
made out of the waste ends of smoked beef and also tripe, dyed with
chemicals so that it would not show white.

The chapter ended with the old man telling Jurgis how each job in the
Anderson plant created different diseases or deformities in the men who
did the work. The men on the pickling counters handled meat that had
been bathed in solutions of acid. The acid slowly ate away their fingers,
joint by joint. The men who worked in the steaming rooms were exposed
to tuberculosis germs that thrived on the moist heat, dim light, and
foul air.

"Worst of any, however," said the old man to Jurgis, "were . . . those
who served in the rendering rooms . . . in which there were open vats
upon a level floor; their peculiar trouble was that they fell into the
vats; and when they were fished out, there was never enough of them
left to be worth exhibiting . . . sometimes they would be overlooked
for days till all but the bones of them had gone out into the world as
Anderson's Pure Leaf Lard."

Brett didn't consider himself an overly sensitive man, but he was
upset. He began forwarding Sinclair's installments to readers at Columbia
University.

*Scalding hogs
preparatory to scraping*

A passage at the beginning of chapter fourteen made Brett's readers stop in disbelief. Not because of what Sinclair had written, but because he seemed to believe that Macmillan would actually publish it.

The passage was an account of how the packing plant where Jurgis's wife worked made sausage.

There was never the least attention paid to what was cut up for sausage; there would come, all the way back from Europe, old sausage that had been rejected and that was moldy and white — it would be dosed with borax and glycerin and dumped into hoppers and made over again for home consumption. There would be meat that had tumbled out into the floor, in the dirt and sawdust where workers had trampled and spit uncounted billions of consumption germs. There would be meat stored in great piles in rooms . . . and thousands of rats would race about on it . . . a man could run his hands over these piles of meat and sweep off handfuls of the dried dung of rats . . . the packers would put poisoned bread out for [the rats]; they would die and then the rats, bread and meat would go into the hoppers together.

Late in September of 1905 Brett canceled Macmillan's contract with Sinclair. The book Sinclair had written was too ugly, too violent, and too politically extreme for the publisher. Worse yet, the book was a lawsuit waiting to happen. A lawsuit Macmillan was sure to lose. So much of what Sinclair had written was preposterous. Even if only a shred of it was true, the packers had more money and more lawyers than Macmillan. Brett told Sinclair he could keep the $500 advance but, said Brett, he felt it professionally, and ethically, incumbent on him to inform the *Appeal* of his decision.

Brett didn't know — and Sinclair didn't know — that the *Appeal* was thinking of walking away from its deal as well. Not because *The Jungle* was too violent but because it had become too dull, too preachy. After Jurgis's son had drowned in the mud outside the family's wretched little house near the stockyards, after Jurgis's wife had been seduced by her boss and then died in childbirth, after her cousin had become a whore (addicted to morphine) to earn money for the family, and finally after Jurgis had become a criminal, then a beggar, then a scab — after all this, the *Appeal*'s readers had begun to lose interest.

The *Appeal*'s original editor, the man whose admirers thought was the new Tom Paine, had retired. The man who succeeded him liked politically correct sex and violence more than polemics. In October, he came to New Jersey to talk things over with Sinclair. Sinclair knew what was at stake. After dinner, he sat the man down by the fire and read him the last, uplifting chapters of *The Jungle*. Sinclair read the story of Jurgis's socialist epiphany with as much passion as he could muster. The man fell asleep. Chapter twenty-eight was the last installment of *The Jungle* that the *Appeal* published.

Munsey's Magazine,
January 1901

A young Doubleday, Page editor named Marcosson saved Sinclair's life. Back in 1902 Marcosson had read, liked, and reviewed Sinclair's fabricated *Journal of Arthur Sterling*, the counterfeit diary of the counterfeit "poet and man of genius" who killed himself. For years, Marcosson had made a living writing mild-mannered articles for a mild-mannered muckraking magazine called the *World's Work*. He yearned to do something more exciting. Which is why, in 1905, the first book Marcosson acquired and edited — and marketed — for Doubleday, Page was Thomas Dixon's sensational and sensationally racist book *The Clansman*. Marcosson engineered newspaper and magazine publicity for Dixon's book that made it a best seller. (In 1915, the filmmaker D. W. Griffith made Dixon's book into the movie *The Birth of a Nation*.)

Sinclair knew about Dixon's book when he walked into Marcosson's office with a typescript of *The Jungle*. When Marcosson asked him what he had, Sinclair said he had "something sensational." Marcosson took *The Jungle* home with him. He started reading it and couldn't stop. "Spellbound" was the word he used when he told his boss Walter Page what had happened to him.

In 1900 Doubleday had published Dreiser's *Sister Carrie* by printing one hundred copies and then ignoring it. In England, Dreiser's book was wonderfully reviewed, and it sold well. In 1903 Doubleday published Frank Norris's posthumous novel *The Pit* and made money. Those experiences, combined with the blockbuster success of *The Clansman*, taught the company a lesson. Marcosson told Page that if he and Frank Doubleday didn't say yes to *The Jungle*, they should have court-appointed guardians named for them.[13] *The Jungle* might or might not be a work of art, said Marcosson, but it would make news.

Page hesitated. He sent a copy of Sinclair's typescript to Chicago, to the managing editor of the *Tribune*. True or not? Page asked. The *Tribune*'s managing editor handed the typescript to a reporter, who happened to be a publicity agent for Armour. "False," came back the report. Inaccurate. Trivial. Exaggerated. Wrong.

Sinclair counterattacked. The *Tribune* was out to get him. Send your own people to Chicago to find out the truth, said Sinclair. Page decided to do just that: he sent Marcosson and the company's own lawyer.

"True enough" came back their report. Page insisted that Sinclair tone down the book's socialist rhetoric — starting with the title. Sinclair agreed to edit his socialist sermons but he refused to change his title.

Doubleday, Page signed the contract for *The Jungle* on January 8, 1906.

Marcosson sent page proofs to the Associated Press and the United Press for distribution to their subscribers. Let the newspapers know, Marcosson said, that they can quote anything they want. The book was going to make headlines. For two reasons.

First, in February 1905, *Everybody's Magazine* — an illustrated monthly with a circulation of 150,000 — had published a series of investigative articles about "the Beef Trust" by Charles Edward Russell. In October 1905 Russell put together a book based on the evidence he'd collected about Armour's and Swift's massive price fixing. Russell titled the book *The Greatest Trust in the World*. Said the reviewer in the *New York Times*, "Accepting Mr. Russell's figures as correct, it must be owned that he seems to justify his ascription of the title."

Second, the same month Russell's book was published, *Collier's* magazine — an illustrated weekly with a circulation of 300,000 — began running articles about "the Great American Fraud," otherwise known as the American patent medicine industry. *Collier's* articles described tonics, syrups, and powders that were either loaded with alcohol or laced with narcotics or had nothing in them but colored water.

Collier's published the last of its exposés on February 17, 1906.

Nine days later, Doubleday, Page sent review copies of *The Jungle* to every magazine and newspaper that AP or UP might have missed. Marcosson sent a special review copy to President Roosevelt. Sinclair sent the president one, too.

A bonfire, seven years in the making, was about to start.

No one person or event had laid the kindling. In 1903 Sinclair had begun his "My Cause" manifesto — his squawk of protest — with the words, "I, Upton Sinclair, would-be singer and penniless rat." Three years later, that penniless rat had rubbed his whiskers together and started a fire that would spread to one of the biggest and most powerful accumulations of industrial capital in America.

Within three months of *The Jungle*'s publication, the book had been translated into seventeen languages and sold enough copies worldwide to make Sinclair a rich man. At the end of June 1906, Congress passed and the president signed into law the Pure Food and Drug Act and the Meat Inspection Act (attached as an amendment to an agriculture appropriations bill). The regulatory and enforcement provisions of these acts were shadows and ciphers of what they might have been had they been passed within weeks of *The Jungle*'s publication. The uproar and debate, public and private, that preceded the bills' passage had as much, perhaps more, effect on the packers (and the patent medicine industry) as the laws themselves.

These events came in clusters that bounced off each other, daily, weekly, and monthly, like metal balls in a pachinko game. Sometimes, they read like excerpts from a political science text, sometimes like case studies from a business school manual, and sometimes like scenes from a comedy of errors.

To begin:

Early in March 1906, as the shouts of public outrage grew louder, an Armour company lawyer paid a call on Frank Doubleday. Doubleday liked selling books as much as any publisher, but he didn't like Upton Sinclair, nor his politics, nor the effect *The Jungle* was having on America's reputation abroad.

Doubleday had just received a telegram from a British newspaper owner and publisher asking to buy British and European rights for *The Jungle*. Doubleday was about to refuse the man when the lawyer from Armour was shown into his office.

The lawyer explained that Mr. J. Ogden Armour had sent him to see Mr. Doubleday. Mr. Armour happened to be in New York. Would Mr. Doubleday care to join Mr. Armour for lunch? Mr. Armour's private railcar was waiting on the tracks at Grand Central.

Doubleday asked the lawyer what it was that Mr. Armour wished to discuss. An advertising contract, said the lawyer. Advertising for what? asked Doubleday. The lawyer answered indirectly. *The Jungle* was having an effect on Armour's British and European sales. Such sales were considerable as, no doubt, Mr. Doubleday knew. (In fact, combined export sales by American packers were more than "considerable." In 1906 American packers sold $100 million worth of "meat products" to Europe alone. Those figures—worth $2.6 billion today—did not include the nine million five-ounce ration cans of beef that the packers had sold to the Japanese army during the recent Russo-Japanese War.[14])

Yes? said Mr. Doubleday. The lawyer continued. If Doubleday, Page would consider limiting publicity for as well as publication of *The Jungle*, here and abroad, Mr. Armour would be grateful. Details could, of course, be discussed during lunch. The lawyer reached into his briefcase. For the moment, though, said the lawyer, Mr. Armour had requested him to present Mr. Doubleday with a small token of his respect and regard. The lawyer handed Mr. Doubleday a large can of corned beef.

Doubleday threw the man out of his office.

"Of all the moral degenerates I ever saw," Doubleday later wrote, "he was the worst." Doubleday gave the British publisher permission to reproduce and sell editions of *The Jungle* throughout the British Isles and Europe. Over the next twenty-six years, in England alone, *The Jungle* went through sixty-seven printings.[15]

A week after Armour's lawyer offered Mr. Doubleday a can of meat, Theodore Roosevelt sent Upton Sinclair a three-page letter. The president had initially sent a note to Sinclair, saying he'd read *The Jungle* and that he agreed the packers had been behaving badly. He suggested Sinclair contact the government's commissioner of corporations. Sinclair wrote back to say that the abuses and degradations he'd described were of epic proportions—the stuff of great novels and great novelists. Tolstoy, Zola, and Gorky never would have talked to any such entity as a "commission of corporations" and neither would he. That prompted the president's three-page letter. Zola was, by all reports, a degenerate; Gorky was leading his followers over a cliff; Tolstoy had a diseased moral nature. As to socialism, foreign or domestic, it was nothing but a collection of weaklings, banded together. If, wrote the president, Mr. Sinclair cared to discuss these matters further he was welcome to visit. The first week of April would be most convenient.

Sinclair accepted the invitation. He felt the wind at his back: new, pure food bills were pending, one in the Senate, one in the House. Harvey Wiley, the Agriculture Department's Poison Squad man, had been called to testify. "Two million children in this country have been killed by poisonous milk," Wiley had said, quoted in the *Chicago Tribune*. "One thousand babies have succumbed to false soothing syrups and pain killers."

In Chicago, the General Federation of Women (representing women's clubs throughout the United States) had asked Jane Addams herself to address a Pure Food Symposium. "With the exception of China," Addams said, also reported in the *Tribune*, "the United States is the only civilized nation that is without pure food legislation . . . such a condition is shameful . . . We must have protection against the adulterated food products with which this country is flooded . . . The fact is, we could have had it long ago if the women of our country had demanded it . . . To say it is none of our business whether people eat poisoned food . . . is not true . . . When we demand national legislation, we are only doing on a large scale what women have been doing individually for a thousand years. In this matter of federal legislation, women all over the country must take it up and agitate the question and demand Congress that it give the nation protection."

On April 4, Sinclair was shown into the president's study. He noticed that *The Jungle*, marked with index cards, lay on a table next to Roosevelt's easy chair. So did *Cosmopolitan* magazine, which had printed in the latest issue a sensational piece of investigative reporting by David Graham Phillips titled "The Treason of the Senate." What Sinclair didn't know, as he looked at the president, was that at least one of the packers (probably Swift) had contributed $200,000 (equivalent to $6 million, today) to the president's 1904 election campaign,[16] and that ten days later Roosevelt would deliver a speech (first, in private and off the record, to the Gridiron Club in Washington, and then, in public, at a ceremony at the House of Representatives office building) that would condemn the articles that *McClure's* and others had published and the books that Russell and Sinclair himself wrote. The president would call them "muckraking."[17]

For the moment, though, Roosevelt needed to find a way to make the packers listen to reason. He hadn't forgotten the canned beef he and his men had been given to eat in Cuba; he knew the size of the packers' export market and he also knew that if the packers didn't change what they did and how they did it they would lose that market. (Roosevelt was right. By June 1906 the year-to-year export of American "tinned meat" had fallen by 85 percent. By August of 1907 the year-to-year decline had leveled off to 75 percent. To be fair, part of the 1905–1906 decline was due to the end of the Russo-Japanese War in 1905.[18]) Worse than being greedy, the packers were complacent. If Roosevelt had to use Sinclair the way a zookeeper used a prod, so be it.

Sinclair, of course, wanted to use Roosevelt as well. He would have preferred an ax to a long pole. Each man understood the other's utility. They reached an agreement.

The Department of Agriculture had already sent a pair of its own investigators to Chicago. Roosevelt told Sinclair he thought their report was a whitewash. Now, said Roosevelt, he planned to send his own team. Would Sinclair care to join them? Roosevelt asked. Sinclair declined; to join the team would be to investigate himself. He was curious, though. Who was the president sending? Mr. Charles Neill, commissioner of labor, said Roosevelt. Sinclair was pleased. *The Jungle* was about wage slaves. Mr. Neill would be assisted by James Reynolds, Roosevelt added. Sinclair was even more pleased. Reynolds was the president's own special investigator. Better yet, Reynolds was a friend of Ernest Poole, the Princeton grad who'd spotted Sinclair when he'd first walked into Chicago's Transit House. Poole and Reynolds had worked together in the same New York City settlement house.

As the meeting ended, Roosevelt asked Sinclair to keep their conversation confidential. Of course, said Sinclair.

The next day, Sinclair sent a telegram to a special investigator of his own, a former newspaper reporter now living in New Jersey. Sinclair had learned that someone in the White House had told a reporter at the *Chicago Tribune* that Neill and Reynolds were headed to Chicago. The *Tribune* had tipped off the packers. The packers had dragooned hundreds of men to scrub everything clean. Sinclair told the New Jersey reporter—a woman named Ella Reeve—that she had to rush to Chicago and line up witnesses to counter the packers. Sinclair said he'd pay for whatever Reeve needed. ("Whatever Reeve needed" ended up costing Sinclair the modern equivalent of $20,000.[19])

On April 11, the *Tribune* published an editorial titled "Investigating a Novel." *The Jungle* is "garbage fiction," the *Tribune* editorial writer said. The book's author "has pretended to describe revolting conditions at the stockyards [that] do not exist, but were woven on the loom of his imagination." The president seems to have taken the book seriously, the editorial continued, only because "it occurred to him that the American export trade of meat would be destroyed if foreigners were led to believe that the novel dealt with facts." The editorial ended by declaring that "the conditions depicted are the product of the distempered imagination and credulous mind of a pseudo social reformer."

Sinclair had begun telephoning and telegramming the White House. Roosevelt spoke with Frank Doubleday. "Tell Sinclair to go home and let me run the country for awhile," he said.[20]

As Neill and Reynolds began talking to informants and exploring the packing plants—always accompanied by guides—the *Saturday Evening Post*, the giant of American illustrated weekly magazines (its circulation nearly equaled *McClure's* and *Collier's* combined), began publishing articles by Ogden Armour himself. The articles were dignified and detailed—turgid too—but they worried Sinclair. (They worried Sinclair even more when he discovered they were written by a *Post* staffer whose boss had once worked for Armour's father.) Sinclair moved to New York, rented rooms in a hotel, hired two secretaries, and began churning out articles for *Collier's* and *Everybody's*.

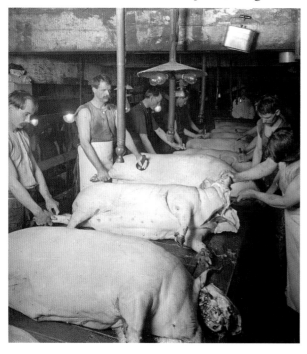

Hogs arranged on moving bench for final scraping, Chicago

After several weeks Neill and Reynolds came back to Washington, amazed by what they'd seen. They briefed the president, but Roosevelt refused to let them put anything in writing. He began to use the threat of their, as yet, unseen and unpublished report to prod the packers and their allies in Congress. Details of what Neill and Reynolds told him began to leak out; as word spread, the president let it be known how much he hoped—for everyone's sake—that the packers wouldn't stand in the way of reform. *Now* was the time, said the president, *before* the Neill/Reynolds report was published, to reach an agreement that would benefit everyone. Neither the packers nor Sinclair saw things as the president did. Sinclair wanted everything revealed immediately; the packers wanted everything put in a box and buried.

In Congress, members of the Senate and the House set about reconciling each other's pure food bills, one with the other. Almost everyone (except the patent medicine makers and the people who added flavors and colors to ethyl alcohol and sold it as whiskey) agreed there should be labels, but no one wanted the labels to be too precise, nor should the labels have dates. A meat inspection amendment passed by the Senate began making its way to the House Agriculture Committee. The committee chairman, a New York State cattle dealer, had gutted earlier inspection measures by agreeing with them, then not funding them. The cattle dealer was ably assisted by a Chicago congressman named "Blond Billy" Lorimer. Lorimer had risen from being a packinghouse worker to being the packers' own elected representative in Congress. (As the meat scandal ran its course, Lorimer campaigned for reelection. At an election rally, Lorimer served twenty-year-old canned corned beef to his supporters. He won, handily.)

Late in May, Charles Neill began to hold private meetings with the packers and their congressional allies. In a series of back-to-back meetings with a congressman, a Union Stock Yards representative, and several senators, Neill described — and the *Tribune* summarized — a few of the things he'd seen in Chicago.

Preparing hams for market, Chicago

"The floors were so filthy," said Neill, "that the blood and grease oozed through and fell upon the good meat that was to be canned."

"Employees walked around in the dirt in which they expectorated and gathered up in their boots any bacilli of tuberculosis which might be flying about and afterwards walked upon the carcasses to be used in interstate commerce."

"A hog which had slipped from a trolley and fallen into a vile place [a latrine] was taken out and without being cleaned was sent along and cut up for food."

"A brand of sausage was anything but sausage."

"The conditions under which the women employees in the cannery department work were deplorable. They were compelled to stand in water much of the time and the temperature of the room was low."

At another meeting — a not-so-secret secret meeting in May — attended by Neill, the president, and Louis Swift, who had recently taken command of Swift & Company after the death of his father, the *Tribune* reported, "Mr. Swift declared emphatically that the condition of affairs Neill and

Reynolds claim to have found did not exist." Mr. Swift went on to say that, "If a commission of men of average intelligence should investigate the meat producing businesses, they would find it conducted in a proper and sanitary manner." Mr. Neill was said to have replied that "he considered himself a man of average intelligence and that as soon as he returned to Washington, after his investigation, he gave instructions that no meat products should be served on his table except fresh beef and mutton."

A day after Neill and the president met with young Mr. Swift, Upton Sinclair invited a *New York Times* reporter to his hotel room for an interview. Since the *Times* (as well as Sinclair) had been thoroughly briefed by Neill himself, the paper chose to print everything it had learned from Neill on its front page and everything it was told by Sinclair on its second page.

Cutting up hogs—removing hams and shoulder, Swift & Co.

Said Sinclair: "In Armour's establishment, I saw with my own eyes the doctoring of hams that were so putrified that I could not force myself to remain near them. The hams were on a working table and a man with a foot pump, which worked on the principle of a giant hypodermic needle, filled them with a chemical that killed the odor."

Said Neill: "The carcasses of hogs which had died of cholera in shipment or which had been smothered in transit . . . were rendered into hog grease which was sold without restriction or precaution . . . portions of this grease were regularly sent to France to be used in the making of a grade of sardine oil."

Said Sinclair, quoting from an affidavit given by a Swift salesman who, for seven years, had free access to the company's packing operations: "Swift & Co.'s 'Cervelat' [brand] sausage is made of beef weasands [windpipes], certain other parts that are not permissible to mention on paper, ends of beef cartilage, etc., and without exception, the cheaper grades of sausage made by Swift & Co. are preserved with 'Curine' which is a combination of borax and some embalming fluid."

Said Neill: "The use of preservatives is universal . . . spoiled meats are doctored . . . smoked meats are imitated by means of artificial coloring and preserved with dangerous chemicals . . . many of the packing house products bear false labels and . . . imitations are made with aniline dyes."

Said Sinclair: "There is no such thing as stopping a sausage machine when one of the operators loses a finger or even a hand. The member goes in . . . and comes out as sausage. Instances of this kind are so common that they cause not the slightest comment. The operators are all uncleanly and many of them are afflicted with tuberculosis. They spit on the meat in preference to spitting on the floor. I have seen this time and again myself."

Said Neill: "The Commission declares that the unsanitary conditions of the packing houses . . . were disgraceful beyond description. The plants . . . resembled huge meat factories rather than slaughterhouses. That is to say that the packing house people regard meat in the same light they might regard dry goods and not as exceedingly perishable food . . . The Commission found

Harper's Magazine,
December 1902

particularly at Armour & Co.'s and at Nelson Morris & Co.'s [packing plants] that the pillars of the buildings were caked with flesh and that the pillars had apparently never been washed since the construction of the buildings. The Commission discovered that the workingmen follow the example of their employers . . . They [the workingmen] are mostly ignorant foreigners or negroes who have no knowledge of the sanitary requirements and care nothing about the quality or the cleanliness of the food they prepare . . . In these packing houses, the meat is dragged about on the floor, spat upon, and walked upon. . . . The packing houses swarm with rats."[21]

After publishing Neill's and Sinclair's accusations, the *Times* sent a reporter on the following day to a packing plant on Manhattan's east side. The reporter spoke with a worker.

"One workman," wrote the reporter, "held up his hands in horror when he was asked whether he ate any of the sausages made by himself and his fellow workers. 'Eat them!' he exclaimed. 'No, indeed! We don't eat them! We go out and get a couple of eggs and toast for our lunch. Maybe we will eat tongue, but never sausage.'"[22]

Meanwhile, in Chicago, a young congressman named Wharton rose to the defense of the packers. Congressman Wharton came from the same district and represented the same interests as "Blond Billy" Lorimer.

"This whole thing is all started from that book," said Wharton in the *Times*, "and I know of my own knowledge that there is no foundation of fact in it. It is made out of whole cloth and is entirely a product of the imagination . . . I live in the packing district of Chicago. I know all about it. I know those packinghouses as well as I know the corridors of the Capitol. I have worked for Swift, pushing a truck in his packinghouse and I know how clean and well kept it was. Why, there is no kitchen of a rich man in this city — or any other — that is any cleaner, if it is as clean, as those places . . . Of course, you know the sort of men many of the laborers in the packinghouses are — foreigners of a low grade of intelligence — and you know how impossible it is to control every individual. If those men happen to want to spit, they are likely to spit, but it doesn't go on the meat. That is nonsense . . . Why, the girls who work there are dressed in white aprons, with white wristlets and white caps and they couldn't work in such clothing if the place was not clean."

A week after Congressman Wharton spoke up for the packers, General Nelson Miles — the commander of the U.S. Army who'd accused the packers of giving his troops "embalmed beef" to eat — spoke with *Times* reporters. "The disclosures about packinghouse products now being exploited are no news to me," Miles said. "I knew it seven years ago . . . Had the matter been taken up then, thousands of lives would have been saved . . . I believe that 3,000 United States soldiers lost their lives because of adulterated, impure, poisonous meat. There is no way of estimating the number of soldiers whose health was ruined by eating impure food . . . I have a barrel of testimony on the subject in the way of affidavits that I collected hen I made my investigation years ago . . . The Investigating Committee . . . refused to hear the 2,000 witnesses I had ready."

The same day Miles spoke to reporters, in early June, the president authorized the release of a written version of the report that Neill and Reynolds had given him after they'd returned from Chicago in April. The Neill/Reynolds report was reprinted, in whole or in part, by every large

Munsey's Magazine,
January 1901

metropolitan daily paper in the country. In the *Tribune*, the report filled five columns, left to right, top to bottom of a page.

Wrote Neill: "The callous treatment of packinghouse workers by their employers must have an influence that can not be exaggerated in lowering [their] morals and discouraging [their] cleanliness . . . The whole situation as we saw it, tended necessarily and inevitably to the moral degradation of thousands of workers who were forced to spend their working hours under conditions . . . which are a constant menace not only to their health but to the health of those who use the food products prepared by them."[23]

Neill made a few modest suggestions. Perhaps it would help if the packers installed sinks in their latrines. Perhaps — once they had installed the sinks — they might provide soap and clean towels as well. It might also be of benefit if the packers provided separate rooms — lunchrooms or dining halls — for the workers to eat the food they brought with them. As of now, wrote Neill, workers who brought their own food had to eat surrounded by what they'd killed, pickled, or canned.

J. Ogden Armour was in Paris on the day the Neill/Reynolds report was published. "It is preposterous," said Mr. Armour, in his hometown *Tribune*, "to believe for a moment that the great Chicago firms, with hundreds of millions of dollars invested in their businesses, are or could be guilty of the sensational charges brought against them . . . No sane man ever would believe the newspaper stories that have appeared on this subject . . . The whole of these so-called revelations have been engineered directly by Mr. Roosevelt himself. The truth is that Roosevelt has a strong, personal animus against the packers of Chicago and is doing everything in his power to discredit them . . . Even supposing that some changes were necessary, do you suppose the best way to go about the matter is to boom it as a newspaper sensation?"

European reaction to the report was less skeptical than that of Mr. Armour.

On June 10, 1906, the *Tribune* printed a "Special Dispatch" sent to it by its correspondent in London. EUROPE THINKS U.S. LACKING IN HONOR was the dispatch's headline. "Entire Continent Aroused Against the Packers / Assert Americans Are Careless and It's Time Some Big Rascals Adorned Prisons."

What followed was as much an indictment of American ethics as it was of American meat: "Much has been cabled about the European effect of the Chicago beef exposures, but it is difficult to give an adequate idea of the worldwide fury and horror created by Upton Sinclair's novel and the daily dispatches to the European press . . . The Old World has come to believe in general terms that American business methods are rotten . . . The administration of justice in the United States is today the subject of open ridicule and contempt throughout Europe."

The dispatch ended with an excerpt from an article that appeared in the British weekly the *Spectator*: "The packers are recklessly selfish. They stop at no offence that promises to serve their purpose. They are grossly oppressive to those they employ. They are familiar with every kind of fraudulent method in disguising the diseased offal it pleases them to sell as meat . . . They have not even tried to conceal their misdeeds."

The House Agriculture Committee did what it could to raise doubts about Charles Neill's credibility. Congressman Lorimer was particularly interested in each and every detail of the hog that Mr. Neill said had fallen into a latrine and then been made into food.

Upton Sinclair telegraphed the committee members, requesting that he be allowed to testify. The committee declined Sinclair's request.

On June 30, 1906, Congress passed the Pure Food and Drug Act and the Meat Inspection Act. The provisions of both acts applied *only* to meat, food, or drugs that were sent for sale across state lines or were sold abroad.

The Meat Inspection Act required that federal inspectors examine animals before they were slaughtered, then examine their meat once they were killed. If the meat was to be canned or processed in any way, it had to be inspected yet again. The federal government agreed to pay for all these inspections. The government's only way to enforce the act was to refuse to label bad meat as "federally inspected."

As to the purity of food products made from meat: Harvey Wiley's Bureau of Chemistry in the Department of Agriculture was given the job of analyzing samples of all food (and all drugs) thought to be impure or deceptively labeled. There were no enforcement provisions.

The Pure Food and Drug Act specified that:

> Food is adulterated, first, if anything has been mixed or packed with
> it which reduces its quality or strength; second if any substance
> has been substituted for it in whole or in part; third if any valuable
> ingredient has been wholly or partially removed; fourth, if it has
> been mixed, colored, powdered, coated or stained so as to conceal
> damage or inferiority; fifth, if it contains any poisonous or injurious
> ingredient which may render it harmful to health; sixth, if it consists
> in whole or in part of filthy, decomposed, or putrid animals or
> vegetable substance, or any part of an animal unfit for food, or if it is
> the product of a diseased animal or one that has died otherwise than
> by slaughter.

The consequence of the events that had been reported prior to the passage of these laws was — as Roosevelt had feared — the collapse of the packers' export sales.

By the end of June 1906 Germany and France had banned the import of *all* American meat products, canned or not. By the end of July 1906 British imports of American canned meat had "vanished." A year later, American exports of canned meat remained 75 percent less than they were even after the Pure Food and Drug Act was passed.[24]

Epilogue

As the beef scandal developed, considerable interest arose as to what the president himself ate. There were reports in the *Washington Post* that he dined lavishly, morning, noon, and night. The president objected: "Instead of a breakfast consisting of oranges, cantaloupes, cereals, eggs, bacon, lamb chops, hot cakes and waffles, President Roosevelt insists that the regular White House breakfast consists of hard boiled eggs and coffee . . . Instead of a luncheon made of such delicious viands as Little Neck clams, stuffed olives, celery, consommé of chicken, fish sauté, eggs a la turque, spring lamb, new string beans, asparagus, mashed potatoes, lettuce, tomatoes, strawberries and ice cream, the President declares that when alone, he always contents himself with a bowl of bread and milk." As to dinner, said the president, in the *New York Times*, "Nine times out of ten, a three course dinner is served."

In May of 1907, in New York, a group of grocery trade reporters convened to sample and pass judgment on a variety of out-of-date canned goods. Their bill of fare consisted of fourteen-year-old "beef stew with potatoes and onions," twelve-year-old "pigs' feet," twelve-year-old "corned beef," eight-year-old "braised beef with peas and string beans," five-year-old cooked shrimp, and four-year-old "roast chicken."

Once the cans were opened, their contents were prepared by an African-American chef who usually cooked on board the yacht of the banquet's host, a grocer named Callahan. The oldest canned food the jury sampled was pea soup from 1880. The newest was shrimp, canned in 1906. Mr. Callahan hoped to prove that canned food, no matter how old, was not just good to eat but fit for a banquet.

A *New York Times* reporter was invited to the grocers' banquet. He took note of the adjectives the jurors used to describe each dish. "The stenographic report," wrote the reporter, "was as thickly strewn with the word 'excellent' as the earth is strewn with leaves in the autumn." "Boned Chicken" was described as "first class." "Tender." "Sweet." The twelve-year-old pigs' feet were said to taste "like suckling pig." "Yes sir," said one of the jurors, "that's what it is, suckling pig. I couldn't recognize the taste at first."

The reporter noticed that wine was served with the meal.

He asked Mr. Callahan, " 'Did the banqueters drink their wine before or after tasting the canned foods?' Mr. Callahan looked straight ahead for a couple of minutes, and then making a motion of his hand as if he were reaching for a bible, upon which to rest it, he replied steadily, 'After.' "

One month later the health commissioner of the State of New York opened his own array of cans: "One hundred and fifty-four samples of so-called roast, corned, dried, and potted beef, potted and deviled ham, chicken and turkey, and canned sausage." The commissioner was particularly interested in contents of the cans marked "luncheon meat." He reported, "Two samples of this product bore labels with the following statement: 'Fine, old English luncheon meat as prepared at Hadden Hall in the reign of Queen Elizabeth.' The contents of the two samples are similar in appearance both to the naked eye and microscopically and consist of large amounts of fibrous tissue and fat, with scattered pieces of skin, glands, hair, and a little muscular tissue."[25]

Finally, the American Meat Packers Association held a banquet in Chicago in October 1907. The hosts of the banquet were the four meatpackers who had been named as members of the so-called Beef Trust.

"The menu was simple, but the manner of service was novel," according to a reporter for the *Chicago Tribune*. "The roast beef and roast mutton were brought in in wooden barrows wheeled by red coated waiters, followed by a procession, single file, of white-gowned and white-capped chefs, fifty in number, carrying their knives and cleavers crossed above their heads. A boar's head was borne aloft in triumph by two waiters dressed after the manner of servants in Sir Walter Raleigh's time. Later, at a fanfare of trumpets, the red coated waiters again marched in procession, carrying other viands."

No cans were opened.

—ML

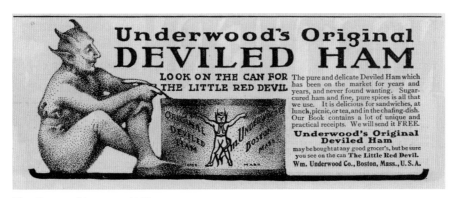

The Century Magazine, *1903*

QUICK FOOD

Lunch Wagons

As early as 1903, food bought from carts and wagons parked outside factory gates began to replace the chunks of bread, meat, and cheese that men had always carried to work in their dinner pails. Not that men stopped carrying their pails. At noon, they'd give their empty ones to apprentices who'd rush off to nearby saloons. The boys returned with the pails filled with beer, ten or twenty pails at a time, swinging on poles, balanced across the their shoulders.

In July 1903 the *Chicago Tribune* sent a reporter—and a photographer—to Philadelphia to do a story about this change in eating habits.

> If the unenlightened will stand in the vicinity of the Baldwin Locomotive Works until the 12 o'clock whistle blows, they will see how the army of 9,000 men, employed [there] get their lunch and how . . . American working [men] . . . In all the large cities [have] found a means of doing away with the dinner pail.
>
> When the whistle blows, the workmen drop their tools before the first blast dies away and dash . . . to the street in search of food.
>
> They do not have far to go, for all around the 14 acres covered by the [locomotive] works, just as close as they can get in the shade of the big, grim buildings, are assembled all classes and conditions of vendors—men, women, and children, white, black, some with

Stained glass Automat facade, date unknown

baskets, others with pushcarts or [wheel]barrows, and still others with horse and wagon.

For half an hour before noon, these sidewalk merchants have been making ready for the rush, for every customer demands the quickest and best service . . . if he cannot get it from one, he passes on to the next.

It is difficult to determine what is not sold in the eatable and drinkable line at these primitive lunch counters:

Oysters, clams, fishballs, meat cakes, sausage, cold meats, sandwiches, dried fish, fried potatoes, pretzels, pies, fruit of all kinds, bread and butter, buttermilk, sweet milk, lemonade, coffee, tea, root beer, and orangeade are only a few of the refreshments to be purchased — and everything is cheap . . .

From 12:00 until 1:00 the sidewalk stands are busy . . . These 9,000 men consume, in less than an hour, 4,000 loaves of bread, 1,000 pounds of frankfurters, 1,000 pints of beer, 208 hams, 23,000 pies, 2,000 pints of milk, 4,000 pints of iced tea, 2,500 pints of coffee . . .

After the whistle announces the end of the lunch hour, the vendors vanish like the mist of a summer morning. Some go home to cook and prepare for the noon hour of the morrow . . . others seek favored corners in the city where business is fairly brisk for the remainder of the day.

What is the cause of this discarding of the long-faithful [dinner] pail?

"Well . . ." said a workman, "the wages of a workman are more than they used to be and it costs little more to eat as much lunch from the curbside 'quick lunches' than it does to bring it from home . . . Our wives have to get up early enough as it is to start us off for work . . . When they have the added work of [preparing] the lunches, it doesn't pay.

"When a man is working hard all morning, he wants something more substantial than a cold lunch . . . No more cold coffee or tea for us. We can get it hot and freshly made from the lunch stands . . . with steaming sausages and rolls and a smoking meat pie — it is food fit for anyone."[1]

Sitting Down to Eat: Cheaply

The very cheapest lunch counters—places that sold food for five or ten cents a plate—stayed open all night. According to the *Tribune*, in Chicago "Until 2:00 or even 3:00 [in the morning] one finds men here, mostly young men, sitting over a cup of coffee and 'sinkers' with dazed and tired eyes. Some of them are homeless . . . others evidently trying to become homeless by dissipating their energy and wasting their health."[2]

A chain called Pittsburgh Joe's was one of the cheapest of these cheap lunch places. In 1908 there were fourteen Pittsburgh Joe's scattered around the edges of Chicago's Loop. Things happened in a Pittsburgh Joe's that rarely—if ever—happened anywhere else: "Two hours after they first met [in a Pittsburgh Joe's at State and Polk], Mrs. Laura Bauer, a widow, 38 years old, and Earl Hight, a youth of 18, became engaged . . . The youth, who was sitting at the counter, asked the widow to pass him a ketchup bottle. She, in turn, requested that he slip the sugar bowl down her way. They smiled at each other.

" 'I just couldn't resist her,' said the youth [to the police officer who eventually arrested them]. 'I thought she was about the nicest looking girl I ever looked at. And then, when she smiled at me after I asked her for the ketchup and I saw [her] front tooth was out . . . I lost my heart. I have a tooth out in front and I guess we were born for each other.'

"The widow's check was lying at the side of her plate and the gallant youth picked it up when he went to pay his own bill. Supper for both cost twenty cents.

"They left the eating house together. On reaching the street, the youth asked the widow if she would have him for better or for worse. She said she would take a chance."[3]

One step up from such places were small, owner-operated lunch counters that opened early and closed late. No matter where they were—in New York City or Charleston, Houston, or Birmingham—immigrant Greeks usually owned and ran them. The Greeks would begin on the street, peddling cheap candy. The money they made from selling cheap sweets was used to buy corner stores—candy and tobacco stores or ice cream and candy stores—located in the busy places they'd noticed while peddling.[4] The money earned from these they used to buy lunch counters, located, more often than not, near streetcar stops and transfer points.[5]

"Of the foreigners who are invading the restaurant field in [this] city," wrote a reporter for the *Chicago Tribune* in 1909, "Greeks are moving to the front as leaders. The Italians may run a sort of artistic café; the Chinese may cater to the fancy trade of chop suey eaters. The Greek caters to the American workman. His meals are . . . plain and wholesome and in general strive to give [his customers their] 'money's worth.' The Greek restaurant keeper is generally a young man [who] . . . takes for his motto 'Small Profits But A Large Trade' . . . He works longer hours and pays his help less for [working] longer hours than American waiters put in . . . The Greek boy who comes over here starts as a dishwasher . . . from his comrades, he picks-up a few English words . . . [after a few years] he is promoted to the rank of waiter. He works as a waiter for a few [more] years . . . by that time he had generally saved $300 [equal to about $7,000 today]. With that, he starts his own restaurant."[6]

SITTING DOWN TO EAT: NOT SO CHEAPLY

The most refined and most expensive quick-lunch place in the country was the Rotunda of the Astor House Hotel, located in New York's financial district.[7] In 1900 more than five thousand brokers and businessmen a day walked into the Rotunda's well-lit and spacious restaurant, ordered drinks at the bar, inspected the food counters, then found seats at one of many service counters. White-aproned, black-jacketed waiters took their orders then returned with their food almost before they had time to unbutton their overcoats.

"Haste, as it has been said, marks the lunch hour in many quarters, but no where so much as in the financial district," so said *Munsey's Magazine*, in 1901. "It must be understood that the [only similarity] the Astor House's Rotunda [shares] with the 'quick lunch' is that it serves as expeditiously as possible . . .

"You may either stand up or sit—and get food at rather high prices. You may make haste or eat slowly, as you choose; you may gobble a sandwich and flee or you may eat a slow, regularly ordained luncheon. Order roast beef, for instance. 'Very good, sir,' says the man behind the counter. There is a clatter of silver, a sudden gush of savory steam, and there, at one's elbow is a whole round of beef. [One is then] confronted by a white aproned man with a thin, keen knife, he will perform at extraordinary speed . . . handing you the exact amount [of your order] with a dish of potatoes at one side. You may still be folding your napkin across your knees . . . It is rapid transit, pure and simple, but you are not pushed to eat it the same way."[8]

Halfway between the Rotunda's fragrant roast beef and Pittsburgh Joe's dazed coffee and donuts were the high-volume, big-city lunch places that served clerks, young businessmen, stenographers, typists (called "typewriters"), and an occasional banker or lawyer.

Again, per *Munsey's*:

> Upon entering a place of this sort, the customer is to reserve a chair by laying one's hat on the seat . . . The chairs are usually of cherry with [a single] wide arm and are set in space economizing rows, A well, just large enough to hold the base of a coffee cup, is set in the center of the wide arm, which is also encircled by a batten which provides against sudden incursions of crockery into one's lap . . .
>
> Having secured yourself a seat, the method is join the press at the [food] counter and seize whatever you may see that suits your fancy. Roulades of pie on plates are stacked upon the counter . . . Intermingled, one finds sandwiches, preserved fruit, crullers, cake, peeled eggs . . . cup custards, and mayhap, fried oysters. To help yourself is the order, then to pay at the cashier's desk as you conscience or honesty dictates. The average cost to each customer is about twenty cents.
>
> There is only a row of young women behind the counter to help you. In one place, the system of making the [customer] his own waiter . . . is carried out to such an extent that a tray is handed to you when you enter the place. There are other places where no chairs are provided. You join a procession and grab food as you move along. In there "restaurants" there are not even employees in charge of the counter. All that is left to the customer . . .
>
> At quick lunch places, hurry seems to be magnified . . . It is a struggle to get to the counter, and, after the struggle, one seems to eat in the same fashion.

In Boston, Philadelphia, and New York the big banks and insurance companies operated in-house dining rooms and lunchrooms to shelter their employees from the lunch rush outside.

In Chicago, Sears Roebuck turned its basement into a warren of restaurants: a low-priced, thousand-seat cafeteria operated next to a high-priced, linen-napkin, table-service dining room. International Harvester set aside the entire top floor of its Chicago headquarters to serve its staff, including an executive dining room, which offered a choice of sirloin or porterhouse steak for sixty cents (equal to about $14 today), a café that served a three-course "complete meal" for twenty-five cents, and a matched set of smoking rooms and ladies' lounges offering views of Lake Michigan.

Other Chicago companies—Western Electric, for example—provided their administrative staffs with box lunches prepared by caterers who delivered hundreds and hundreds of lunches to buildings throughout the city. In 1905 eight Chicago catering companies delivered an average of ten thousand box lunches a day. The largest of those catering companies was owned and operated by a woman who'd been in the business since 1890.[9]

THE LUNCH PROBLEM, PART ONE: EATING BAD FOOD TOO FAST

WHY WE ARE A NERVOUS PEOPLE was the headline of a wonderfully illustrated article that appeared in the *Chicago Tribune* a few months before *Munsey's* described the elegant efficiency of the Astor House's Rotunda.

> You climb onto a high stool, fighting for space at the counter with men whose elbows are at your face.
>
> Sixty-two male citizens, perched on similar stools [arrayed] around the [counter's] hollow square feast rapidly on pie and "dairy dishes." Inside the square, eight heroic women in uniforms of black and while, fight to protect the towering pyramids of pie and donuts . . . The men [on the stools] are soldiers with but ten minutes respite from the daily battle which is never ended.
>
> The instant you succeed in struggling to the top of a stool, one of the beleaguered [women] inside the square rushes forward. She juggles in the air for a fraction of a second then a stoneware plate, a glass of water, a knife, fork, and spoon, and a paper napkin bang and clatter on the hardwood counter before you.
>
> At the same instant, her face, which is a living interrogation point, catches your eye.
>
> "Hurry up and order," it commands without speaking a word. "This is a quick lunch room, and time is even more precious than pie."
>
> "Pork and beans, pie and coffee," you say quickly, trembling lest you delay the game.

Haim's

Quick Lunch Restaurant,

358 BOWERY.

31. Dec. 1906   **NEW YORK.**

BILL OF FARE.

EGGS, OMELETS, ETC.

Two Fried Eggs with Coffee or Tea..............10	Plain Omelet with Coffee or Tea..............10
Two Boiled Eggs with Coffee or Tea..............10	Ham Omelet with Coffee or Tea..............15
Two Scrambled Eggs with Coffee or Tea........10	

DAIRY DISHES.

Rolls, Butter and Coffee 5	Crackers and Milk.. 8
Oatmeal and Milk.........5	Milk Toast............10
Force, Malta Vita or Power and Milk.........5	

SANDWICHES.

Ham, Roll..........3	Salmon Roll..... 3
Cheese..........3	

GRIDDLE CAKES AND TOAST.

Wheat Cakes with Maple Syrup...........................5

   „   „   „   Coffee........................7

DESSERT.

Home Made Pies of all kinds..........5 cents.

Rice Pudding.. 5	Tapioca Bread Pudding 5

COFFEE, TEA, ETC.

Coffee or Tea.. 2	Ice Cold Glass of Milk ..2 & 3
Cocoa....................3	

Daily menu, Haim's Quick Lunch Restaurant, New York, 1906

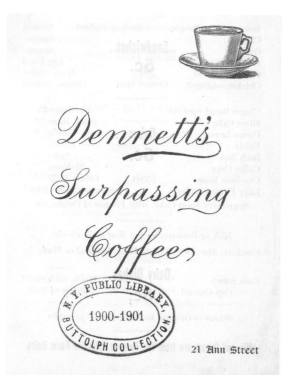

21 Ann Street

*Daily menu, Dennett's
Surpassing Coffee, New York,
1900*

"Pork and!"

Up at the front of the room, a [frantic-] looking woman is cooking fifteen dishes on fifteen separate fires . . . her ears are strained to catch the shrill orders of the [women] inside the besieged pie counter. Half a dozen voices are shrieking at once . . .

"Come again," sings the cook in a shrill falsetto.

"Pork and!"

"Mince it!"

The cook is a wonder worker. Like a cork, she bobs to the surface of the "short orders."

"Rare cut! Mince it!" she warbles them in a burst of triumphant melody: "Take away your 'Pork and'!"

You drink a pint of ice water and look around you.

Through the narrow door in the front, men are projected [out] onto the street as if by a catapult; at the same time, other men are sucked in as if an air pump was at work . . . Always at rush hour, the women inside [the counter's] hollow square face a solid, unbroken phalanx of rapidly moving jaws.

Sixty-two jaws beat time to the music.

Sixty-two glasses and coffee cups clink against the hardwood.

Higher, carrying [through] the air, rise the shrill, nasal sopranos of [the women clad in black and white] . . .

"Come again!"

"Take your pork chops!"

Your "Pork and" lies untouched upon the counter.

In low whispers which are perfectly audible under the high-pitched uproar, two men on adjoining stools discuss business between bites.

"My commission will be two fifteen. He's gone over to the bank now to get the money. Got to get back in five minutes to meet him."

With that, he leaps off the stool and rushes down the narrow aisle to the door.

When you turn back to the counter, [your] "Pork and" has disappeared. The garrison [behind the counter] is quick to take

Dennett's

25 PARK ROW.   25 PARK ROW.

BILL OF FARE.

LITTLE-NECK CLAMS

Chowder, Fulton Market Style............15

Half Shell............15	Steamed............35
Stew............20	Broil............30
" Milk............25	" Baltimore Style......30
" Boston............25	Roast, Pan............30
Fry, Small............20	" Shell............35
" Large............35	" Fancy............35

Fish Cakes............15
" " with one fried or poached Egg......20
" " " two " " " Eggs.....25

EGGS AND OMELETTES

Boiled Eggs............	(2)....15	(3)....20
Fried Eggs............	(2)....15	(3)....20
Scrambled Eggs............	(2)....15	(3)....20
Poached Eggs, plain............	(2)....15	(3)....20
" " on Toast............	(2)....20	
Plain Omelette	(2)....20	(3)....25
Ham "		(3)....25
Ham and Eggs............		25

DESSERT

Special Attention is Called to the Quality of Our Pies.

Pie, per cut, (All Pies in Season)............5
 Crullers............5
 Prunes............
 Corn Starch............
 Cup Custard............5
 Chocolate Eclair............5
 Assorted Cakes............5
 Ice Cream............10

We have introduced a Perfect Apparatus for FILTERING our DRINKING WATER, whereby we can and do ensure an Entire Immunity from Microbes or the Slightest Defilement.

OTHER HOUSES:

25 Park Row,		13 South 9th St.,	
4 & 6 Beekman St.,	N. Y.	19 " " "	Phila.
143 & 145 Nassau St.,		529 Chestnut St.,	
140 East 14th St.,		1311 & 1313 Market St.,	
12 Myrtle Avenue,		306 E. Baltimore St.,	Balto.
353 & 355 Fulton St.,	B'klyn.	312 W. Baltimore St.,	
30 Liberty St.,		241 Washington St., Boston.	
195 Fulton St.,		783 Market St., San Francisco.	

(**OVER**)   S. S. SWAIM, GENERAL MANAGER.

Daily menu, Dennett's, New York, 1900

advantage of the slightest lack of attention on the part of [their] besiegers. Pie and coffee and a red check lie before you . . .

"Yesterday," says the proprietor, "we fed 838 people between 11 and 2 o'clock!"

You are shot out into the quiet street where there is only the clang of the streetcar gong and the roar of the city to soothe the ear.

From behind you, out of the half open door, sounds a parting wail: "Take away your wheats!"[10]

The medical consequences of this way of eating had been familiar to Americans since the time of the nutritionist Sylvester Graham (1794–1851). The Kellogg brothers of Battle Creek, Michigan, were about to grow rich and famous because of it. From the *New York Times*: "The Prevalence of 'The American Disease'—dyspepsia—is largely due to the quick lunch habit of our businessmen and women. The inferior food, catch-as-catch can service, the noise, the hurry, even the heavy, permanent odor of the average quick lunch restaurant, all conspire against good digestion waiting upon appetite."

Dyspepsia led to other misfortunes. From the *Chicago Tribune*: "No girl should marry a man with a quick lunch habit," was the advice of the director of Chicago's Health Department. "The quick lunch habit causes indigestion, indigestion engenders ill nature, ill nature makes a man miserable . . . someone has to suffer for it, [so] he scolds his wife . . .

"The places where quick lunches are served are responsible for more divorces, wrecked homes, and domestic trouble than anything else. When a man scolds his wife and finds fault at home, it nearly always can be laid at the door of the quick lunch restaurant.

"We think that we are civilized, but the way people eat at lunch counters is worse than barbarous. A savage wouldn't think of mistreating himself that way."

In 1905 an American entrepreneur named James Wyman "convinced capitalists that the British wasted too much time at table, especially [during] business hours, and that they would flock to an [American-style] quick lunch place. Wyman opened a beautiful restaurant at 63 Strand." The restaurant's menu included donuts, wheat cakes, cranberry pies, and oysters stewed, sauced, or fried. Wyman hired American waiters to staff the place. "Americans in London fell upon his neck and wept with joy. The British avoided him," wrote a reporter for the *Tribune* in 1905.

Wyman's quick-lunch oasis closed in a year. He was undeterred. "Wyman formed another company and opened a waffle palace, putting $30,000 into it [in 1905, $30,000 was equivalent to about $750,000 now]. He argued that no one could escape the seductive attractions of the waffle."

Wyman's waffle palace closed in three months.

Two years later, the *Chicago Tribune*'s London correspondent asked the great British caterer and restaurateur Joseph Lyons why he thought Wyman's quick-lunch and waffle efforts had failed.

Lyons presided over a food service empire that included 120 London teashops, serving some three hundred thousand customers a day. Lyons also owned and operated more than half a dozen of London's most expensive and exclusive restaurants.[11]

Lyons's answer to the *Tribune* was brief. "The American," said Lyons, "spends five minutes eating his meal and twenty minutes picking his teeth. The Englishman spends twenty minutes eating and five minutes picking his teeth . . . We eat slowly and sparingly in the middle of the day . . . We eat much less than the Americans . . . The portions served in American restaurants, if placed before our customers, would sicken them by their size."[12]

A few months later Lyons was in New York trying to find an American publisher for a crime novel he'd written about robbing the Bank of England. (The novel had been published in England and caused a sensation.)

Once again, a reporter, this one from the *New York Times*, asked Lyons to describe the difference between the way British and Americans ate. "From my experience," said Lyons, "a man can't go slowly here. Look at your 'quick lunch' people who swallow their noonday meal in a hurry . . . These are, I suppose, what you call 'the hustlers,' the downtown men possessed of wonderful energy. To me it is a waste. You are a nation of dyspeptics and the 'quick lunch' is to blame. This 'hurry up' style of eating was tried in England . . . it proved a failure. People there don't want to swallow their food in chunks."[13]

The Lunch Problem, Part Two: Waiters

Most of the people who could afford to eat in restaurants didn't like waiters. In particular, they didn't like tipping them. From the beginning to the end of the decade, newspaper columnists, reporters, and letter-to-the-editor writers kept asking the same sort of rhetorical question: "Why should we continue to tip the waiters, and not the hod carriers, the bricklayers, the motormen, or even, say, the clerks who wait on us in stores?"

"Tipping has become an abominable nuisance all over the world," according to a 1908 *New York Times* editorial. "Nobody wants to give big tips except vulgar persons who fancy they gain respect by such a show of questionable generosity. The worst of tipping is that it has grown to such proportions and become so general that even a native born American who cherishes the idea of freedom and independence is not ashamed to accept a gratuity."[14]

The *Chicago Tribune* in 1905 reported:

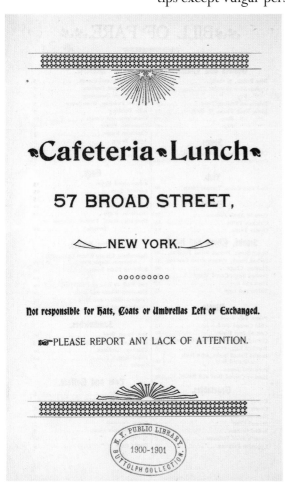

Daily menu, Cafeteria Lunch, New York, 1900

When a man enters a restaurant, he is ordinarily met with effusive, tip-seeking cordiality and ushered with profound civility to a seat . . . The waiter comes and sizes up his customer. If the customer looks like a ten cent tip, he receives ordinary care: the waiter stands by . . . for perhaps thirty seconds, then steps across the room to ask another waiter how the race at Sheepshead came out. He returns, receives his orders — and disappears.

Twelve minutes later, he returns with a knife, a fork, and spoons. If you have ordered soup, he invariably forgets the soup spoon. He refills the glass with water, and disappears again . . . after a while . . . he returns with the food. It is absolutely necessary for him to forget the napkin, the butter, or the cream . . . should he even remember all three, he will have forgotten the salt, the pepper, or the vinegar.

Having served these things, he will disappear again. No one has ever been able to discover what becomes of a waiter at the time he is wanted.[15]

Again, the *New York Times* in 1909: "The crude waiter of today is always there when one does not want him and never on hand when one does. Occasionally, he is a prowler: he stands nearby, surveying the dish the patron is eating as though he were counting every mouthful and internally ejaculating: 'Hurry up!' . . . He seems to be counting the moments 'til his customer had bolted his food, called for his check, tipped him — the supreme moment from his standpoint — and given his place to somebody else who will hurry up and tip him in turn."[16]

The primary reason being tipped was "the supreme moment" for most waiters was because they were miserably paid.

As you may recall: in 1909, a year of economic stability following the aftershocks of the Panic of 1907, a "street laborer" earned $1.50 a day, a semiskilled manual laborer earned $1.75, and a skilled worker $2.44.[17]

Compare these wages with the $1.42 base pay (without tips) that a white man working as a restaurant waiter with a "good job" earned in 1905. Then, compare these wages with the average base pay of an African-American waiter, working in a hotel in New York, Chicago, or Memphis. At the best places, a black waiter was paid 83 cents per day. "It is only the most aggressive [black] waiter who manages to average as much as fifty cents a day in tips." Black waiters working behind the counters of quick lunches earned no tips at all.

No matter the race of a waiter, he earned what he earned by working twelve to sixteen hours a day, seven days a week.

"If I had a son," said a veteran waiter in Chicago, "who wanted to enter this business and there was no other way of keeping him out of it, I would have him confined to an asylum until his foolish desire was starved out . . . Anyone could do better shoveling snow than acting as a waiter. There is absolutely no business where a man's environments are so demeaning, where the work will cause him to lose so large a share of his self respect, and where there is so little chance of anything better in the work of a waiter."[18]

"Of course the real responsibility for the tipping system rests not on those who give or those who collect tips, but on the dignified proprietors of hotels and restaurants."[19] Such "dignified proprietors" were content

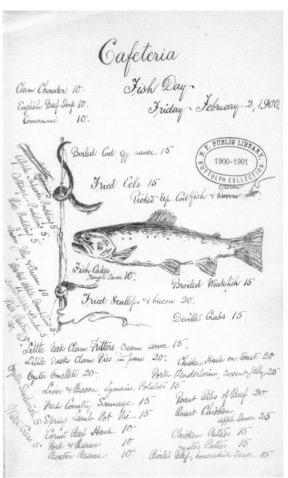

Daily bill of fare, Cafeteria Lunch, New York, 1900

to have their customers pay twice: first for their food and then for their service. Whenever reformers suggested that employers raise the base pay of their service staffs, the employers reminded them: "The abolition of the tipping system would simply mean . . . an increase of from twenty to twenty-five percent of every item on the bill of fare."[20]

Waiters grew tired of this shell game, in which the responsibility for paying them a living wage shifted back and forth between the people they served and the people who employed them.

The result: waiters formed unions. Then they went on strike.[21]

THE BIG STRIKE

The most significant — the biggest and most publicized — waiters' strike of the decade happened in Chicago in 1903. The waiters who began the strike were men who had the most to gain and the least to lose: black men employed by a chain of downtown Chicago restaurants called Kohlsaat's.

H. H. Kohlsaat was the man who owned and operated the chain. H. H. had opened his first "bakery lunchroom" in 1880. By 1891 he'd grown rich — rich enough to buy a controlling interest in a Chicago newspaper (*The Inter Ocean*) that was "an arbiter of upper class taste," according to Richard Schwarzloge in "Newspapers" in *The Encyclopedia Chicago*. He bought two more papers after that and he opened more lunchrooms. President McKinley appointed H. H.'s brother a federal district judge. President Roosevelt moved his brother to the federal circuit court.

The point: Kohlsaat was more than just a rich restaurant owner. He and his brother were influential power brokers in a very Republican part of a very Republican country. Most significant, all the waiters who worked at Kohlsaat's were black. When all five hundred of them went on strike, thoughtful people in Illinois and Washington paid attention. They understood that whatever the outcome of the strike it would have as much to do with race as with class. In fact, the outcome of the strike had just as much to do with gender.

No one knew if H. H.'s business managers saw the 1903 strike coming. Kohlsaat's waiters were models of smiling, diffident service, perfect "darkies," dressed in white jackets and bow ties, pouring coffee, taking orders, nodding "Yes, sir," then hustling back to their customers with wheat cakes in the morning and Irish stew at noon.[22]

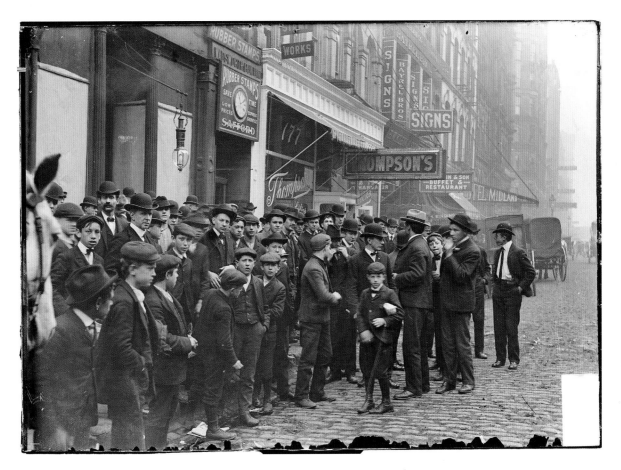

The Kohlsaat's strike began in the first week of May of 1903 when the manager of a Kohlsaat's (referred to as the "Treamont branch" on Dearborn) fired forty-five waiters for what he first said was "incompetency" and then described as embezzlement in the *Chicago Tribune*.

The "colored waiters' union" demanded that the men be reinstated. Kohlsaat's refused but let it be known that it was willing to hire union waitresses to take their place. All five hundred of the company's waiters walked out during the lunch hour rush.

> The action of the strikers forced the thousands of patrons of [Kohlsaat's] restaurants to seek out other eating paces. Late in the day, the company tried to fill the places of the strikers with white help, but the waiters' union checkmated the move.
>
> About 3 o'clock, twenty union waitresses entered [the Treamont branch] and took seats at the counters.

Crowd of men and boys lining the sidewalk and street in front of Thompson's restaurant during a waiters' strike, Chicago, June 4, 1903.

"We don't serve ladies there," said the head waiter.

"I guess you'll serve us," interrupted one of the girls — and he did.

As the [new] waitresses brought the coffee, pie, and cake, [the union waitresses] threatened them if they did not stop work. One of the pickets refused to leave her seat and drank six cups of coffee [while trying] to convince the one serving her to quit.[23]

The company called the police.

The union withdrew its pickets, then called a strategy meeting. If Kohlsaat's didn't reinstate the men, the union voted to ask the engineers of the Steam Power Council to quit work. If the engineers did, Kohlsaat's main bakery would lose power. Without bread or rolls or pie or cake the whole chain would have to shut down.

The union issued a statement: "The Kohlsaat company has always hired colored men and will have to continue to do so." The union listed four Kohlsaat's, employing a total of 215 men, that its pickets had closed down.

Meanwhile, the company sent instructions to a labor agent in Milwaukee to start hiring white girls. He signed up a hundred of them. The company reserved two railway cars to bring them to Chicago. When the girls arrived the next afternoon, police escorted them to a hotel where the company had rooms waiting for them. Union waitresses tried to talk to the girls but the police threw them out of the building.

A week passed.

The Chicago Federation of Labor tried to arrange a settlement.

The company decided it had won the strike. It issued a victory statement: "At a conference held this afternoon, the Chicago Federation of Labor, the colored waiter's union, and the Kohlsaat company [announced] the strike was settled. All the strikers will return to work [tomorrow], but the company will employ girls in [its Treamont branch]. It will employ colored help at its other restaurants, as long as they are competent . . . The men discharged [from Treamont] will not be taken back in our employ."[24]

The settlement — if there was one — vanished the next day. It was replaced with calls for a general restaurant strike.

"Twelve thousand waiters, cooks, and hotel employees will demand an increase in pay before the close of the week . . . Their action threatens to tie up the restaurants of the city and force people to carry lunch baskets when they leave home in the morning."[25]

The union that issued the call — "the Hotel and Restaurant Employees and Bartenders International" — was a union that no one, not the Chicago Federation of Labor and not the Restaurant Keepers Association, had ever heard of. These were its demands:

> For workers in restaurants: working for one week, not exceeding 66 hours per week: $12.00 for first class help; $10 for second class. In restaurants, working for six days, not exceeding sixty hours, $10 for first class and $9 for second class. In hotels: $40 a month. In clubhouses: $50 a month. In summer resorts: $40 a month. And in summer beer gardens: $12 a week.
>
> For waitresses: those employed seven days a week: first class: $8; second class: $7 a week. Those employed six days a week: first class: $7; second class: $6. Lunch and supper girls: five hours a day: 85 cents. Three hours a day: 65 cents.[26]

Some restaurant chains (chains that competed with Kohlsaat's) settled quickly. Other places — particularly large, German restaurants (with such names as the Edelweiss and Vogelsang's) that had never employed union help — kept operating.

At a big Chicago restaurant called King's, according to a *Tribune* reporter, "The cooks and waiters abandoned their tasks [just before noon]. The men and women at the tables saw hope of luncheon vanish. The waiters folded up their aprons and put them away in their dressing room. The cooks walked out of the place without so much as taking care to prevent the cooking foods from being ruined. Roasts were abandoned to dry and burn . . . Steaks scorched and smoked over fires."[27]

Eight days after the general strike began, the Chicago Federation of Labor endorsed it. Of the eleven hundred restaurants affected, only eighty-six small and medium-size places had settled with their workers. The Restaurant Keepers Association, representing twenty-two of the city's biggest and most expensive restaurants, refused to negotiate a general agreement. Kohlsaat's, because of its size and prominence, was a member of the association.

"Little progress has been made in the settlement of the strike of the colored waiters that has kept the H. H. Kohlsaat's restaurant closed for some time [ten weeks to be exact]. The proposition made by the company that the colored men who were replaced by girls [at Kohlsaat's Treamont branch] be employed by a new [Kohlsaat's] at Wabash is said to have been considered unfavorably by the [colored waiters' union] which demands that the girls be discharged."

On the eighteenth day of the general strike, Samuel Gompers, the president of the American Federation of Labor, convinced the Waiters, Bartenders, and Hotel Workers International to agree to arbitration.

The International issued a statement: "The joint board of the union will ask all employers to reinstate all strikers and discharge the non union help that has been imported." The International might as well have asked the bosses to fly their workers to the moon.

Three days later, all eleven hundred restaurants (including all seven Kohlsaat's) in the Loop reopened. Customers packed the dining rooms of the big hotels. "The managers were smiling and happy, while the waiters had more work than they could attend to, with the resultant abundance of tips. All the dining rooms were brilliantly lighted and every table filled with guests."

Not everyone was so happy. Only a few restaurants had rehired strikers. There were more people looking for work than there were jobs.

"Crowds of men and women who found their places had been filled when they applied for work . . . appeared at the union headquarters, demanding to know what provision had been made for them. Indignation ran high . . . A mass meeting . . . was called.

"The members of the joint board [of the union] tried to pacify the crowds by telling them they would be reinstated in ten days. This they rejected and refused to believe . . .

" 'The board has played us,' exclaimed [a Sherman House hotel porter] who had found his place filled. 'We joined the union in good faith . . . it called us out, and now we are out of a job with no prospect of getting work.' "

At Kohlsaat's, the company's business manager promised the colored waiters' union to raise waiters' pay. When the union asked him to put what he said into writing he refused. All five hundred of the company's waiters walked out again.

"When asked to continue to work during the [noon] rush hours, they laughed and, gathering on the sidewalk, taunted all those who entered the restaurants."[28]

The International's joint board became alarmed. Kohlsaat's waiters might set off another general strike — an unauthorized one — that would give the restaurant owners an excuse to walk away from whatever arbitrated settlement would be reached.

The International needn't have worried.

After six weeks of meetings, presided over by a civil court judge, the Arbitration Board granted the International only a fraction of what it had wanted. The union had demanded pay increases of up to 40 percent. The board granted it only 10 percent.

"As the reading of the [arbitration] report progressed," reported the *Chicago Tribune*, on August 23, 1903, "the union men and women became incensed . . . It is expected that the strike that tied up the majority of the big restaurants in the city will be renewed tomorrow morning."

The August 25, 1903, *Tribune* published an editorial entitled "Foolish Colored Men."

The colored workers in Chicago who have gone on a hopeless strike are doing themselves and their race an injury. They are making it more difficult for Negroes to work.

For years, the colored people have gradually been driven out of occupations which they, at one time, almost monopolized. Once, they were found in most of the barber shops. [Once], they had ready employment as coachmen and butlers. They have been pretty much forced out of these fields . . .

There was a time when they were preferred as waiters, but the time has gone by . . . In most places, they are set aside in favor of whites. In view of this, it is folly for colored men to act in such as way as to hasten the process of [their] displacement.

It was a great mistake for the colored cooks and waiters to take part in the [general strike that began in June]. They were seduced into it by the white employees who knew that their chances of winning would be much smaller if the negroes remained at work. Many colored men lost good places because of the strike.

The second strike [the one that began again at Kohlsaat's] in which negro employees are taking a prominent part, will cost them their jobs and will convince many restaurant keepers . . . that . . . it is better to give the preference to white labor.

The blacks are victims of an outrageous race prejudice in many quarters. The most effective way for them to combat that prejudice is for them to be steady, trustworthy, faithful workers who do not repudiate arbitration rewards.

Two days later the *Tribune* published a report that amounted to an obituary notice for black waiters: "Waiters Beaten / Negroes to Go /

Restaurant Keepers Turn Attention to Replacing Black Men / White
Girls Are Hired."

> With the waiters' strike practically broken . . . the Chicago Restaurant
> Keepers' Association has begun a determined effort to remove negro
> waiters from downtown eating houses.
>
> Yesterday, 100 girls were hired in Milwaukee to help displace the
> negroes in the Kohlsaat's restaurants . . . Agents of the employers are
> at work in St. Louis, Indianapolis, and other western cities, securing
> girls who are willing to come to Chicago.
>
> Since the negroes have joined the union, the restaurant owners
> say they have been indolent, often insolent to patrons, and practically
> worthless as waiters.
>
> "The day of the negro in the downtown district is over," said
> president F. B. Barnheiser of H. H. Kohlsaat Company last night.
> "Within a short time, not 10% of the negroes now employed within
> the Loop will be at work. They have themselves to blame, for the
> proprietors, exasperated by their conduct, have decided to employ
> only white men and women.
>
> "With an eye to justice, however, the Kohlsaat Company will place
> the few negroes who remained loyal to in it one restaurant, while
> white waiters will be employed in the other establishments."
>
> Other restaurant keepers plan to follow [Kohlsaat's] example.[29]

Hiring white girls made many people happy. Employers knew they
could pay them lower wages than they paid men — white or black.
Customers, especially white men but also white women, who ate in
restaurants that had once employed men felt free to give waitresses lower
tips or no tips at all. In the *Chicago Tribune* of August 1903: "Inquiry
among the waitresses in the largest dining rooms employing women
brought out the fact that, comparably speaking, the waitresses get few
tips, and only a small portion of those come from men patrons."

Waitresses tolerated this for a while.

Then they went on strike. In August of 1910 the *Tribune* reported:

> The battle of the plates, which began at noontime on Friday, when a
> dozen women waitresses "struck" at the restaurant of Mrs. Theresa
> Mahler, leaving hungry Chicago Board of Trade Brokers half-starved,
> was transferred to a . . . courtroom yesterday.

Five of the striking [waitresses] appeared dressed in their best to vouch for their union's business agent, Miss Anna Willard, who crooked her finger and called the strike.

Miss Willard was arrested after Mrs. Mahler had turned a riot call and a wagon load of policemen had been called to the restaurant.

Mrs. Mahler . . . charged Miss Willard with inciting a riot. "She called my restaurant a 'scab dump' . . ." declared the proprietress with flashing eyes.

"First she entered my restaurant and started to yank the aprons off the girls. Then she told them to march out—and out they went! Such work! Telling everyone who passed that my restaurant was a 'scab dump' and not to eat there."

Miss Willard stood silent and smiled derisively . . . When her turn for speechmaking came, [she] simply demanded a jury trial.[30]

THE LUNCH PROBLEM SOLVED:
THE INVENTION OF MODERN FAST FOOD

If fast food is defined based not only on the food itself but also on the way the food is served and the setting and circumstances under which it's eaten then two restaurant companies share the credit for having invented modern fast food during this era. Each company aimed to solve the same set of problems: first, lunch as a crowded, rude, dyspeptic experience that customers had to endure and, second, lunch as a fraught process in which the customers felt they were at the mercy of waiters and waitresses who themselves felt they were at the mercy of their employers.

One of the companies—a quick-lunch chain run by two brothers—was called Childs. The other, known as the Automat, was a restaurant setting dominated by a self-service, food-delivery system ("a fresh food vending machine") invented in Switzerland, built in Germany, and then imported to the United States by Joseph Horn and Frank Hardart.[31]

The Childs brothers, William and Samuel, opened their first quick-lunch restaurant in New York, on Cortlandt Street, in 1889. Horn and Hardart opened their first, fifteen-stool lunchroom across the street from Wanamaker's department store in Philadelphia in 1888. The Childses solved the "crowded, rude, dyspeptic" problem within a year of opening their first place. Horn and Hardart made the customer/waiter/employer triangle disappear simply by eliminating their waitstaff.

Food—good tasting, well prepared, simple, and satisfying—was the foundation of both companies' success. In the case of Childs: uncomplicated food—wheat cakes or Boston baked beans or roast beef hash—made from the very best ingredients and served in a place as clean and bright and fresh and open as the kitchen of the big New Jersey family farm where the brothers had grown up was the basis of its fortune. Wonderful coffee ("gilt-edged coffee," Horn and Hardart called it) that wasn't boiled, then clarified with eggshells, then strained (the way everyone else made it) but was freshly ground and freshly brewed, using the French drip method that Frank Hardart had learned while slaving away at a little lunch counter in New Orleans, made and kept Horn and Hardart's reputation.[32]

Central warehouses, where ingredients were stored under the best conditions, and central kitchens, where hot foods and baked goods were prepared in bulk, using standardized, strictly enforced recipes, were strategies that both companies shared. Central inventory control and central commissaries enabled both companies to achieve two goals at once. They controlled food quality and uniformity and they shrank the size (and changed the nature) of their outlets' kitchens while increasing the size of their seating areas, where customers ate and paid.

Neither company developed its food delivery and customer service strategies out of thin air. What was unique about these companies was how, by combining procedures that hadn't previously been combined, they created new ways of serving old-fashioned food.

CHILDS

William Childs was fifty-eight when he let himself be interviewed, for the first time in his life, by a reporter from *American Magazine*. The year was 1921. William and his brother had been in the restaurant business for more than thirty years. By then, there were more than one hundred Childs restaurants in cities from New York to Los Angeles and Montreal to New Orleans. Underwritten, in part, by a syndicate of Standard Oil investors, Childs' ubiquity was based on a strictly enforced consistency (later replicated by McDonald's). Every Childs looked very much like every other Childs; every Childs served the same food (with slight regional variations) as every other Childs, at the same prices. People who didn't usually eat at Childs

*Childs Restaurant, 1900,
Byron Company*

when they were at home ate at Childs when they were traveling. Clean, safe, moderately priced, good but not fancy food was what everyone expected when they walked into a Childs. It was William Childs's job (Samuel managed the company's real estate and investment operations) to make sure no one was disappointed.[33]

"Did you ever stop to think," William Childs was asked, "that several thousand young men [just like you and your brother] . . . opened restaurants in New York City without ever being heard from beyond a five block radius? What did you give the public that it hadn't been used to getting?"

Mr. Childs sat for a long time in thought, his hand crossed in his lap.

"That's not an easy question," he said at last. "Naturally [Samuel and I] had certain ideas and ideals—and they were pretty much the same as we have today.

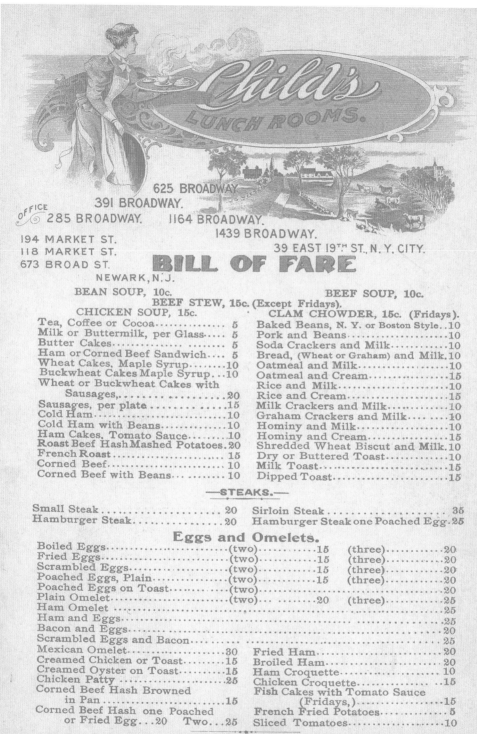

Child's LUNCH ROOMS.

625 BROADWAY
391 BROADWAY.
OFFICE 285 BROADWAY.   1164 BROADWAY.
1439 BROADWAY.
194 MARKET ST.
118 MARKET ST.   39 EAST 19TH ST. N. Y. CITY.
673 BROAD ST.

BILL OF FARE

NEWARK, N. J.

BEAN SOUP, 10c.   BEEF SOUP, 10c.
BEEF STEW, 15c. (Except Fridays).
CHICKEN SOUP, 15c.   CLAM CHOWDER, 15c. (Fridays).

Tea, Coffee or Cocoa	5	Baked Beans, N. Y. or Boston Style	10
Milk or Buttermilk, per Glass	5	Pork and Beans	10
Butter Cakes	5	Soda Crackers and Milk	10
Ham or Corned Beef Sandwich	5	Bread, (Wheat or Graham) and Milk	10
Wheat Cakes, Maple Syrup	10	Oatmeal and Milk	10
Buckwheat Cakes Maple Syrup	10	Oatmeal and Cream	15
Wheat or Buckwheat Cakes with		Rice and Milk	10
Sausages,	20	Rice and Cream	15
Sausages, per plate	15	Milk Crackers and Milk	10
Cold Ham	10	Graham Crackers and Milk	10
Cold Ham with Beans	10	Hominy and Milk	10
Ham Cakes, Tomato Sauce	10	Hominy and Cream	15
Roast Beef Hash Mashed Potatoes	20	Shredded Wheat Biscut and Milk	10
French Roast	15	Dry or Buttered Toast	10
Corned Beef	10	Milk Toast	15
Corned Beef with Beans	10	Dipped Toast	15

——STEAKS.——

Small Steak	20	Sirloin Steak	35
Hamburger Steak	20	Hamburger Steak one Poached Egg	25

Eggs and Omelets.

Boiled Eggs	(two)	15	(three)	20
Fried Eggs	(two)	15	(three)	20
Scrambled Eggs	(two)	15	(three)	20
Poached Eggs, Plain	(two)	15	(three)	20
Poached Eggs on Toast	(two)			20
Plain Omelet	(two)	20	(three)	25
Ham Omelet				25
Ham and Eggs				25
Bacon and Eggs				20
Scrambled Eggs and Bacon				25

Mexican Omelet	30	Fried Ham	20
Creamed Chicken or Toast	15	Broiled Ham	20
Creamed Oyster on Toast	15	Ham Croquette	10
Chicken Patty	25	Chicken Croquette	15
Corned Beef Hash Browned		Fish Cakes with Tomato Sauce	
in Pan	15	(Fridays,)	15
Corned Beef Hash one Poached		French Fried Potatoes	5
or Fried Egg...20 Two...25		Sliced Tomatoes	10

The Milk used in this establishment is fresh from my own Dairy every morning.

The Proprietor is not responsible for personal property left or exchanged unless checked by the Superintendent.   *17 Jan. 1900*

Bill of fare, Child's Lunch Rooms, New York and New Jersey, 1900

"What is the restaurant business anyway? I asked myself. And the best answer I could work out was that it was merely housekeeping without the problem of shelter. So we determined to make the food as close as possible to that served in the best homes. We used a lot of family recipes—and still use them. All our rice pudding, for example, is prepared just as Mother used to make it for us boys."

Serving food like Mother used to make (especially if she and her boys lived in one of "the best houses") might have contributed to Childs success, but it was more than their mother's rice pudding that made the brothers rich.[34]

William understood this. "Absolute cleanliness was our goal," he said. "Lighting in those days was a compromise between gas and electricity. Most popular priced restaurants appeared dismal. We put in the large, glass fronts we have today; white glass [porcelain tile] walls, and white [marble topped] tables.

"The place had to look clean, smell clean, and *be* clean. White shows dirt more quickly than any other color, but it also advertises cleanliness."

Long before the food and drug scandals that culminated with the passage of the Pure Food and Drug laws in 1906, William and Samuel understood that their restaurant had to sell purity and cleanliness along with the griddlecakes and sandwiches.

William continued, saying, "Another thing to eliminate was the smell that hovered in the air of many restaurants. We installed exhaust fans which changed the air every two minutes by forced ventilation.

"Nearly all restaurants had men waiters—but people were used to having women wait on them at home. We hired attractive girls, paid them more wages than they could get elsewhere, and maintained discipline. Our young women did not wear jewelry, chew gum, or enter into unnecessary conversation."

The Childses did more than demand good manners from their waitresses. They dressed them in white—white dresses, white shirtwaist blouses, white aprons, accented only by black bow ties or black ribbons around their necks. A Childs waitress looked less like someone's sister and more like a nurse working as a maid.

The *American Magazine* reporter listened to all this, then began to ask William a series of questions—questions so broad, so general, so anthropological that no one might have been able to answer them before Childs became a national chain that paid close attention and kept careful records of the kinds of foods its outlets sold and when and where they sold them.

The reporter's next question was a modest one: "You are continuously learning new things about people's tastes, I suppose?" As one question followed another, William's answers became more broadly analytic. His answers, read today, reveal how much yet how little has changed since he and Samuel opened their first restaurant with money William had earned delivering milk from a horse and wagon in the farm country of New Jersey.

"Taste is less variable than you might imagine," William began. "People in all parts of the country eat pretty much the same thing, season to season, year after year... Our managers estimate that 40% of our customers have the same lunch, day after day... You would be surprised to know how the individual records of our far flung group of restaurants correspond.

"Naturally, there are minor differences. Boston is the only city where we have to list pie *and* beans on our breakfast menu. Also, more oysters are served in Boston than anywhere else... In the South, there is a marked demand for smoked ham and bacon... Crackers and milk is a popular lunchtime dish, East and North, but the South and West show little fondness for this item. The Middle North, around Minneapolis, is particularly partial to fresh meats... Nine out of ten young boys who eat in our places are sure to order griddle cakes.

"Beans are very popular in Boston, but our sales sheets show that downtown New York holds the record for consumption of this popular dish... It's hard to say why lower New York holds the supremacy. Our managers attribute it to the fact that the thousands of girls employed in the busy offices order beans because they are cheap, and ready for instant service...

"In New Orleans, we serve several dishes — mostly Creole products — that are not found elsewhere on our menus. Favorite among these is a cream cheese[35] which is much the same thing as the old, country 'pot cheese' most of us are familiar with."

"What is the commonest order at your restaurants?" asked the reporter.

"Coffee," William answered. "By an overwhelming majority! Corned beef hash is a favorite among solid foods. Boiled ham and beef divide the honors in meats. Chicken soup leads its field and oatmeal is the most popular hot cereal, both summer and winter. Potatoes are the most largely eaten vegetable, with beans a good second.

June, 1907

(Fridays) Fish Cakes with Tomato Sauce..........10

LITTLE NECK CLAMS.

Half Shell	15	Fry, Large	25
Stew	20	Broiled	30
Fry, Small	20	Pan Roast	30

Steamed Clams...................30
Clam Chowder (Fridays)......15

SANDWICHES.

Ham	5	Roast Beef	5
Corned Beef	5	Minced Ham	5
Boned Chicken	5	Fish Cake (Friday)	5

Oyster 5

SALADS

Potato	10	Chicken	25

EGGS, OMELETTES, ETC.

Two Boiled Eggs	15	Bacon and Eggs	25
Two Fried Eggs	15	Ham and Eggs	25
Two Scrambled Eggs	15	Scrambled Eggs and Chipped	
Poached Eggs	15	Beef	20
Poached Eggs on Toast	20	Ham Omelette	20

Plain Omelette....................15

PASTRY AND DESSERT.

All Pies in Season	5	Tapioca Cream Pudding	5
Crullers	5	Chocolate Eclairs	5
Stewed Prunes with Cream	5	Cream Rolls	5
Apple Sauce	5	Napoleons	5
Baked Apple	5	Bath Buns	5
" " with Cream	10	German Coffee Cake	5
" " (large) in bowl		Lady Fingers	5
with Cream	15	Ice Cream Vanilla	10
Corn Starch, Chocolate	5	" Neapolitan	10
Corn Starch, Vanilla	5	Cup Custard	10
Rice Pudding	5		

NOT RESPONSIBLE FOR PERSONAL PROPERTY
UNLESS CHECKED BY THE MANAGER.

Daily menu, Childs', New York, 1907

Childs Restaurant, 1906,
Byron Company

"Out of every $100 spent in a typically located restaurant, about one-fifth, or $20, goes to beverages . . . The others range something like this: Griddle cakes, $16.50; Hot dishes, ready-to-serve, $13.00; Desserts, $12.00; Egg dishes, $9.50; Sandwiches, $4.25; Oysters, $3.50; Cereals, $2.75 . . . salads and cold dishes are at the bottom of the list."[36]

The reporter then asked William a question that people still ask today: "Is there much difference between the orders of men and women?"

"A little," William said. "Men go in for more meats, potatoes, and eggs; women are inclined to eat more soups, salads, croquettes, and desserts. At the end of the meals, the chances are in favor of the men ordering pie and the women ordering ice cream."[37]

Hidden behind William's answers about pie and ice cream and hash and baked beans was a business and marketing strategy as perceptive and potent as the Childs brothers' decision to sell cleanliness along with their food.

If Childs' uniformity and ubiquity were precursors to McDonald's, and if Childs' pancakes "fresh off the griddle" were the ancestors of IHOP's, then what William said at the end of his interview anticipated the "location" strategy of Starbucks.

"We never locate a new place without carefully counting and studying street traffic," William said. "We know that from three to fifteen percent of the people passing out the doors will stop in to eat.

"Dense traffic of a low grade will yield only 3%; the average location will yield 7%; but it is only a strategic location that will bring in as high as 15%.

"The ideal location taps a great traffic artery along which people are constantly moving to shop, transact business, see the sights, and attend theaters."

William and Samuel's strategy of locating their restaurants in the busiest, most prominent parts of cities made Childs — with its big windows, white walls, high ceilings, and cavernous interiors full of hungry people — icons of modern life. Whatever William wanted to believe about the prosperous, farm-kitchen origins of the cultural phenomenon that he and his brother created, the hard-edged reality of their restaurants was very different.

This is what the architectural historian Lewis Mumford said:

Lured into the void of a modern American lunchroom by the vision of thick disks of golden batter basking on an iron grill, one is struck immediately . . . by the cacophonous chorus of china and metal. From the polished tiles of the white interior comes a frigid glare . . . It is difficult not to associate this surgical immaculacy with that of the ward in the better sort of hospital. The cleanliness is, in fact, blatant: the restaurant is like a soap that not merely removes dirt . . . but adds a gratuitous odor of antiseptics . . . to call attention to its performance.

If one looks carefully at the floors, the cutlery the tables, the chairs, and the rest of the fixtures, every article is excellent, and its excellence is due to the fact that it has been made by a machine . . .

If there are no surprises in [such] a modern scheme of decoration and equipment, there are likewise no disappointments. The whole structure is as neat, as chaste, and as inevitable as a demonstration in Euclid.[38]

Horn and Hardart

Compared with the Childs brothers, who built the counters of their first restaurant themselves, furnished the place with secondhand chairs and tables, and risked William's milk-route money on their success or failure, Horn and Hardart's Automat began very differently.

Joseph Horn's family were well-to-do factory owners in Philadelphia. (The family business manufactured and sold surgical instruments.) When, at the age of twenty-seven, Horn told his mother—a widow who'd raised seven children on the income from the family business—that he wanted to start a restaurant, his mother bought him a ticket to tour the country to see for himself how restaurants were run.[39]

The story goes that in Boston Horn came upon a one-of-a-kind restaurant called Thompson's Spa that became the inspiration for the "waiterless restaurant" Horn and Frank Hardart eventually opened. Thompson's was a warren of fifty mahogany-paneled big and little rooms, spread across four storefronts. Waiters shouted their orders into speaking tubes; basement kitchens sent up the food on dumbwaiters. All this was clever enough, Horn thought, but the way Thompson's delivered coffee to its customers thrilled him: a central reservoir sent hot coffee—through silver pipes!—to faucets in the different rooms. The man who designed and owned this spa was an engineer who'd studied at MIT. Horn wasn't the first or last visitor to ask how it was all done, but no one—not Horn's waiter, nor the MIT engineer, nor the engineer's sons who ran the place—would tell him.[40]

When Horn came back from his tour, he asked his mother to loan him $1,000, then put an ad in a local paper looking for a partner. Horn got only one answer: three words, scribbled on a scrap of paper, stuffed in an envelope with a boardinghouse return address on it. Frank Hardart had sent it. He'd been working in a quick lunch called Joe Smith's when he'd seen Horn's ad. He tore the corner off a bag of sugar, wrote, "I'm your man" on it, and mailed it.

The two men met, shook hands, and their partnership began.

Twelve years passed.

Hardart's French drip coffee built the partners' reputation. They opened more lunchrooms, always on busy street corners in commercial neighborhoods. The lunchrooms made money. (When Frank Hardart died in 1918, at the age of sixty-eight, he left an estate the equal of about $4.2 million today.)[41] Restaurant supply salesmen came calling. In 1900,

Automat, New York, 1900s

a man selling a self-contained "waiterless restaurant" made by a German company called Quissana presented himself to the partners. All he had to show were artist's sketches and engineering drawings. The partners expressed interest.

Ray Stannard Baker, the American journalist, had seen such "waiterless restaurants" while in Germany. He wrote about them in *Seen in Germany*, published in 1902.

"There are several of these curious restaurants in Berlin," wrote Baker.

Two very fine ones in *Friedriech Strasse*—and they are also found in other parts of Germany. They are large, brilliantly fitted rooms with metal and glass walls which contain many pockets and slots.

Supposing you wish a glass of beer and a sandwich? You drop a twenty *pfennig* piece in the proper place, and, having set your glass underneath a spout, you turn a handle and immediately your glass is foaming full.

Then you cross the room to the sandwich department where, through a glass wall, you see all varieties of sandwiches in stock. When you have selected the kind you wish, a coin in the slot will cause it to drop out on a little shelf and then to a plate or onto your hand.

Should you desire coffee, milk, salad, cold meat, preserves, and, in come cases, warm dishes, they are all to be had by the dropping of a coin . . . The food furnished is well-cooked and fresh . . .

One would think that such institutions would in no wise attract the leisurely German . . . but they are quite as popular as our own quick lunch restaurants, being especially crowded in the evenings.

The Quissana salesman may not have been as articulate as Baker but the man's drawings and plans were enough to send Frank Hardart to Germany to see for himself. Hardart hadn't been back to Germany since his family left Bavaria when he was thirteen. He'd been raised poor, then lived poor in America, working and cooking and washing dishes in shabby little restaurants until his partnership with Horn changed his life.

Hardart was fifty-one, with money to spend, when he saw his first Quissana machine selling food and drinks in Berlin. Quissana representatives told him that one of the machines would cost him and Mr. Horn $30,000 (a huge sum, equal to about $750,000 today), and that it would take a year to build, test, and ship. Hardart placed an order immediately.

The Quissana company did what it had been paid to do but the ship carrying the machine collided with another ship and sank. The order was insured, so the company began building another machine. A year passed.

It turned out that Mr. Horn and Mr. Hardart weren't the only restaurant keepers visited by the Quissana salesman. Early in 1902 a man named James Holcomb opened an Automatic Café at the corner of Broadway and Spring Street in New York. The story goes that Holcomb paid more than twice as much as Horn and Hardart did to buy and install an extravaganza of beveled glass, mirrors, onyx, and colored tiles replete with German proverbs. Holcomb's "slot machine" café sold more than just ham sandwiches and baked beans. A man with a handful of nickels could buy himself a dish of lobster Newburg,[42] or — if he was so inclined — a gin fizz or a highball.[43] Coffee and beer came out of separate spigots, each with its own hand crank. Sandwiches, wrapped in wax paper, could be had by pulling a lever that opened a small windowed box. Hot dishes — including lobster Newburg — arrived by dumbwaiter from a basement kitchen after customers inserted tokens they'd bought with more nickels.

Meanwhile, in Philadelphia, Horn and Hardart's second Quissana machine arrived in time for them to open their own Automat on Chestnut Street, in June 1902.

Philadelphia's *Evening Bulletin* announced the happy news: "The horseless carriage, the wireless telephone, and the playerless piano have been surpassed . . . Artistically, [the Automat] is a glittering . . . combination of plate glass, marble tiling, weathered oak wainscoting, and hammered brass fittings. Practically, it is a boon to thousands of hungry businessmen and women."[44]

James Holcomb's New York extravaganza went out of business in 1904. A year later, Horn and Hardart opened their second Philadelphia Automat. In 1907 they opened their third; in 1912 they opened their fourth. None of Horn and Hardart's Automats sold beverages other than coffee and tea.

Each time the partners opened a new Philadelphia Automat, they refined its vending operations. They replaced Quissana's beverage spigots with dolphin-headed spouts, copied, in miniature, from a fountain Horn had seen in the ruins of Pompeii while on vacation.[45] Quissana's trap-door, windowed boxes (connected by dumbwaiters to basement kitchens) were replaced with heated (or cooled) metal boxes fitted with turntables that could be spun and refilled by service workers, hidden behind the boxes in a kitchen area where prepared food was kept ready.

As to the food itself, the quality of everything served by every Automat (and by all the lunchrooms that the partners operated) was governed by Joseph Horn's favorite saying: "There is no trick to selling a poor item cheaply. The real trick is to sell a good item cheaply."[46]

The partners bought the best ingredients available at the best prices they could negotiate. Everything—baked goods, entrées, soups, and salads—was prepared by a central commissary under the command of a head chef. *Everything* was then tasted *every day*, at lunch, by a panel that included the partners, their head chef, their chief engineer, and a small group of restaurant managers and headquarters staff. Between bites or sips the panelists tasted and evaluated black coffee that came, one day to the next, from a different Automat. Over time, procedures that emphasized quality, consistency, freshness, and uniformity were codified in a "Manager's Rule Book." The holding temperature and sixty-minute life span of a batch of coffee before it had to be discarded and fresh coffee brewed; the 120-minute life span of a batch of fresh juice (once fresh juice was added to the menu); the number of times every day each dining table had to be wiped clean; the precise placement of condiments on each table's lazy Susan—everything from portion size to presentation to disposal (or donation to shelters and feeding centers for the homeless and poor) was regulated and enforced. Behind every Automat's glass-fronted food displays were crews of servers, behind them were crews of hot and cold food and beverage managers, and behind them all were the partners themselves, sampling and screening everything from the rolls to the butter to the plates on which the rolls and butter were served.

In 1911 the partners began to scout the New York market. First, they opened two lunchrooms that served nothing but coffee and baked goods and closed before dinner. Next, they looked for land: one lot for a central commissary, a second lot for their first New York Automat. Brokers for the partners located a site on Eleventh Avenue and Fiftieth Street for a new commissary. The lot belonged to the Astor estate but the estate was prohibited from selling Astor property to a company (the partners had, by then, incorporated). Frank Hardart and his son solved the problem by buying the lot themselves—then selling it to the partnership.

As to the restaurant site, brokers found a site at Forty-sixth Street and Broadway, fronting on the Great White Way. A subway stop at Forty-second Street and another at Forty-ninth served hundreds of thousands of riders a day; the adjacent theater district drew large crowds of tourists.

The neighborhood itself was inhabited by workers and clerks who lived, paycheck to paycheck, in boardinghouses and cheap hotels.

The partners made their move.

They hired a firm of Philadelphia architects who gave them what they wanted. The facade of their new restaurant had the symmetry of a bank building or a district post office. Into this facade the architects cut a huge, thirty-foot rectangle, two stories high, flanked on either side by two-story, Palladian-style arched openings. Into the facade's rectangle and flanking arches, the architects fitted gigantic stained-glass windows, protected by filigreed ironwork. The size of these windows was remarkable, but their brilliant, colored intricacy was even more so. The man who'd designed them—the Philadelphia glass sculptor Nicola D'Ascenzo—had also designed windows for the Folger Shakespeare Library in Washington, D.C., and New York's Cathedral of Saint John the Divine.

Inside, beneath a carved plaster ceiling, lit with pearly electric bulbs and ornamented with fruit and leaves and neo-Gothic figures that might have decorated the pillars of a church whose worshippers celebrated the pleasures of food, customers dined at round tables topped with Carrara marble. The floor beneath their feet was an expanse of small white tiles, inlaid with a pattern that suggested the intersecting circles made by raindrops on a pond.

"Along the side and rear walls stood the Automat mechanism—not just machinery, but machinery with splendor, its ornate wooden framework sparkling with mirrored surfaces, its uppermost edges alternating between swelling arches and horizontals, so that the entire room was enveloped in an ennobling, continuous rhythm . . . Here was efficiency enshrined, daily necessity given an atmosphere of glory."[47]

And what was served amidst this splendor?

Baked beans

Fishcakes

Fresh rolls and butter

Beef stew

Salisbury steak with mashed potatoes

Apple pie or pumpkin pie

Ice cream

Coffee or tea

—ML

042936. WINDOW IN GIRLS' RESTAURANT, NATIONAL CASH REGISTER, DAYTON, O.   DETROIT PHOTOGRAPHIC CO.

HER FOOD

WORK OR STARVE

"I was born in the South, in Tennessee," Jane Williams began. She was twenty-five, she said, when "my father died suddenly and poor — and my brother followed him soon after. Then came the beginning of the hard times . . .

"I learned typesetting and stenography and tried school teaching . . . I found few opportunities in the South. I drifted out to Texas and then, last January, to Chicago. I had written . . . some articles for southern papers and magazines. I had read proof and held copy. I felt surely in Chicago congenial work could be found . . .

"I made the rounds of the publishing houses and employment agencies in vain. At the latter, I was told I was 'too old' to hope for a good position, that young girls alone were in demand . . . a temporary position at $6.00 per week was all I could find."

It was 1903 when Miss Williams told her story to the *Chicago Tribune*. The country was in the teeth of a recession that began in September 1902 and finally ended in August 1904. The six dollars she earned doing temporary work would have bought her about as much as $161 would buy her now.

"It may be easy to live on $6.00 per week when you're used to it," she said, "but I found it hard."

Two dollars weekly went for my tiny hall room.
  None too much of it was left for my food.

Window in girls' restaurant, National Cash Register Company, Dayton, Ohio, 1902

99

Every day of the four weeks I held that $6.00 position, I dined on buckwheat cakes, syrup, and a cup of coffee for 15 cents. I found I could keep up best on that diet. I needed the coffee to keep me awake. I soon grew so weak and tired. For breakfast I had simply a cup of coffee — with an uncooked cereal in my room for supper. These were easy times and luxurious, however, compared to those that came later...

At the end of the month, I found myself out of a position and with less than a dollar in my pocket...

During my five weeks without employment, I earned $2.50 by miscellaneous jobs of typesetting... How did I manage? Well, I was careful.

I faced starvation many times. Nobody knows the thoughts that can come up in a human heart while tramping the streets, cold, hungry, exhausted, looking for work, with well fed, prosperous, uncaring fellow humans on every side...

Two nights and two days were the longest I ever went without food, but I tell you my thoughts were rampant during that period, and they were not pleasant ones. Suicide? Why yes, of course. I thought of it, but I'm not a coward... "If I drop dead on the streets, I'll die an honor to the paving stones I drop on," I told myself. I told one woman who — and I'd only just made her acquaintance — stood by me with sympathy and encouragement — as well as practical assistance now and then.

As for food, I did with little.

Occasionally, when I had a little money, I treated myself to a solid meal of wheat cakes and syrup... I found how to manage a long time without fainting on a single cup of coffee.

A place called the Penny Lunch kept her alive. "I never saw another woman in it, but I was treated nicely... At this restaurant, you could get two slices of fruit cake or one of 'black cake,' a kind of ginger cake, or a cup of coffee or a glass of milk, each for a penny. Once or twice, when I had a little money or was unusually hungry, I treated myself to a five cent meal there. For a nickel, they gave you three slices of fried bacon, some Irish potatoes, bread, and a cup of coffee or a glass of milk. You don't know until you try how good such food can taste — with genuine hunger for a sauce."

After five weeks, Miss Williams found another temporary job, "holding copy," as she called it. She repaid the fifteen cents she owed the penny restaurant ("Where they trusted me," she said), and the forty cents she owed the milkman.[1]

Thousands of women and girls — farmers' daughters, small-town teenagers, women of varying ages cut adrift by family misfortune — streamed out of the rural South, Northeast, and Midwest and into the great cities in the 1890s and 1900s, looking for work. They joined thousands of young immigrant women, some sent ahead in groups by families who expected them to establish themselves in America while supporting relatives back home, others crowding into tenements with parents and younger siblings. These women, both native- and foreign-born, saw opportunity not, as in years past, as housemaids or governesses, but in the cities' burgeoning shops, offices, and factories.

What they found, when they arrived, was a ladder of opportunity, but only some of the rungs were available to anyone. A small-town girl might imagine herself working as an elderly lady's companion or as one of the new, glamorous-sounding "hello girls" who ran telephone switchboards, but unless she was white (a definition that, in 1900, excluded not only African Americans and Latinos but also Jews and Italians and Greeks), had a secondary education, and spoke fluent, grammatical English, or could make use of family connections, the options available were both less lucrative and less genteel.

At the bottom of the heap was laundry work, which was arduous, wet, and, thanks to the use of limb-crushing mangles for pressing linens and open flames for heating flatirons, dangerous. Then there was sweatshop labor sewing or finishing garments, piecework that could earn a quick and accurate seamstress a decent living but provided less than subsistence wages for anyone else who tried it. Slightly better was light factory labor — rolling cigars, dipping candy, binding books, trimming hats — though working conditions, safety, and pay varied widely by city and employer. Many employers hired only those who had done the same work before. There was also waitressing, which offered the theoretical chance to earn tips — and, perhaps, to strike the fancy of a well-heeled customer — followed by department store clerking and clerical work in offices.[2]

Employers who paid higher-than-average wages or had reputations for good working conditions — the largest department stores, Childs restaurants — could insist on hiring only the experienced. A first-timer was usually forced to accept a position at a less attractive workplace for much lower "learning wages," or to take temporary factory or retail jobs during pre-holiday rushes, only to be laid off as soon as demand ebbed.

Few of the women who migrated to cities to work understood that it could take weeks or months to find any job at all, or that starting wages might be as low as $2 or $3 per week—far from the $9 or $10 that newspapers in Boston, Philadelphia, Chicago, and New York reported were necessary for a woman to survive on her own in a rented room with modest meals.[3] Rooming with relatives or sharing a bed in an unheated room with one or two other girls could leave enough money for carfare, basic clothing, and food. But if a woman had no family or friends in the city, and if she refused to enter domestic service or take shelter in a big city's restrictive "homes for working girls" (dormitories run by the Young Women's Christian Association or local missionary societies, and infamous for rigid curfews, bad food, and disapproving matrons), sacrifices had to be made.[4]

Dorothy Richardson, a twenty-something woman from small-town Pennsylvania who called herself "Rose Fortune," chronicled her search for work in New York City in the early 1900s. Her experiences were serialized in several newspapers and magazines before being published, in 1905, as a book titled *The Long Day*. Her account makes clear how hard the struggle to keep body and soul together, housed, and fed could be for working women living on their own.

"I have been in New York almost a month," she wrote in 1903, after she'd abandoned hope of finding work quickly as a reader to invalids or as a receptionist, "and have not yet found a job that will enable me to live. I have only two dollars left . . . Even the little dairy lunch room has become a luxury to be indulged in only for an occasional hot stew at the end of the weary day. My breakfast of rolls and coffee, boiled on the landlady's kitchen range, is eaten from the top of an empty flour barrel . . . With breakfasts at an average cost of three cents each, and dinners at fifteen cents (I now forego lunch entirely), I figure that a perfectly healthy, normal girl can keep body and soul together, at least for a time. For me, however, that time is fast drawing to an end."[5]

In her lean first month in the city, Rose had two brushes with homelessness. She lost all her belongings in a rooming-house fire and had to stay at a "home for young women" that doubled as an orphanage. Days later, a coworker who'd invited her to share a room turned out to have an intrusive "gentleman friend" and a drinking problem, and Rose fled into the night, spending the early morning hours huddled in a twenty-four-hour quick-lunch restaurant with a homeless woman from the neighborhood.[6]

Rose Fortune eventually found her way into a series of blue-collar jobs. She glued decorative paper onto ladies' hatboxes; she made artificial poppies from silk and wire; she tried—and failed utterly—to sew women's underdrawers; she made little velvet jewel cases; she shook out wet laundry as it came, stiff and twisted, off the wringers.

In each place, Rose Fortune learned the small satisfactions and many travails of manual labor. She also discovered a problem with which her sisters in labor all over the country were already familiar.

A WOMAN'S LUNCH

For women working in urban laundries, factories, and workshops, the midday meal was a problem on at least three counts: no time, no money, no suitable place to eat. The lunch bell rang at noon and, once it did, everyone had thirty minutes in which to find, purchase, and consume the midday meal. At some factories, that could mean a stampede down the staircase to the nearest quick-lunch counter. More often, working girls trying to meet $8 in weekly expenses on a $4 paycheck brought bread-and-butter or cold meat sandwiches from home, wrapped in paper and tucked into a repurposed pasteboard box or a skirt pocket. They ate their lunches at their stations or huddled in an empty corner of the workroom.

That approach assumed the presence of leftovers. A young woman living alone in a "light housekeeping" studio—a single, rented room with an alcohol lamp to make tea and a wooden crate for food storage—might have 15 to 20 cents a day available for food after rent and carfare to and from work. Fifteen or twenty cents bought a modest evening meal—pork and beans, hotcakes, a bowl of murky stew—in a lunchroom, and a breakfast of coffee and rolls, eaten in her room.

Many girls improvised. Lunch might be nothing at all, an apple from a street vendor, a handful of candy from the corner store.

At the workshop where she made silk poppies, where the time allotted for lunch was a luxurious full hour, Rose Fortune saw another solution.

At 11:15, a little girl, wearing an immense flower-laden hat and carrying a large market basket, comes and asks us what we want for lunch. She has a long piece of pasteboard and writes as the girls dictate. I can buy anything I want, Bessie explains—bread and butter, eggs, chops, steaks, potatoes, canned goods—for which I will find ample provisions for cooking over on the gas stoves where the rose makers heat their pincers. When the little girl is gone I learn that she is the runner, and that this is one of her tasks.

"How far does she have to go to market?" I inquired.

"Over to First Avenue."

"Isn't that pretty hard work for such a small girl? Isn't her basket very heavy?"

"Oh, yes; but all the little girls are anxious for the job. They're only too glad to get the ten per cent commission the grocers always allow them."

It lacks but a few minutes to twelve when the child returns, panting under her heavy load, her face dripping with perspiration . . .

"How much did you clear today, Emma?" somebody asks.

"Twenty-one cents," the little girl answers, blushing as red as the poppies.

When Miss Higgins [the supervisor] slips her tall, willowy form into a stylish jacket and begins to pin on her stunning hat it is a sign that the lunch hour has come. One hundred and twenty girls pop up from their hiding places behind the hedges, which have grown rapidly since morning. In a trice tables are cleared of flowers and foliage, and cups and saucers and knives and forks produced from mysterious sources. In the "machine end" stewpans and spiders and pots and kettles are put over the fires. Bacon and chops sputter, steak sizzles, potatoes, beans and corn cook merrily. What was lately a flower garden has become a mammoth kitchen, filled with appetizing sounds and delicious odors. White-aproned cooks scurry madly. It is like a schoolgirl's picnic.[7]

The picnicking of the flower makers turned out to be the exception that proved the rule. More often, Rose Fortune's noontime experiences were meager: the improvised sandwich, supplemented by a square of spice cake or a delicatessen pickle. At the Pearl Laundry, where she worked as a "shaker," the work was so backbreaking, so numbingly repetitive, that no one could have withstood an entire twelve- to fifteen-hour shift on a sandwich alone: "If your job is shaking the wrinkles out of towels and sheets, this in itself is violent exercise. The air is hot and damp because you stand near the washers. You are hurried at a furious rate. When you finish one lot you have to roll heavy baskets, and dump them upon your table, and then go on shaking and shaking again, only to do more heavy loading and dumping."[8]

After a couple of days of lunching on sandwiches, pickles, and donuts, Rose and her coworker, a one-eyed girl, were dropping at their counters from nausea and exhaustion, until they were rescued by one Mrs. Mooney, an "ancient crony" among the laundresses.

"It's them pickles and them rotten cold lunches you girls eat," declared Mrs. Mooney, who was fond of talking on the nutritious properties of food. "Now I says, the Lord only give me one stummick, and when that's wore out he'll never give me another, and I can't never buy one with no money, and I never put anything in that stummick at noon but a good cold beer and a good hot plate of soup, and that's what you ought to do." Mrs. Mooney and another old lady took Rose and her friend to Devlin's, a saloon three blocks away, where a pint of beer and a bowl of soup cost a nickel. With only thirty minutes for lunch and three blocks to walk, the women had no time to change shirtwaists or pin on hats—they trooped into the street with their sleeves rolled up and their damp aprons still tied around their waists.

For modest, small-town Rose Fortune, entering a saloon, let alone hatless and in sodden workclothes, was doing the unthinkable. But hunger and thirst and Mrs. Mooney's determination won out: ". . . we filed in the 'ladies' entrance.' The room was filled with workmen drinking beer and smoking at the little round tables, and when they saw us, each man jumped up, and grabbing his glass, went out into the barroom. Commenting on this to Mrs. Mooney, she explained as we seated ourselves:

"'Sure, and what'd ye expect! Sure, and it's a proper hotel ye're in, and it's decent wurrkin'-men that comes here, and they knows a lady when they sees her, and they ups and goes!'"

Tasting the hot soup, Rose "instantly determined never again to blame a working man or woman for dining in a saloon in preference to the more godly and respectable dairy-lunch room. We all ate ravenously, and I, who never before could endure the sight or smell of beer, found myself draining my 'schooner' as eagerly as Mrs. Mooney herself."

As for Mrs. Mooney: "'My! But that braces me up,' she declared, sighing deeply and licking the froth from her lips; 'it's almost as good as whisky.'"[9]

Never Let a Man Treat You to Dinner

Whatever you are, do not join the class of girls who hint for gifts from men and then boast of having "worked" the man. Do not "work" any man for your luncheon, for candy, for theatre tickets, for jewelry or clothing. Be very careful to refrain from expressing a wish for anything of this sort when you are talking to a man.[10]

If Rose relaxed her standards of propriety to eat lunch with Mrs. Mooney in a saloon, there was another Rubicon she didn't cross. Plenty of young working women in similar straits did the harsh arithmetic of their household budgets and concluded that there was no way to pay for food, clothing, and shelter, let alone an occasional Sunday matinee or evening out, without a little outside help.

Enter the gentleman friend. The workplaces women came into were filled with obliging men, young and not so young, married, single, or somewhere in between, who were happy to show a hardworking girl the town or buy her a hot meal or a nice new dress. They might be seeking wives or more temporary company. And there were bosses and foremen who might offer a pretty girl restaurant lunches or even a promotion, the quid pro quo implied but present. At the Pearl Laundry, Rose caught the eye of the lanky foreman, who in their first conversation of any length told her of his eighteen-dollar-a-week salary (more than four times what Rose and her friend were making) and boasted that his eventual wife would stay home and never have to do laundry, since his was cleaned by the Pearl, a perk of the foreman's job.

Rose caught the eye of the foreman's boss too. The boss "when he came to me lingered a moment and uttered some joking remarks of insulting flattery, and in a moment he had grasped my bare arm and given it a rude pinch, walking hurriedly away." Moments after the pinch, the boss sent the foreman to tell Rose she had been promoted to the "wrapper's counter," which paid more and was located away from the swampy washrooms. Rose was advised to refuse the promotion by "the rest of my companions, who repeated diverse terrible tales of moral ruin and betrayal, more or less apocryphal, wherein the boss was inevitably the villain." After a handwritten, emphatic note of warning from the foreman, she took the stories seriously, leaving the Pearl for good.[11]

Muckraking journalists such as George Kibbe Turner of *McClure's* followed the threat of predatory men a step further, writing exposés of a thriving white slave trade. Turner described how "cadets"—teenage procurers drawn mostly from the ghettos of New York's Lower East Side—would congregate at the five-cent dance halls frequented by immigrant working girls, win their trust by dancing with them and treating them to two-penny sodas, and then bundle the women off to brothels.[12] Another *McClure's* article claimed such practices were commonplace in all large U.S. cities, and not only in cheap dance halls: "Those who recruit women for immoral purposes watch all places where young women are likely to be found under circumstances which will give them a ready means of acquaintance and intimacy, such as employment agencies, immigrant homes, moving-picture shows, dance-halls, sometimes waiting-rooms in large department stores, railroad stations, manicuring and hairdressing establishments."[13]

Most attention from male strangers was less sinister, if not altogether innocent, like the situation confronting Theodore Dreiser's Carrie Meeber. Carrie was hungry, feverish, inadequately dressed for the Chicago autumn, and failing in her efforts to find work when she ran into the dapper traveling salesman Drouet, whom she'd met for the first time on the train to Chicago. Drouet took Carrie to the "old Windsor dining room" on Monroe Street, where the tables were draped in white linen, the silver was immaculately polished, and sirloin steak with mushrooms cost $1.25 (equivalent to $25). After plying her with steak, asparagus, stuffed tomatoes, and coffee, Drouet offered to take Carrie to the theater. She demurred, but he pressed on her forty dollars for new clothes and shoes, meeting her reluctance with "Aw come, Carrie . . . what can you do alone? Let me help you."[14] That she accepted his help, and the sexual relationship that followed—and that she profited from both—was a matter of scandal when *Sister Carrie* first appeared in 1900. But what was scandal to middle-class readers was a fact of life for many working women living on their own.

As a factory worker who relied on a "gentleman friend" for her Sunday meals explained to the New York Factory Investigating Committee in 1915, "Why! If I had to buy all my meals I'd never get along."[15]

Best Lunch for the Business Girl

"I'm down and out," said the stenographer, as she walked home with a companion after office hours. "I'm afraid I'll have to give up my job, and what shall I do?"

"What's the matter?" asked her friend. "I'll bet it's your lunches! Aren't you dizzy and your head queer, and your temper or nerves ready to strike fire like oil-soaked cotton?"

The stenographer smiled freely. "Sounds as if you'd been there yourself."

"I have. What did you have for lunch?"

"Didn't eat any. The chief wanted a paper copied at that time, and I had dyspepsia, anyhow."

— New York Times, 1908

Not every woman working in Boston, Chicago, New York, or Philadelphia was toiling in squalor for below-subsistence pay. By the mid-1900s someone visiting Wall Street or Boston's State Street or Chicago's Loop after a decade away would have noticed a dramatic change: women were suddenly everywhere in urban downtowns — and not just tired factory workers, underfed shop clerks, or the ladies of leisure who were the shop girls' customers. Such women had been familiar sights on city streets for some time, but suddenly the sidewalks of Manhattan and Baltimore and St. Louis and Los Angeles were filled with an army of smartly dressed, self-confident women: the office girls.[16]

As businesses became larger and employers realized that they could increase productivity by having workers specialize, the once jack-of-all-trades (and overwhelmingly male) job of office clerk came to be replaced by pools of stenographers, "typewriters," bookkeepers, cashiers, switchboard operators, and shipping clerks, working in separate departments. Already by 1900 certain specialties — stenographer, typist, telephone operator — were predominantly occupied by women, and across specialties the number of clerical positions being created in cities was tremendous. Women were thought to be especially suited to these positions by virtue of their greater manual dexterity, attention to detail, and sociability.[17]

Women were increasingly better educated, too. By 1900 girls were completing high school at a significantly higher rate than their male classmates. Women with high school diplomas or some college had the knowledge of spelling and grammar employers needed in their clerical staffs. New business "colleges," business classes offered in public schools, and night courses taught girls and women typewriting, shorthand, and other office skills.[18]

As in virtually every occupation, women who worked in offices were paid less, often far less, than male counterparts. But, once trained, a stenographer, typist, or telephone operator could expect starting wages of $8 to $10 per week, with private secretaries and the most experienced transcriptionists making $25 or more per week. Compared to teaching, the other major career path open to women with secondary education, office work offered more social freedom: no school boards monitoring one's conduct after hours, no instant dismissal at marriage.[19] And compared to the physical risks of factory work, and the endless standing and abuse from customers and supervisors endured by waitresses and shop girls, the working conditions of a typewriter or telephone operator "hello girl"—regular hours, convivial coworkers, the relative clean and quiet of an office—seemed attractive.[20]

Business welcomed women workers, too, but as women flocked to city business districts, the problem of lunch emerged once again. Office girls usually had time to sit down for a meal, but few if any places to eat were convenient, affordable, and met middle-class standards of feminine delicacy. "Business girls" were hired for personality and appearance as well as skill; the ideal young woman of the era was energetic, cheerful, and, above all, "dainty" in every way. Dainty women needed dainty food, but where to find such sustenance outside the home?[21]

Saloons like the one Rose Fortune had visited with Mrs. Mooney dotted most downtowns but, with their clientele of gruff workingmen, were unthinkable for business girls. The moderately priced, sit-down restaurants that had sprung up in urban financial districts to serve middle managers were also male preserves, full of heavy food and cigar smoke. Dainty food was consommé, chicken salad, an éclair; a businessman's lunch was bean soup, roast beef and potatoes, steamed pudding. A restaurant owner in Washington, D.C., told a *Post* reporter during a lunch service in 1903: "If it were not for the men we would never sell a piece of meat—at this time of the day particularly. Somehow women rebel at the thought of beefsteak, preferring something dainty . . . A man will come in and order a cooked luncheon and finish with a piece of pie. A woman may take a sandwich and some sweet thing, either cream or fancy cake, but never pie."[22]

The quick-lunch counters that were appearing in cities in the early 1900s were cheap, and it was possible to order just soup or a sandwich and a cup of coffee without risking a waitress's contempt, but many middle-class girls were reluctant to eat in them. Unless the lunchroom made a point of offering separate facilities for men and women, a crowded quick lunch could mean rubbing shoulders with staring male strangers. Even worse, the food served in such places was widely thought to be hazardous.

First-person accounts by women who worked in the quick-lunch restaurants confirmed people's worst fears about the standards in such places. The journalist Maud Younger went undercover to waitress in a succession of quick lunches, then wrote a three-part series for *McClure's* about her experiences.

"Once, I dropped a ham sandwich on the floor, right in front of the head-waitress. I looked up at her questioningly, because I had never seen an incident of this kind, and I was not entirely certain of the accepted policy in such a case. 'Change it,' she said quickly. She knew I would not change it, and I knew that she knew I would not. But I took it all up, went to the counter, and said to the man there. 'Change it.' He looked at me and then at the sandwich and back again at me. Then he rearranged the same ham on the same bread, and I sallied forth a second time to present the reconstructed sandwich to my customer. It was interesting to observe her eating it with relish."[23]

Gradually, entrepreneurs saw the unmet demand for a reasonably priced lunch that matched the tastes and sensitivities of women office workers. In the big cities, catering firms sprang up to provide affordable box lunches to office workers and tourists. Demand for box lunches was brisk. Costing about ten cents each, the lunches typically contained "a bun meat sandwich, a section of pie, fruit of some sort—either a banana, a peach, a pear, or plums—a pickle, and a small cake or doughnut." Not quite the pinnacle of daintiness the female lunch clientele sought but close, for customers the food was fresh and carefully packed.

For women producing and selling the lunches the business was attractive. As the *Tribune* pointed out, apart from finding an agent to sign up potential clients, start-up costs were modest: any clean workspace near a business district would do, the raw ingredients and packing materials could be obtained cheaply, and the owner and a few employees (who might be relatives) could set up a production line and rapidly assemble dozens of lunches in the early morning, sending them out for delivery by nine or ten. A large lunch catering business would need to hire deliverymen, but the smaller ones could contract with newsstands outside the big office buildings; newsagents would sell the lunch boxes for a small commission. The *Tribune* estimated that "Even the novice who has contracts for but two or three buildings or enterprises, which use but 200 boxes daily, is still able to make from $4 to $6 per day clear."[24]

In New York, an African-American woman known only as "Aunt Mary" ran a successful business providing up to three home-cooked meals per day for a reasonable weekly rate: $5 per week for dinner, less for lunch or breakfast. The meals came in portions sufficient for two people, packed in a cloth napkin–lined basket and delivered by young boys, who would rush with the baskets on streetcars from Mary's house to customers' apartment and hotel rooms.

Mary became known for the quality of her ingredients, for which she shopped personally early each morning. Her clientele included wealthy families who lived in hotel suites during the New York social season. Those families could afford hotel dinners but were glad to pay one-fourth the cost and avoid the heaviness of restaurant food — provided the delivery boys were discreet about the contents of the baskets. Mary's operation also developed a following among single office women, who could divide the meals with roommates or save leftovers for lunch the following day. Said one such "bachelor girl": "I really feel as if I were living once more. No more dining alone at horrid restaurants where people look at you as if you were the tag end of a misspent life. No more boarding house tables where they look coldly as the dinner at you if you are late. No more going out in the wind and rain so tired that you don't care, and finally buying a can of tomato soup and coming home so exhausted that you had rather go to bed hungry than eat it. It is the greatest scheme ever invented."[25]

Candy store owners, noticing the crowds of office women buying bonbons at midday, set up counters with seats and began to offer simple, mostly liquid refreshments — cocoa, egg creams, bouillon and crackers. Reported one shopkeeper in Chicago: "These girls come in and sometimes get only an order of bouillon, but even more often the regular bill of fare for them is bouillon, chocolate soda, and an order of crackers. This amounts to 25 cents, and the same thing will be ordered each day, never changing the soda for a frappe, which is 15 cents and would total more.

"Of the bouillons here, tomato is a long way the favorite and leads chicken and clam by half again the number of orders.

"Hot chocolate is a favorite with the lunch girl, and there is one place in town where a cup of hot chocolate is served with a cozy little compote of fancy crackers — all for 15 cents. It is excellent chocolate and makes quite a luncheon, and what seems especially to appeal to the business girl, is the one little cake which is always placed among the crackers."[26]

By the 1910s some of the candy store counters would morph into full-fledged restaurants, serving salads, sandwiches, cakes, and ice cream to a mostly female clientele. One of the most famous, the Schrafft's chain, originated as a Boston candy company and expanded to include stores with cafés in New York City and Syracuse. Owner Frank Shattuck, with the advice and oversight of his sister Jane, created restaurants with dignified, elegant decor, white tablecloths, and menus based on "American home cooking . . . for secretaries and stenographers who must watch their pocketbooks."[27]

At some large businesses employing many women, executives understood that comfortable, affordable dining facilities on the premises would improve efficiency. In Chicago, the president of the Telephone Exchange opened a café serving free hot meals for his switchboard operators. As reported in the *Tribune*: "Heretofore the switchboard operators have been obliged to bring their lunches with them or leave the building at the noon hour. President Sabin, however, came from San Francisco, where his telephone company has fed its own employés at its own expense for many years. He immediately transplanted the idea to Chicago soil, and intimated at the same time that better service would be obtained from the employés as soon as the first meal had been tasted. General Superintendent S.J. Larned says already that President Sabin was right."

At the Telephone Exchange café's grand opening, the women "said a last goody-by to their lunch boxes and cold snacks, and attacked the hot meal with too evident satisfaction." After a lunch of bouillon, whitefish, roast beef, cherry pie, and ice cream, the delighted switchboard operators returned to their posts with a chorus of "Hip, hip hooray, and a tiger for President Sabin!"[28] The Metropolitan Life Insurance Company in New York opened a dining room with a section set aside for its women workers and met with similar success. Wanamaker's department store in Philadelphia and Saks in New York offered their saleswomen dining rooms where they could get hot lunches and dinners at cost.[29]

Meanwhile, women's philanthropic associations came to the aid of their working sisters by setting up "lunch clubs," cafeteria-style establishments for women only. (Men could eat in them as guests of members. Later in the decade, many lunch clubs opened membership to both men and women.) The clubs charged a small monthly membership fee, and then just enough per meal to cover the costs of the club's rented space, food, and service. The food was the main attraction, but some early lunch clubs also offered "homelike" amenities for the working woman living on her own: libraries stocked with books, newspapers, and comfortable armchairs; writing rooms with rows of desks, where a girl could purchase stationery and postage stamps; and "rest rooms" outfitted with beds and couches, where the weary could take a nap.

The most famous of the Chicago lunch clubs was the Noonday Rest, founded by the Klio Association, a women's club whose affluent members were interested in good works. The Chicago clubwomen took their inspiration from the Boston minister and progressive activist Edward Everett Hale. Hale's "Lend a Hand" service club had organized a noonday rest for Boston shop girls and factory women in the early 1890s, and it had quickly filled to capacity.

The Klio Noonday Rest opened on East Monroe Street between Wabash and Michigan Avenues in 1895, closed briefly during a power struggle among Klio Association trustees, then reopened in early 1896. In addition to offering Noonday Rest members buffet lunches and handsome dining and rest rooms, the ladies of Klio sought to provide cultural improvement, courtesy of some of their college-educated officers. In the late 1890s, a woman named Mrs. Sherwood delivered weekly lectures on art and literature, and the Rest offered regular classes in "French, Spanish, physical culture, English, elocution, and music by masters of the arts."[30]

"We go in for culture over here, and study," a Klio Noonday Rest member told a *Tribune* reporter in 1907. By then, the lunchtime lecture series had expanded to include some less lofty topics.

"Care of the Feet — Its Influence on Beauty."

"The Best Exercise for Yourself."

"Cultivate a Sense of Humor — It Oils the Machinery of Life — It is a Beautifier."

"How to Live Forever — the New Cult."

"How to Prevent Divorce."[31]

Despite the problems caused by infighting among association officers, the Rest enrolled six hundred working girls as members in its first month of operations. Membership quickly grew to more than two thousand members, necessitating a waiting list and expansion to roomier quarters on Monroe.[32] The Rest attracted the attention of the newspapers (the *Tribune* compared it, not entirely in jest, to the private clubs of Chicago millionaires), and at least one celebrity. The stage star Ellen Terry visited the Rest in December 1901. Joining the working girls in the lunch line, Terry "ate shrimp salad at five cents per order and pronounced it the best she had ever tasted."[33] The Rest was so wildly successful that the following year a rival club, the Woman's Social Economic Association, declared its intentions to open a similar club for young men.

As the popularity of the noonday rests became clear, they sprang up in other cities. The *Boston Globe*, apparently unaware of Dr. Hale's early efforts, reported plans for a lunch club for both men and women to open in the city in 1902. By 1904, in New York, "an enterprising syndicate, seizing upon the idea furnished by certain philanthropic Chicago women who had established a number of 'noonday rest and lunch clubs' for working girls in the Windy City, founded, as an experiment, a women's lunch and club room at 100 Nassau Street. By the middle of August the speculators were forced by the number of applications for membership to open a second lunch and club room at 43 Broad Street. Within the last month, they have had to add the serving of dinners to their daily programme at the Broad Street place and to enlarge the capacity of the establishment in Nassau Street."

New York lunch clubs, like their Chicago counterparts, charged a twenty-five-cent monthly membership and admitted nonmembers for a nickel. "Once inside, steam tables, set with excellent food at low prices, offer to the girls a choice of soups, fish, meats and vegetables. Further up on long tables spread with cold dishes present a wide variety of salads, breads, sweets, and the indispensable pickles. Meats are only 8 cents a portion, vegetables 4 to 5 cents, salads 5 cents, biscuits 2 cents, breads 1 cent, sandwiches 5 cents, tea, coffee, and cocoa 3 cents, milk 4 cents, and most of the desserts, including ice cream, 5 cents."[34] Members seated themselves. They set their own places and bused their own dishes.

Shortcomings became apparent as lunch clubs multiplied. To keep costs low, organizers often located them in cheap, second-floor walk-up space. Club members mobbed the narrow, steep stairways during the lunchtime rush.[35] On May 1, 1907, the Lotus Lunch Club in Chicago caught fire shortly before noon, when seventy-five patrons and twenty-five employees were in the room. The fire, which started in the building's basement, spread upward and quickly blocked the stairs and elevator. The only means of escape for people trapped in the club was "a small window at the back, which opened on a fire escape leading to the alley."

According to the *Boston Globe*, "About 80 persons were caught with only this chance of safety. Most of these were women, and they made a frantic rush for the window, fighting fiercely in an effort to escape. Those who first stepped on the fire escape were almost immediately pushed off, and they fell to the alley, 20 feet below. Before they could get out of the way, others fell or jumped upon them. The women piled upon one another in a mass, from which they were dragged by men from neighboring stores, but every one of those who came out of the rear window was injured in some manner, except the last half dozen, who were rescued by firemen."[36]

It was miraculous that no one died in the Lotus Lunch Club fire, but investigations by journalists and building inspectors in the weeks after the fire revealed that dozens of clubs in Chicago and New York were firetraps. Housed in 1870s-vintage wooden buildings, many clubs had no fireproofing, fire escapes that ended one or two floors above the ground to deter thieves, and windows partially blocked by iron railings or bars.[37]

Despite the hazards, the popularity of the lunch clubs endured, which led to another problem: a "noonday rest" at the peak of lunch service was anything but restful. A visitor to a club serving both men and women described the scene in 1909.

A sign located at the foot of a winding stairway in one of the busiest parts of Chicago had on it the picture of a hand pointing upwards. Words on the sign indicated that at the top of the stairway a lunch club would be found. Up the stairs were rushing helter-skelter men and women, all in the greatest possible hurry to rest.

Behind a long counter filled with trays and platters and bowls of eatables that emitted savory odors stood three women with huge ladles in their hands and these they were manipulating with a speed that spoke of long and varied experience. They seemed almost to work by intuition, putting on each plate as it was shoved out to them the desired amount and kind of food . . .

With the before mentioned visions in mind of relaxed persons leisurely eating and sipping it came as something of a shock to notice that all, girls especially, ate sitting close to the table with both hands ready for use. When their left hands were not in the act of carrying something to their mouths they were on the table, lightly clinched, thumbs up, and in readiness for emergency. The food, instead of disappearing gradually, went with lightning rapidity.

A visit to another lunch club's rest room revealed that "most of the chairs were gathered into groups and the groups consisted of girls talking away as fast as they could talk."[38]

Grace Clarke, a reporter for the *Chicago Tribune*, quoted a "saleswoman of unusual ability" who avoided the lunch clubs, saying, "I simply cannot wait on myself." Wrote Clarke, "The part, which sitting back at a quiet and orderly table and being waited on in a quiet and orderly way, plays in fitting one for the afternoon's work is one which is recognized by all women who study the real use of their lunch and the noon hour."[39]

BOILING SISTERS DO A BUBBLING BUSINESS

The eating demand which is still farthest from being met is a combination of solid food and home cooking with daintiness.
— GRACE CLARKE, *Chicago Daily Tribune*, 1906

Business girls were not the only women seeking clean, peaceful, welcoming places to eat. Ladies of the leisure class, too, were spending more of their afternoons and evenings in town. As late as the 1890s, the social lives of wealthy women had revolved around the custom of calling on one another at home and giving and attending an endless series of luncheons and teas in one another's mansions. By 1900 more and more of those luncheons and teas were being held in the private dining rooms of fine hotels and restaurants, and women were passing their days shopping at department stores, making

Green Teapot Tea Room, 1906, Byron Company

excursions with friends to parks and museums, and attending club meetings. These ladies longed for a new kind of restaurant, one that would provide women like themselves with a warm welcome, delicate food, and a cozy refuge from the bustle of city streets. From this longing emerged the tearoom.

The first tearooms opened in department stores in the 1870s. Islands of quiet, wicker furniture, and potted greenery, they served lunches and tea to women shoppers, children, and the occasional husband.[40] By the 1890s society women began to open their own, freestanding tearooms in shopping and hotel districts. These women had not only the capital to rent and furnish attractive spaces but a built-in clientele of friends. Some women opened their tearooms as a hobby, inspired by visits to "tea houses" in England, but as often as not the proprietresses had experienced some "financial reverses," perhaps were recently widowed, and were investing a portion—sometimes all—of the family assets in the hope of being able to maintain a comfortable lifestyle.[41]

Town and Country reported in 1906: "These places are not 'cheap' in any sense. The furnishings are artistic, and the china, linen and furnishings of the very best. They represent quite an investment and are run by gentlewomen, as a rule, who are not as wealthy as they have been in other days . . . Here you may obtain excellent viands, and at five o'clock, tea is served with the best bread and butter and the usual accompaniments of sandwiches, etc., which are characteristic of the English."[42]

The first few society ladies who opened tearooms in New York failed to sustain their business—either because, as one reporter suggested, they lacked financial management skills or simply because they tired of the project. No matter: a fad of late-afternoon tea drinking, bolstered by the urban habit of dining ever later in the evening and the growing popularity of temperance, supported the tearoom phenomenon. By mid-decade New York, Chicago, Washington, D.C., Boston, and San Francisco each had a handful of tearooms, owned and run by women.[43] Some owners followed their customer base to summer resorts, setting up seasonal tearooms in colonies such as Newport and Ogunquit.[44]

Tearooms gained a following as much for the cozy atmosphere they provided as for their food and (nonalcoholic) beverages. Owners chose themes that allowed them to put fashionable bric-a-brac to good use. There were Dutch tearooms, with big open hearths, copper kettles, and "rows of Dutch plates and prints." There were colonial tearooms with Chippendale desks and silver candlesticks. There were Oriental tearooms, with Chinese and Japanese porcelain, shoji screens, and wall hangings and employing kimono-clad Asian waitresses. There were garden tearooms: "On Fifth Avenue . . . one has but to mount a few steps to pour tea under the vine-covered trellis of a picturesque pergola whose outdoor influence is a welcome foretaste of early spring. Here abound broad columns, and over latticed archways Southern smilax and bamboo are intertwined, each green wicker table beneath accommodating a party of congenial spirits. Above the tables outdoor baskets of growing blossoms are swung, and at the end of the vista are a few garden seats and a piece or two of good outdoor statuary."[45]

Successful tearooms became renowned for their house specialties, often based on family recipes: homemade waffles, extra-crisp English muffins, Lady Baltimore cake. Whatever the specialties, their luncheon and teatime menus invariably met the "daintiness" standard—small sandwiches, salads, perhaps chicken à la king or croquettes. A few served breakfast.

By keeping prices high, the early tearooms ensured an affluent and ladylike clientele. As tearooms multiplied, some began to gear menus and prices to middle- and upper-middle-class professional women, especially during lunch service. In Chicago, tearooms became so popular with office girls that they began to draw male coworkers and bosses.

"That the Chicago man is loyal to mother's salad, mother's doughnuts, and mother's recipes for pies in spite of all the marvels that the French chef can hold out to him is shown by the invasion of what are called, or what used to be called, women's eating places in Chicago," wrote Grace Clarke in 1909.[46]

Valentine's Tea Room, 1906, Byron Company

With the invasion came demand. " 'Men want seats by themselves in which they can talk over their business,' said the manager of the tearoom at one of the shops . . . When the room was first opened it was intended exclusively for women, and men who asked why hat racks were not provided for them were frankly told that they were not catered to. The simple cooking and daintiness of the women's service appeals to them, however, and since they come in such numbers it may be that we will give them what they demand now, which is a place to smoke."[47]

In every city where they appeared, tearooms became a favorite haunt of private school and college girls home on holiday, "young buds" who met in the tearooms to gossip and read each other's tea leaves.[48] These young women took the "tearoom habit" with them to Smith, Vassar, and Wellesley. Tearooms began to open in the towns surrounding many women's colleges.

More than a few of those college girls decided to try their hand at running their own tearooms after graduation. And why not? There was a waning but still persistent belief that finishing college left a woman unmarriageable—fully 75 percent of women in the generation graduating before 1900 had remained single.[49] Columnists fretted that the increasing number of women college graduates threatened the traditional family and doomed young women to spinsterhood, as men sought partners who would not pose an intellectual challenge. For their part, women graduates understood that they might need to support themselves. With their options still limited, some college-educated women entered law, medicine, teaching, or settlement work.[50] Others saw in the tearooms a rare opportunity to go into business for themselves.

One recent graduate described how she'd gotten her start: "I took stock of the capital with which I was to step into the world and earn my own living. My stock taking showed perfect health, my college education, and $300, my share of my father's estate after the expenses of my college course had been paid. In spite of the protests of my friends I decided to become a business woman instead of entering one of the professions. I believed that a well-conducted tearoom in a college town where there was nothing of the kind would pay well, so I proceeded to open one."[51]

Her hunch paid off. The tearoom met its expenses on its first day of operations. As days became weeks, the place continued to draw crowds. Within two weeks she and an Irish girl she had hired to wait tables in a "fresh cap and apron" were serving a steady stream of faculty and

students. The graduate "determined no longer to heed the shaking heads of my friends," who had fretted about the financial risk she had taken.

There were growing pains. The first expansion of the tearoom and staff drew complaints: from college boys who felt the new room she'd added, with its simpler furnishings and bow-tied male waiter, was "second class" and lacked the charm required to impress a date, and from professors, who huffed when obliged to wait for their food at busy times. But the graduate persevered. When the end of the academic year caused a precipitous drop-off in business, "I kept the same number of employees and had them put up preserves, jams, sirups and pickles for use the coming season. I knew it would not only be economical, but also a great drawing card, especially with certain of the professors, to be able to state that everything served was made on the place and under my own supervision."[52]

The graduate was joined by others. As women who'd finished college returned to their hometowns or moved to new cities, they seized the

Daily menu, Tea, Congress Hotel, Chicago, 1908

chance to create tearooms where none had existed. In Los Angeles, the "Misses Morris," Mildred (Columbia) and Harriet (Smith), opened the city's first tearoom, the Copper Kettle, on New Year's Day 1908. In their first eight months of operation, they served fifteen thousand customers. The *Los Angeles Times* called the Copper Kettle "the center for all the genuinely interesting folk in art, literature, and fashion who visit or dwell in this land of 'little rain and much sunshine.'" The popularity of the Kettle and its "fascinating" Japanese furnishings led to a lucrative mail-order business, with the Morris sisters selling curiosities such as Japanese vases and "bronze-colored baskets with gay opium tassels" to women around the country.[53]

By mid-decade tearooms and teatime had established themselves as an important element of the lifestyle of women with leisure time and disposable income. *Harper's Bazaar* reported in 1908, "To-day, at the tea hour — and as often at high noon — smart carriages are drawn up in front of the tea-room; within, the merry tap of high heels on polished floors mingles with the fresh odor of violets and the rustle of many skirts. It is the fashion to drink tea in New York!"[54]

Luxury hotels capitalized on the tea fashion and made it their own. Though the tearooms run by women and the tearooms run by hotels served dainty food to genteel, mostly female customers, the resemblances ended there. The cozy rooms run by women were oases of quiet civility, but the palm courts where the grand hotels served tea were big, lively, very public places where "the smart set" went to see and be seen. Set under vaulted archways or beneath elaborate mosaic ceilings, with orchestras providing live musical accompaniment, hotel palm courts offered an ideal stage for preening. Small tearooms might draw customers eager for tea and biscuits "like mother used to make," but the cups of Earl Grey (or, in some cases, the cocktails, hidden in china teapots and dispensed into innocent-looking teacups) served in the hotel palm courts were a pretext for the true repast: the array of dresses, jewels, lapdogs, and bachelor escorts on display.

Prominent society tea drinkers attracted crowds of celebrity watchers. In New York in 1907, "two American heiresses and their titled fiancés were a magnet for a gigantic throng during the tea hour at the Plaza yesterday afternoon. Miss Gladys Vanderbilt and Count Laszlo Széchenyi sat at one table in the tearoom, and Miss Theodora Shonts and the Duc de Chaulnes were guests at a party given by Mrs. A. H. Goodwin, a few feet away. The corridors as well as the tearoom itself were thronged during the tea-drinking of these celebrities.

Hotel Astor, roof garden, 1905, Byron Company

"At four o'clock crowds began to assemble in the hotel corridors and within . . . half an hour the corridors were impassable. Visitors took possession of bellboys' benches and every available chair. Meanwhile the Fifth Avenue dining room filled up. The palm-trimmed tearoom was so filled that the glass doors were closed. The crowd was undismayed and courteously stormed the doors. The broad shoulders of M. Pearl, the maître d'hotel, were necessary to resist a flying wedge of well-dressed women . . .

"At five o'clock Mrs. Goodwin was waiting in the corridor for the Misses Shonts and the Duke. She could not look over the hats of the hundreds of women there, so one of the assistant managers stood by her side to offer assistance. At last Miss Shonts, in purple cloth, appeared with the Duc de Chaulnes. A table had been reserved, but the approach to the tea room was clogged, so the party was escorted to their places by means of the ground floor pantry."[55] Miss Vanderbilt and the count similarly had to be smuggled past the throng, through business offices on the hotel's first floor, but the reporter managed to see enough to admire the heiress's dress of "raspberry satin."

The Plaza and the Waldorf-Astoria in New York, the Copley Plaza in Boston, and their competitors in other major cities knew what they were doing when they provided some special amenities for their most conspicuous consumers.

Hotel Plaza, southwest corner of 59th Street and Fifth Avenue, 1907, Byron Company

"The tea room of the Plaza is patterned after the informal rooms in the Ritz in Paris and the Carlton in London, and with this novel atmosphere of easy chairs and tabourets the women foresaw corresponding privileges. They believed they could bring their beloved canines to the tea room. Very soon the strains of Nathan Franko's orchestra, bearing chunks of Puccini's compelling music, were interrupted by barks and growls and [the] cooing [of] pet names . . . In fact, one sociable pup would often scrape up an acquaintance with another sociable pup, providing their mistresses were on calling terms. Informal tea is all very well, but the dogs were too aggressively Bohemian." The Plaza's manager solved the problem by turning a bellhop into a dog attendant, who "checked" the ladies' lapdogs into a converted coatroom.

"It was necessary to provide a place for the transient dogs," said Mr. Sterry last night. "We simply couldn't have them running about, and as we realize how deeply attached their mistresses are to them, we have opened a check room. There has been no revolt against the check room. The [bell]boy is careful, and the dogs have bits of carpet on which to lie down. It is so much the fashion for smart women to take their dogs to tea that we have been obliged to make the afternoon comfortable for them. It is simply a case of meeting a modern exigency."[56]

A Table of Her Own

The economic necessity which has forced women out of the home and into the world of business has completely annihilated the old idea that a woman should eat only in the privacy of her own household or in the homes of her friends, has created the absolutely new social phenomenon of women eating in public, unescorted by men, by the tens of thousands, and has given rise to a new phase of the restaurant business.[57]

There are five million women earning their living in this country, and it seems strange that feudal customs should still exist here as they do in the older countries. I believe that women should be served in the restaurants, and I hope I will be able to make others think so, too.[58]

On a Sunday evening in August 1900, Rebecca Israel walked into the Café Boulevard at Tenth Street and Second Avenue on Manhattan's Lower East Side. She was quiet, neatly dressed, and alone, in search of dinner. The Boulevard served central European and French food to a largely central European, Jewish clientele. Jewish, but not kosher: the Boulevard's Sunday, six-course table d'hôte dinners started with Blue Point oysters, moved on to consommé or bisque, which was followed by a fish course of lobster or perch, an entrée of stuffed cabbage or sweetbreads, and then a main course: Austro-Hungarian roast, stew, or goulash. Dessert might be sweet-cheese strudel or linzer torte. It was a menu—and a restaurant—with old world style and new world ambition.

Unfortunately, there would be no six-course dinner for Miss Israel that night. The proprietor, Ignatz Rosenfeld, had a strict policy against serving unescorted women. Despite Miss Israel's polite objections she was turned away at the door.

Rosenfeld's refusal to serve Rebecca Israel reflected a belief, still widespread in 1900, that the better restaurants were masculine territory, places where men could do business over a roast beef lunch

Palace Hotel Restaurant AND Ladies Grill Room.

BEERS ON DRAUGHT.
Eastern Beer 10 per glass, 20 per stein.

EGGS IN EVERY STYLE.   FRUIT IN SEASON.

Coffee or Tea and Rolls or Cold Bread for one 20

RELISHES.
Radishes 10   Pickled Stuffed Peppers 25   Olives 15   Stuffed Olives 30   Sardines 25
Chow Chow 15   Pickled Beets 20   Pickles and Chutney 20   Santa Cruz Pickled Onions 15
Anchovies 25   Pickled Walnuts 20   Bloater Toast 25

EASTERN OYSTERS.
Oysters on the half shell	30	Butter broiled ... 50
Fancy roast on toast	40	Pan roast ... 40
Fry	50	Milk stew ... 40
Oyster patties	50	Plain stew ... 40
Dry broiled on toast	50	Boston fancy stew ... 50
Dry broiled	40	Box stew ... 40

CALIFORNIA OYSTERS.
Raw	25	Pan roast ... 30
Stew, milk or plain	30	Oyster cocktail ... 25
Fried	50	Fancy roast on toast ... 40
Brochette on toast	40	

CLAMS.
Little neck clam stew 30   Clam fry ... 50
Little neck clam, half shell 25   Clam fritters ... 50
Clam broth 50

COLD MEATS.
Ham 25   Tongue ... 25
Roast pork 25   Lamb ... 30
Roast beef 25

SOUPS.
Green Turtle with Amontillado 15   Consommé 15

FISH.
Broiled Smelts, Colbert 25
Potatoes Hashed and Browned

ENTREES.
Stewed Wild Duck with Noodles 25   Glaced Ham with Mashed Vegetables 25

VEGETABLES.
Artichokes 10   Small Onions 10

ROAST.
Beef 35   Veal 30   Lamb 40

GRILLED TO ORDER.
Veal Chops plain, for one	35	Porterhouse for two	1.25
Veal Chops breaded, for one	45	Porterhouse, with Mushrooms, for two	1.50
Beefsteak for one	35	Extra Porterhouse	2.00
Beefsteak with Tomato sauce, for one	40	Mutton Chops [special 40] for one	30
Beefsteak with Bacon do	45	Lamb Chops [special 50] do	40
Beefsteak with Mushrooms do	50	Pork Chops do	40
Hamburg steak do	40	English Mutton Chop do	30
Small Sirloin, for one	50	Extra English Mutton Chop do	50
Sirloin steak with Bacon do	60	Broiled Chicken, half do	75
Sirloin steak with Mushrooms do	65	Welsh Rarebit do	40
Sir'oin steak, for two	80	Golden Buck do	50
Extra Sirloin	1.60	Ham and Eggs do	40
Small Tenderloin, for one	50	Broiled Kidney do	30
Tenderloin steak, Tomato sauce, for one	55	Sausages do	30
Tenderloin steak with Bacon do	60	Ham do	25
Tenderloin steak with Mushrooms do	65	Bacon do	25
Tenderloin steak, for two	80	Ham Omelette do	50
Châteaubriand	1.50	
Devilled Bones, Spare Ribs, etc.	30	Game in season, grilled or roasted.

SALADS.
Crab 25   Shrimp 25   Chicken 25   Potato 15   Lettuce 15   Water Cress 15
Cold Slaw 15   Chicory 15   Romain 15

CHEESE.
Roquefort 15   Neufchatel 15   Greyére 15   American 10   Brie 15   Edam 15   Sierra 15

No orders served for less than 20 cents.   Extra service 25   Corkage $1.00 per bottle

October 20, 1900.

Daily menu, Palace Hotel Restaurant and Ladies Grill Room, San Francisco, 1900

or socialize with one another over oysters and canvasback duck. The ban on unescorted women in restaurants wasn't universal, and it wasn't airtight: women had free run of the tearooms and palm courts. They could eat lunch together in the ladies' dining rooms of large hotels. They could take evening meals in humble places like the quick-lunch counters without incident — if they didn't mind the food or sitting cheek by jowl with overcoated strangers. Most of New York's French and Italian table d'hôte restaurants — humbler places than the Boulevard — seated women without escorts, though given their reputations as "bohemian" haunts, full of debauched artists and writers, it took courage for an unaccompanied middle-class woman to venture into one of them.

When it came to fine-dining establishments six o'clock was the witching hour. After that, women risked being turned away unless they were the invited guests of men. In the largest hotels, women arriving to dine (alone or in groups) without men might be tucked out of sight in private dining rooms. Now and then — and upredictably — women who were registered guests at a hotel might be permitted to eat alone in one of the hotel's main dining rooms. In such cases, the *Chicago Tribune*'s etiquette columnist Elizabeth van Rensselaer advised, a woman "can suitably order her meal by 7 o'clock if not before. A woman who dines alone at the fashionable hour between 7:30 and 8:30 at a large hotel will find herself an unpleasantly conspicuous figure." Van Rensselaer also warned unescorted women not to be seen ordering wine with their meals or to sit alone in the evening in hotel palm gardens, "where the orchestra plays and late diners sip their coffee or liqueurs."[59]

Van Rensselaer was hinting at an old way of thinking: a woman out in the world and looking for an evening meal might be a "public woman" of another sort entirely.

. . .

After Ignatz Rosenfeld turned Rebecca Israel away from his restaurant, she sued him for discrimination. The basis for her suit was the State of New York's civil rights bill of 1895, which provided that "all persons within the jurisdiction of this State shall be entitled to the full and equal accommodations, advantages, facilities, and privileges of inns, restaurants . . . and all other places of public accommodation and amusement, subject only to the conditions and limitations established by law and applicable alike to all citizens." Though the law had been meant to protect African Americans from being refused service at hotels and restaurants, Miss Israel and her lawyers saw its potential for women.

Israel's suit took three years to churn through a series of appeals. In 1903 the New York State Supreme Court dismissed her suit. Justice Greenbaum held that "all rules or regulations barring out a certain class of intended patrons are admissible and perfectly lawful if they are equally and impartially enforced against all comers . . . Mr. Rosenfeld, in wishing to defend his place against an invasion of women unescorted by men, was perfectly within the law in enforcing a rule of the house."[60] In 1903, that amounted to full and equal accommodation.

Four years passed. Then, in July 1907, Harriot Stanton Blatch and her friend Hettie Wright Graham arrived at New York's Hoffman House for dinner. The hotel had a fashionable roof garden. Blatch, the daughter of Elizabeth Cady Stanton, was a noted suffragist and writer, a Vassar graduate who also held an honorary master of arts degree. Graham was a Quaker from Long Island who had recently returned from doing settlement work in Appalachia, where she'd helped Berea College in Kentucky start a community-based weaving program.[61]

The friends had just come from a lecture at the University Women's Club. The evening was oppressively hot and a meal in the open air seemed the right sort of refreshment. Though "they debated the advisability of going to the roof garden for their meal," it was just a few minutes past six. The lobby clerk assured them that they could be served. When the elevator brought them to the roof, an attendant took their parasols and gestured to some empty tables.

Then the trouble began. A waiter approached to ask whether they had an escort or were registered as overnight guests of the Hoffman. When Mrs. Blatch replied, "No," the waiter refused to seat them. The headwaiter sent them on their way.

Back in the lobby, Mrs. Blatch demanded to see the manager. "I am very sorry," said the manager, "but that is the regulation of the house, and we cannot make any exceptions in its application. We do this for the protection of just such ladies as you are. We do it to keep out objectionable women; women of the type you would not like to have dining in the same room with you."

"I have never been bothered by objectionable women," responded Mrs. Blatch. "When I have been annoyed it has been by men. I do not suppose you make any effort to keep objectionable men out."[62]

She sued.

Progressive magazines and women's associations rallied to her cause. The New York Equal Suffrage League passed a resolution endorsing her suit and encouraged its members to attend the trial.[63] An editorial in the *Independent* declared, "There ought to be a law revoking the license of a hotel or restaurant that refuses to receive women on the same terms as men. A still more efficient measure would be for all self-respecting women to refuse to patronize, even with masculine accompaniment, any place that insults their sex by such a rule."[64]

At the trial, testimony focused on whether Mrs. Blatch and Mrs. Graham had been offered a table in the indoor "ladies' dining room." The defense claimed that the manager and maître d' had offered them such an alternative, which should have been sufficient, but that the women had insisted on dining only in the roof garden in order to "make a test case." Mrs. Blatch and Mrs. Graham denied this. They had simply been turned away, they said.[65]

The all-male jury found in favor of the Hoffman House. Mrs. Blatch appealed the verdict, and in early 1908 a New York State assemblyman introduced a bill declaring that "women, whether alone or accompanied by escort, shall be entitled to equal accommodations with men at hotels, restaurants, barber shops, theatres, public halls, and in public conveyances."[66] Mrs. Blatch's appeal and the legislative effort failed, but the suit and the bill revealed a shift in at least some people's thinking. By 1908 the fact that respectable women such as Mrs. Blatch and Mrs. Graham could not dine without a male escort was beginning to be seen for what it was: an antique, preposterous, and ultimately untenable custom.

For their part, hotel and restaurant managers were ambivalent about the idea of women dining alone. A few months before Mrs. Blatch walked into the Hoffman House, the Waldorf-Astoria had posted a notice on the bulletin board in its lobby: "Ladies without escort will be served in the restaurants hereafter at any hour."

The problem, a *Times* reporter wrote, was that "it did not seem to be a question of a woman's right to dine when and where she pleased, but rather one of her eligibility and right to the title of lady. The management of the Waldorf said: 'It has always been a rule of this house to entertain ladies — real ladies.' "

"But what is a lady? Is it determined by dress or manner or — or accent?" asked the reporter.

"Why, my dear Sir, why, a lady, my good fellow, is a — um, lady — hey?"

At Delmonico's, a night manager answered the same reporter's question about serving unaccompanied women by saying, "Oh, no, we discourage it. But if the lady is known to us, it is all right." When asked to define a lady, he replied, "Well, a lady is one you can tell easily. You can tell by the way she sits, by the way she orders, by the way. Oh, man, a lady is a lady, don't you see?"

The reporter then posed the question to Mr. Regan, general manager of the chic Knickerbocker Hotel, who responded, "My good Sir, a lady is — is — Now see here, a woman who may not be a lady comes in here. She sits down and she realizes that there are fine people around her. She immediately sits up and says to herself: 'Hm! This is the place where I've got to behave myself.' "[67]

Of course, Rebecca Israel, Mrs. Blatch, and Mrs. Graham *weren't* ladies, if ladies were the fashionably decorated companions of prosperous men. They were something unfamiliar: well-educated, financially stable women who made their own way in the world. They had their own professions, their own pocketbooks, and their own politics and preferences. Hotel and restaurant men schooled in the ways of high society didn't know what to make of them.[68]

When Harriot Blatch filed suit against the Hoffman House, she told reporters, "I do not think a restaurant owner has the right to deny a woman a meal at any hour. There are numbers of women working as physicians and in other professions. They should be permitted to eat wherever they choose and whenever they choose."[69]

"Wherever" and "whenever" women chose to eat varied from social class to social class.

From their posts in the most arduous jobs in laundries and factories, to office jobs and the professions, women entered a working world that was not fully prepared to receive them. Women, through their growing presence as workers, proprietors — and ultimately as paying customers in even the most elegant establishments — eventually secured with their pocketbooks what Israel and Blatch could not secure through the courts: restaurant tables of their own.[70]

— LS

AU CHAT NOIR

Hotel — Restaurant

TABLE D'HÔTE

32 WEST 28th STREET

⸙ and ⸙

551 WEST BROADWAY

Half block from Bleecker L station.

New York

HESSE BROTHERS, Prop's.

OTHER PEOPLE'S FOOD

Teddy Roosevelt became president in 1901 because an anarchist shot William McKinley. Three years later Roosevelt ran for the office (against a well-mannered, rather high-minded Democrat) and won by two and a half million votes.

In February 1905 he went to New York to celebrate. He was the guest of honor at two dinners. One, a Lincoln's Day dinner at the Waldorf-Astoria, was a twelve-course banquet served to eighteen hundred guests.[1] The two hundred ladies present were seated separately, served separately, and permitted to join their husbands only after the men had coffee and cigars. Standing beneath a blazing electric sign from which shone the words "With Malice Towards None / With Charity to All," Roosevelt delivered a forty-five-minute sermon about equal opportunity and equal justice for "the black race." As the president rose to speak, "a hush ensued that would have let the lightest whisper be heard" in the vast room.[2]

The second dinner was a Valentine's Day celebration for four hundred people, all of them Hungarians, most of them Jews, men and women packed elbow to elbow, in the main dining room of the Little Hungary on East Houston Street.[3] At the end of the meal, as guests sipped their tokay, a New York congressman named Sulzer — a Democrat no less — rose to introduce Mr. Roosevelt. "This is the first time, I believe," said the congressman, "that a President of the United States has ever visited the people of the East Side of New York, sat at their table, and broken bread with them."[4]

. . .

Table d'hôte, Au Chat Noir Hotel and Restaurant, New York, 1900

The two dinners — the Waldorf extravaganza and the Little Hungary love-fest — might as well have been scenes in a gastronomic, social-psychological "Tale of Two Cities." The Waldorf banquet was — as all such banquets were — a ritual of power, imported from France. Its twelve courses — from its *Pomplemousse avec cerise* to its *Glace assortés* — were sacraments of dynastic/ruling class culture.

At the Little Hungary, the meal began with cream of snail soup (*Csiga Leves*), followed by paprika chicken and spaetzle. A *Sorbet a la Kossuth* served as a palette cleanser before roast Long Island duckling and cabbage and apple strudel (*Kapostzes Retes Apple Strudel*) were served. Two Hungarian wines (a *Kobanyal* and a *Sashegyi*) and a *Moselblumchen* accompanied the meal.

For the Jews who erupted in "cheers that made the old walls of the Little Hungary literally shake" as Mr. Roosevelt spoke his first words — "Thank you . . . my fellow Americans" — the food evoked memories that such food often does when eaten by people far from home.

Mr. Roosevelt himself had memories of his own.

In 1894, when he was a New York City police commissioner, his good friends Jacob Riis (the Danish immigrant reporter and photographer responsible for *How the Other Half Lives*) and James Reynolds (the distinguished director of the University Settlement House on Delancey Street) took him out to the Little Hungary. "They told me," Mr. Roosevelt was quoted as saying, "that we would have a good dinner and good music. Both prophecies were true." The Little Hungary became one of his favorite restaurants.

The moment Mr. Roosevelt was elected governor, the New York Hungarian Club sent him a dinner invitation. In 1899, at the Café Budapest, the club's president, Marcus Baum, rose to toast their honored guest: "To his Excellency, Theodore Roosevelt, president of the United States." The audience rose and clapped and cheered and whistled. Mr. Roosevelt sat and grinned his toothiest grin. "Governor," Baum continued, "we might as well arrange the celebration now. Will you allow us to give you a dinner when you become president?"

"Certainly I will," answered Mr. Roosevelt.

A few days after Roosevelt won the 1904 election, Mr. Baum went to Washington to remind him of his promise. "The president recalled his promise and agreed to set a date for his coming." He settled on February 14, St. Valentine's Day.

Speaking from the Heart

Cream of snail soup followed by cabbage and apple strudel were not the kinds of food that most Americans ate, let alone enjoyed, in 1905. But the four hours that Mr. Roosevelt spent at the Little Hungary were filled with more than the pleasures of good food and wine — or the delight that politicians always feel when they hear themselves being cheered.

"The President had one of the greatest times of his life," reported the *Times*. And why? Mr. Roosevelt's memories of his own before-and-after may have accounted for his happiness. But "the greatest times of his life"? What else — besides nostalgia mixed with wine — had made him feel that way?

There were many Americans living in cities then who enjoyed eating immigrant food in immigrant restaurants. They liked it because it was cheap and because it tasted good to them. They also liked it because such food, eaten in such restaurants, provided them with experiences that made them feel more alive.

Of course, there were many more Americans who hated immigrants and loathed their food.[5] High-minded lady social workers and domestic science practitioners devoted themselves to teaching immigrant mothers and daughters how to cook and eat like good Americans — how to eat more beef, drink more milk, eat more bread (and less pasta or masa), and serve simpler (and less spicy) meals, closer in color, content, and flavor to the plain food of New England's Puritan fathers. Such kindhearted ladies believed that teaching immigrants how to cook and eat properly was equivalent to teaching them to read and write and speak English.[6]

The question remains, what kinds of experiences — what states of heart and mind — did eating immigrant food in immigrant restaurants provide Americans who went there to enjoy themselves?

The newspaper account of Mr. Roosevelt's visit to the Little Hungary provides some answers.

Mr. Roosevelt traveled to the Little Hungary in a cavalcade two blocks long, guarded by squadrons of mounted police. Immediately in front of and behind his carriage were cabs packed with detective sergeants and special police. A Secret Service agent rode next to the coachman atop the president's carriage; another sat inside with Mr. Roosevelt. At every intersection — from the house at Forty-ninth Street and Madison where the president and his family were staying, down to Houston Street — foot patrolmen blocked traffic.

Fear prompted these precautions, but instead of assaults there were cheers.

As the cavalcade swept down [Fifth] Avenue, north-bound coachmen gave way for the on-coming carriages, waving their whips in salutation and, now and then, [shouting] from full lungs a cheer for the President . . . At 28th Street, [where] a horse car [i.e., trolley car] had been held up [by police], the driver stood at his horses heads, uncovered. He waved his cap wildly and yelled, "Three cheers for President Roosevelt! Our Teddy! The People's Friend!" A messenger boy or two and an old gentleman answered [the driver's salute] and the President, catching sight of them, leaned far out and waved . . .

The caravan turned east toward Avenue A and onlookers turned into crowds, big, thick, and noisy. People carried candlelights on poles and waved them in greeting.

They drove the police out of their way, shouting "Roosevelt!" with as many variations of accent as there are nationalities settled in the streets that were once homes of the wealthy of New York.

The cry of the many was not wolf-like, although there [were] many who hunger there. In fact, a boy had died yesterday from starvation . . . a few minutes' walk from [the Little Hungary] where the feast was spread. And the cheering was not that of native-born Americans, but an exultant roar of "Roosevelt!" and "Teddy!"

The policemen and the Secret Service men might as well have been asleep at home in so far as the safety of the President was concerned. The mob following his carriage was his protection as he went through the streets that are noted for cafes and clubs where the most radical Socialists and Anarchists discuss their theories . . .

A small boy, bearing one of the many red [candle] lights, lost his footing and slipped under the feet of the cavalry policemen directly at the door of the President's carriage as it was about to turn onto First Street. He was up in a second, wildly waving his red flame to shout in the President's face, "*Vive le President!*"

"*Vive les Etats-Unis,*" shouted back the President as a mounted officer pulled the boy away from further danger of heels and wheels. A minute later, a very fat enthusiast repeated the act of the boy with a similar miraculous escape from harm. As he gathered himself, he

CRISTOFORO ✳ COLOMBO

29 MULBERRY ST.

RESTAURANT

Bernardoni & Soffredini

✣ BILL OF FARE ✣

ZUPPE.

Orecchie di prete —

Pastina in brodo	5	Minestrone 5 all'ordine	10
Riso in brodo	5	Risotto	5
Minestrone	5	Pasticcio	5

FRITTI.

Cervello all'ordine	10	Pesce *e Marinato*	5
Cotolette alla Milanese	10	Anguilla	5
Fritto Misto	10	Calamai	5

fritto di Carciofi

BOLLITI.

Manzo	5	Pollo	10

Bacalà in Bianco

UMIDI.

Rognone	5	Fegato	5
Stufato	5	Pesce	5
Fricassea di Vitello	5	Anguilla *arrosto*	10
Trippa	5	Calamai	5
Fricassea di Pollo	10	Polpette	5

ARROSTI.

Pollo	10	Agnello	10
Vitello	10	Maiale	10
Bistecca	10	Manzo brasé *con Spinaci*	10

INSALATE.

Lattuga	5	Fagiolane	5
Indivia	5	Fagiolini	5
Cicoria	5	Cavolfiore	5

25. Mch. 1900 FRUTTA   FORMAGGI   CAFFE'

Stampato da Frugone & Balletto, 178 Park Row, New York.

Bill of fare, Cristoforo Colombo Restaurant, New York, 1900 cried out, "*Hoch! Hoch! Hoch! Lieber Roosevelt!*" He was pulled away before he could hear Mr. Roosevelt remark that it was evident that there were other than Hungarians in the neighborhood.

In narrow First Street, the crowd wedged closer to the carriages and was running wildly, bearing aloft [their] red lights. Someone struck up "The Star Spangled Banner" and it was at once a mighty, inspiring chorus . . .

The people fell over one another in the wild rush . . . The street was ablaze with red light . . . They impeded the progress of [the president's] carriage, although there were mounted policemen in front, on either side, [and] behind it. They were close to him as he waved his high hat and smiled. The President was radiantly happy . . . It was evident that he had no thought of danger.

Then something disastrous nearly happened. Three hundred patrolmen had cordoned off the streets within two blocks of the restaurant. The president and his entourage swept down Houston Street toward the Little Hungary like waterbirds headed for a landing on a lake.

As [Roosevelt's] carriage came up to the curb, he swung open his door to get out at the old entrance he had known when, as Police Commissioner, he used to dine at the place.

In the years that had passed, the restaurant had grown so that the old entrance was now a small affair. [As the president opened the door to get out], he was twenty feet from the new and grander entrance . . .

Secret Service Man Thorne, whose duty it is to see that the Chief Executive comes to no harm, was equal to his responsibilities. As the President opened the carriage door, he caught him firmly, forcing him back. The President weighed something over 200 lbs, the Secret Service man not over 150, but he managed to hold Mr. Roosevelt back.

"Thank you, Mr. Thorne," said the President as he alighted safely at the proper entrance . . .

Then he spied a policeman—Louis D. Bohm, formerly Private Bohm of the Rough Riders.

"Hello, Louis!" shouted the President.

"Hello, Colonel!" said the policeman as he came to a full, military salute.[7]

All this — the cheers, the crowds, the delight, the close calls, and the last-minute near disaster — preceded the food, the wine, and the speech that followed.

"Not a set speech," President Roosevelt twice assured his listeners. What he chose to say was more personal — and more revealing — than the sermon he'd delivered the night before. At the Waldorf, he'd been flanked by senators, cabinet secretaries, chief magistrates, university presidents, generals, admirals, and the richest men in the land. The gathering at the Little Hungary was different. "Allow me to speak as an old friend among old friends," Mr. Roosevelt said.

Before considering what this "old friend" had to say, recall the circumstances of his speech: (1) A little boy and a fat man had nearly been run over before his eyes; (2) Nearby, in the neighborhood where another little boy had just starved to death, men spent their days in cafés, arguing about ideas — the same ideas that had inspired the man who'd shot McKinley; and (3) Having reached his destination, drunk with cheers, Roosevelt had come very close to breaking his neck as he'd stepped out of his carriage.

Inside the sanctuary of the Waldorf accident, illness, injury, and death had been kept at bay. Outside, on the streets leading to the Little Hungary, life was precarious. In fact, the first man the president met as he stepped out of his carriage had reminded him, with his salute, of how close Roosevelt and all his Rough Riders had come to dying in Cuba.[8]

After dessert was served and toasts were made, Mr. Roosevelt rose to speak. He rambled and repeated himself but the people who heard him thought it "one of his happiest efforts."

"I have seen a good deal of your lives," Mr. Roosevelt began. "I have come to know your efforts, your toil, your happiness, your success," he said. "But success, once gained . . ." He paused. "It is a great mistake . . ." Again he paused. "Oh — is there any mistake so great? — as to measure success only by what glitters? What counts . . . . is not the things of the body but of the soul."

As Roosevelt searched for words, the ones he found had a spiritual and emotional warmth. "I doubt it would be possible," he said, "to find a more typically American gathering than this. For Americanism is not a matter of birthplace, of ancestry, of education, or of creed . . . It is a matter of spirit that is in a man's soul . . .

"I am sure . . . if you look back on your own lives, what makes you feel proudest . . . are memories . . . not [of] days of ease, but [of] effort . . . when you are doing all that is in you for some worthy end. And . . . the worthiest end is to care for those closest to us . . . to live so that they are happy and not sorry that you are alive. After this, the best thing is to be able to handle yourself [so] that . . . when the end comes . . . your fellow men are a little better off for your having lived. That much is open to all."

Then President Roosevelt said something he'd never said in public.

"The greatest prizes come by accident," he said. "And no human being knows this better than the one who has won one of them. The greatest prizes, I say, are won by accident."

After this, he wished his audience good night. "No meeting I have attended since I became President has given me more genuine pleasure that this." Secret Service men and detectives formed a corridor for his exit, then blocked anyone from following him.

The speech Roosevelt gave at the Little Hungary sounded a bit like a eulogy — the speech of a man assessing the value of his life in retrospect. Twice, as he rambled, he spoke of "the soul" and "the end." Finally, he confessed, "The greatest prizes are won by accident."

Duty, honor, and country, equal justice and equal opportunity had comprised the sermon he'd preached the night before. Everyone at the Waldorf believed they deserved to be there. Effort, not accident, willpower and not fate had made them who they were. "We are the very best of the very best," they thought. "We are just like Mr. Roosevelt and he is just like us." Roosevelt said nothing to disillusion them.

But in a roomful of Hungarian Jews — on St. Valentine's Day, no less — Roosevelt felt safe enough to talk about accident and final judgment. He may have willed himself and his men up San Juan Hill but troopers had died all around him, and it was another man's death that had elevated him to office.

In fact, the very day he'd chosen to eat and drink and laugh at the Little Hungary was the twenty-first anniversary of the day his mother and his wife had both died, within hours of each other, in the house where they and Roosevelt lived.

The president had chosen to celebrate Valentine's Day at the Little Hungary because it was a place where he could speak his heart — a heart that lived with ghosts. Not to be alone with those ghosts, to be alive and happy in a room full of friends and food and wine, had been his "genuine pleasure."

Other Americans used other immigrant restaurants for their own reasons. They didn't carry the same burdens, the same memories as Mr. Roosevelt, but when they walked into Italian restaurants, or Lebanese cafés, or Chinese chop suey joints, they came for more than the food. In the first decade of the new American century, immigrant food, eaten in immigrant restaurants, fed different kinds of hungers, satisfied different parts of America's soul.

IMMIGRANT ZONES

Americans began crossing into immigrant zones to enjoy themselves—in benign and not so benign ways—starting in the 1840s.

The largest and oldest such zone in the east was New York's Kleindeutschland (By 1909 "Little Germany" encompassed four hundred city blocks, from Division Street north to Eighteenth Street, from Third Avenue to the East River. Only Berlin and Vienna had more German speakers within their borders.)[9] The zone's taverns and beer gardens (both large and small), its wine bars,[10] its wonderfully provisioned delicatessens,[11] and its moderately priced restaurants with their generous portions attracted working-class, middle-class, and moderately well-to-do New Yorkers.

The "Regular Dinner or Supper," served on January 8, 1900, by the Schulz Restaurant on Second Avenue cost the equivalent today of $5. The restaurant's bill of fare began with noodle soup, followed by a choice of roast sirloin of beef, roast leg of veal, potted roast beef, boiled beef with horseradish sauce, Reinbraten ("kosher roast"), fried calf's liver with onions, hasenpfeffer (rabbit stew) with potato balls, or hamburger steak and onions. Desserts included a choice of sponge cake, fruit pie, *Charlotte Russe* (vanilla Bavarian cream on top of lady fingers), and snowballs (molded and steamed white cakes served with a sweet fruit sauce). Potatoes (roasted, mashed, or fried), a vegetable (stewed tomatoes or string beans or sauerkraut or mashed turnips) plus coffee or tea were included with the meal.

Schulz's served dinner and supper from 11 a.m. until 9 p.m. It charged the equivalent of fifty cents extra if a customer wanted to substitute roast chicken or turkey for any of its daily entrées. Sauerbratens (sweet and sour pot roasts), schnitzels (veal cutlets, cut thinly, dipped in eggs and bread crumbs, then fried), goulashes (beef braised with onions and tomatoes, seasoned with paprika and garlic, served with sour cream) were other entrées commonly served by places like Schulz's.

By 1910 German food appeared on the lunch, dinner, and after-theater, supper menus of *American* restaurants throughout the country. Schnitzels and goulashes (sometimes labeled "German," sometimes "Hungarian," sometimes not labeled at all), knockwursts and frankfurters (labeled "imported"), sauerkraut and pickled beets, German potato salad, German potato pancakes, and the cured, sliced meats called "cold cuts" appeared on the bills of fare of medium-priced restaurants from New York to San Francisco.[12]

The immigrant zone that Theodore Roosevelt entered on Valentine's Day 1905 had more people living in it than Baltimore and Boston had at the beginning of the new century. Six hundred thousand Europeans and Asians worked and slept, ate and drank, grew old and died confined to an area of 1,400 acres.[13] Within that zone were country-of-origin enclaves (the newspapers referred to them as "colonies" or "quarters"). Within these enclaves were regional settlement blocks. For example, Sicilians lived on Elizabeth Street; Calabrians and Neopolitans kept to Mulberry Street; Genovese settled around Little Five Points; northern Italians occupied Bleecker Street west of Broadway.

As it was in New York, so it was in San Francisco.

Immigrant neighborhoods — and their restaurants — were so close together that an adventurous man "might well imagine himself possessed of the magic carpet told of in the Arabian Nights Tales as he is transported, in the twinkling of an eye, from country to country. It is but a step across the street from America to Japan, then another step to China. Cross another street and you are in Mexico, close neighbor to France. Around the corner lies Italy, and from Italy you pass from Lombardy into Greece. So it goes until one feels he has been around the world in an afternoon . . . finding all the peculiar characteristics of the various countries as indelibly fixed as if they were thousands of miles away . . . You find that each [group of immigrants] has brought the best of its gastronomy for your delectation."[14]

Chicago's immigrant zones were just as close together as San Francisco's and New York's, but in two Chicago neighborhoods immigrants from different countries mingled with Americans of different classes.

One neighborhood — a food and entertainment district west of the city's Loop, running along Halsted and West Madison Streets — served

Dishes to Order

Sirloin Steak	.50
Extra Sirloin Steak	1 00
Tenderloin Steak	.65
Single Porterhouse	1 00
Double Porterhouse	1 50
Steak mit Hindernissen	.60
Chateaubriand	1 25
" a la Bearnaise	1 50
" " Jardiniere	1 50
" with Mushrooms	1 50
Filet Mignon, plain	.60
" aux Champignons	.80
" a la Bordelaise	.75
" with Truffles	1 00
Hamburger Steak	.40
" with Egg or Onions	.50
Lamb Chops (three)	.40
" " " a la Jardiniere	.50
" " " breaded, Tomato Sauce	.50
Veal Cutlet	.40
" with Tomato Sauce	.50
Wiener Schnitzel, naturelle or breaded	.40
" " Tomato Sauce	.45
" " Sardellen	.50
Kalbsschnitzel a la Holstein	.50
Kaiserschnitzel	.60
Sweetbreads on Toast, French Peas garni	.65
" with Mushrooms	.75
Broiled Philadelphia Squab on Toast	.75
Half Broiled Spring Chicken on Toast	.75
Whole Broiled Spring Chicken on Toast	1 50
Wiener Backhuhn	.75
Fried Spring Chicken a la Maryland	.90
Chicken Saute a la Marengo	.80
Chicken Croquettes, French Peas garni	.50
Chicken Croquettes a la Reine or financiere	.60
Chicken Patties	.50
Chicken Liver with Mushrooms	.50
Calf's Head a la Vinaigrette	.40
" " en tortue	.50
" " a la poulette	.50
Calf's Brains with Brown Butter	.40
Calf's Brains breaded, Tomato Sauce	.40
Lamb's Fries breaded, Tomato Sauce	.40
Veal Kidneys, broiled	.40
Veal Kidneys, stewed, Sauce Madere	.40
Bratwurst with Sauerkraut	.40
Frankfurter Sausages	.30
" " Sauerkraut or Salad	.35
Imported Frankfurter " "	.40
Pig's Knuckle and Sauerkraut	.40

Rarebits

Welsh Rarebit	.35
Golden Buck	.45
Yorkshire Rarebit	.45
Long Island Rarebit	.45

Eggs, Omelettes, Etc.

Egg, boiled 2	.25	Omelette, with Cheese	.40
Eggs, fried 2	.25	" with Mushrooms	.50
Additional Egg, extra	.10	" with Peas	.40
Eggs, poached 2	.30	" with Kidneys	.50
" scrambled 3	.30	" aux fines herbes	.40
" with Mushrooms	.50	" au Rum	.40
Ham and Eggs	.40	" au confitures	.40
Bacon and Eggs	.35	German Pancake	.30
Omelette, plain	.30	French Pancake	.30
" with Ham	.40	Potato Pancake	.30

Compots

Stewed Prunes	.15	Imp. Zwetschen	.15
Currant Jelly	.10	Apples or Oranges	.15
Imp. Preisselbeeren	.15	Nuts, Raisins	.20
Apple Sauce	.15	Stewed Apricots	.15
Preserved Cherries	.15	Stewed Huckleberries	.15
" Peaches	.15	Stewed Raspberries	.15

Cold Dishes

Appetit Silz, per box	.30
Pates de foie gras	.50
Eels in Jelly and Radish Salad	.30
New Matjes Herring with New Potatoes	.35
Marimirter Herring	.25
Caviar, per portion	.50
Anchovies	.25
Pickled Lamb Tongue	.30
Sardines	.30
Sardellen	.40
Sardellen Leberwurst	.40
Raw Hamburger with Egg	.45
Raw Hamburger a la tartar	.50
Cervelatwurst Sausage	.40
Bologna Sausage	.35
Roast Beef, Mixed Salad	.45
Fricandeau of Veal, Mixed Salad	.40
Half Cold Chicken, Mixed Salad	.60
Cold Turkey, Cranberry Sauce	.60
Corned Beef and Salad	.35
Beef Tongue, Mixed Salad	.40
Boiled Ham, Mixed Salad	.35
Pickled Salmon, Cumberland Sauce	.50
Half Long Island Duck, Apple Sauce	.60
Westphalian Ham, Asparagus	.60
Smoked Nova Scotia Salmon, Cucumbers	.60
Kieler Sprotten, Ruehreier	.45
Appetit Broedchen a la Terrace	.30
Club Sandwich, Mayonnaise	.25
Pot Cheese and Chives	.25
Royans a la Bordelaise	.35
Pig's Knuckles in Gelee	.35
Home Made Sulze, Sauce Vinaigrette	.35
Schweinsrippchen in Gelee a la Terrace	.40
Berliner Rollmops	.30
Cold Veal Cutlet, Mixed Salad	.45

Sandwiches

Appetit Broedchen a la Terrace	.30	Corned Beef	.10
Roast Beef Sandwich	.20	Swiss Cheese	.10
Tongue	.15	Cervelat	.15
Roast Veal	.15	Sardine	.15
Caviar	.20	Raw Meat	.15
Salmon	.20	" with Egg	.20
Sardellen	.20	" Sardellen	.20
Turkey	.20	" Tartar	.30
Westphalian Ham	.20	Roquefort Cheese	.15
Club Sandwich	.25	Brie Cheese	.15
Boiled Ham	.10		

Cheese

Pot Cheese with Shives and Caraway Seeds	.25	Neuchatel	.25
Brie Cheese	.25	Muenster	.25
Camembert	.25	Swiss Cheese	.20
Roquefort	.25	Cream "	.20
		Kloster "	.20

Half portion served for one person only . . 15

Coffee, Tea, Etc.

Coffee, cup	.10	Milk, per glass	.10
Pot for two	.25	Cream, small pitcher	.10
French Coffee in Machine	.50	Dry Toast	.10
Chocolate, cup	.15	Butter Toast	.15
" Pot	.25	Milk Toast	.25
Cocoa, cup	.15	Toasted Crackers	.10
" Pot	.25	Soda Crackers	.10
Tea, per cup	.10		
" Pot	.20		

very order given. By doing so you will avoid all mistakes.

Daily menu, Terrace Garden Restaurant, New York, 1901

Chicago's working poor and its underclass. A *Chicago Tribune* reporter wrote in 1908:

> With hundreds of all night restaurants and lunchrooms and scores of nickel and dime theaters, several vaudeville and dramatic houses, and numerous dance halls, the district immediately west of the river is the liveliest in Chicago on a Saturday night . . .
>
> Streetcars and elevated roads carry thousands of pleasure-seekers from every one of the two score nationalities which make up Chicago's population . . . Men and women and children of all ages and descriptions seek and find their friends and acquaintances here . . . The crowds of foreign-born and native American citizens intermingle and defy all attempts at classification . . .
>
> The restaurants and lunchrooms [of the district] are the first to arrest attention . . . They run from the five-cent quick lunchrooms to the type of restaurant where one can get a meal "as good as any one in town." In respect to color and atmosphere, they run from [the] hobo's den to [the] bohemian café where literature and art, poetry and philosophy are discussed in Greek and Russian . . .
>
> In the matter of food, these restaurants vary greatly. With coffee and sinkers [donuts] as a starter, there are many places where spaghetti is all the go and garlic is the prevailing odor. Jewish chop suey and lamb a la Athens are dominant on Halsted between Harrison and Twelfth Streets . . .
>
> Here, the young working men and women [hurry] to and from the theaters and nickelodeons. In spite of the cold [and] slushy weather, white skirts are rustling and the fluttery girl makes for the dancehall with a happy laugh . . . Penny arcades are crowded with men and children. Particularly sensational and suggestive pictures have three or four men waiting for their chance to drop a penny in the machine and see them . . . On every corner, you will find some man trying to sell you something. There, a woman will tell you your fortune for a nickel, while here, a young man . . . having had his legs cut off by a street car [sits and begs].[15]

An entirely separate district—a six-block Restaurant Row, east of the river, on Randolph Street, adjacent to the Loop—served an "Arabian Nights Tale" of cuisines to thousands of middle-class diners, day and night. From the *Tribune* in summer of 1909:

An accurate count showed that [there were] thirty-nine different eating establishments [on Randolph] between Michigan and Fifth Avenues. Six different nationalities are represented by these establishments and 27,000 diners are accommodated by them every day of the year . . .

The daily clientele of these places vary from 75 to 2,500 in number; the customers range from Chinamen with chop suey tastes to Orthodox Hebrews who touch only "koshered" meat . . . The social status of the individual diners runs from bedraggled tramp to millionaire clubman. Rich or poor, high or low, yellow, white, or black . . . Regardless of race, station, occupation, religion, political view, party affiliations, or size of pocketbook, just so long as you have the price, be it five cents of fifty dollars, when you want anything to eat, you are sure to find it on Randolf . . .

The nationalities represented along the "Row," in order of their relative popularity are: American, German, Chinese, Kosher . . . Hungarian, and Italian. Of these, the number seeking American fare stands . . . [at] 12,800 [diners per day]. The lovers of Teutonic fare follow a close second with 12,000 diners [sitting] down everyday in front of dishes prepared by chefs . . . who learned their art in the Kaiser's domain.

Next in popularity, strange to say, come the Chinese, for no less than 1,850 citizens who have developed oriental tastes make their way daily . . . to appease their hunger in Mandarin style. An additional 500 are about equally divided between the practical gourmands who can only be satisfied with the heavy dishes of the Magyar's domain . . . and the abstemious Jew with his aversion to all . . . meat that has not been killed by a rabbi's hand. Another 100 seek the spaghetti and ravioli of an Italian food expert.

Midway in the block is located a "family restaurant." An appeal here is made to the "intelligent eater," high grade food being served at a moderate cost. The service is supplied by experts from abroad, the specialty being German bakery products, pastry, and coffee. According to the proprietor, no race can compare with the German in the area of preparing food for the table.

"It is not only the cooking," said he, "but the skillful combing of dishes which gives the German bill-of-fare its high qualities. The phlegmatic Teutonic race, with their patience and painstaking habits, are better adapted to this than any other. For generations, they have studied their trade and can provide results unequalled by others."[16]

Family restaurants that served food "unequaled by others" weren't the only public institutions that the "phlegmatic Teutonic race" bestowed on America.

Taverns (called *lokales*) that served *lager* beer were another.

The quality of the lager itself attracted Americans, but it was the setting and circumstances in which Germans served their lager, the social and emotional atmosphere that accompanied its enjoyment, that drew Americans to "Germantowns." Americans went to German taverns and beer gardens not just to drink but to be happy in a way that may not have been entirely new to them, yet was . . . different. The Germans called this particular kind of happiness *Gemütlichkeit*. "Good natured, good temper" is one way to understand it.[17]

Germans in American drank their lager as they did in Germany: they drank it sitting down. The American/Yankee custom of drinking while standing was considered antisocial and uncivilized. Furthermore, the American custom of doing nothing but drinking and talking and then drinking some more they considered unhealthy. "A man who doesn't eat while drinking is likely to become a drunkard"[18] was what German tavern keepers and their regular customers (their *Stammgasten*—from the words *Stamm*, meaning "main stem" or "family," and *Gast*, "guest") believed.[19]

Germans also believed in taking their time. They considered the Yankee habit (that is, the English/Irish ale/gin/whiskey habit) of walking into a bar, ordering a drink, throwing it back (instead of sipping it), then ordering again and again until a man walked or stumbled out into the world to be a misuse of a substance whose effects—from happiness to tranquillity to torpor—could best be enjoyed if they were prolonged.

To this end, German émigrés promulgated an old-world tavern culture that used food and drink to produce a comfortable, convivial kind of high. German taverns welcomed not only single men and men in groups but men accompanied by their wives and children. "A German saloon was as much a family institution as an Irish bar was a man's world."[20]

The best example of such tavern culture—its food and drink and openness—was a legendary place called the Atlantic Garden in New York's Kleindeutschland. A brewer named William Kramer opened the Atlantic in 1858 and kept it running until 1911. One hundred feet wide and two hundred feet deep (its front entrance was on Bowery, its back doors on Elizabeth Street), it featured a central hall that was (based

Hotel Astor, 1904, Byron Company

on engravings) at least three stories high. The Atlantic could—and did—accommodate twenty-five hundred people on a cold, winter's night.

The earliest (and perhaps the best) description of the place appeared in a book called *The Night Side of New York*.[21]

> The Atlantic is rightly named for the beer consumed there nightly is of oceanic proportions . . . Entering first the bar room, a large, low-ceiling, square room with a bar on either hand, groaning with a variety of dripping kegs, piles of crystal glasses of all dimensions and variety, loaded with sausages . . . with cakes and bread, brown and shiny, contorted and twisted, patted and molded as only the German brain could devise; green, fresh-looking salads, dripping with oil, dimpled with red beets and scarlet [radishes], salads of fish, salads of meat, salads of herring,

Hotel Astor, rathskellar and wine cellars, 1905

salads that the Devil and Dr. Faustus only know the ingredients of . . . we . . . scan the goings-on of the tippling congregation . . . The bar keepers are all fat and very busy . . . light-haired boys with round, flushed faces like bloated red cabbages; hungry looking attendants, very bow-legged and swarthy, rush in and out, in a perpetual state of frenzy, screaming and sweating, with a pyramid of glasses . . . It is a very busy night and the wooden mallet of the keg-tapper is ever echoing . . . Let's follow the wake of that wadding Dutchman . . . let us follow him to where the strains of [a] band emanate.

Pressing through a wide, open, glass door, we behold a would-be enchanted garden. It is enclosed at the sides, [while] overhead a high, vaulted roof shuts out the stars and the night air . . . Its walls are all painted . . . to portray a blooming garden scene — Alas! — It's the portrayal of a dismal cemetery . . . melancholy daubs of a peacock or two give the idea of buzzards hovering over the pesty place of the dead . . . At the farther end of the garden is a raised platform, boarded with a dozen stunted and sickly dwarf trees . . . to help-out the conception of an earthly Eden.

At the left is a big box on rafters suspending aloft the musicians [who play a medley of popular music and classical melodies]. On the right are [booths] for shooting, with spring gins, the flaming bodies of ferocious Turks and Zouvres . . .

The garden is very well stocked with bearded Germans, female Germans, youthful Germans, fat Germans, thin Germans . . . every description of Germans . . . their chattering and husky laughing is buzzing in every direction . . .

We said that there are present, females — [but] they are not gaudily dressed, not painted . . . These are wives and daughters; they are with their families . . .

The majority of Germans drink deep, but very slow. They seldom get noisy or hilarious, but they are always boisterous, loud talkers — and gesticulation is their characteristic . . . Their [foaming] cups are sipped in slight draughts, then, with a chorus of grunts, they rest [their drinks] on the table and turn their heads around upon the scene, like languid weather cocks — a look at the music, a slow nod to a familiar face.

Who else — other than friends and family — did these deep drinkers see as they looked about them?

"Though the greater part of [the Atlantic's] patrons are Germans, every other nationality is represented there: French, Irish, Spaniards, Italians, Portuguese, even Chinamen and Indians."[22]

CONTINENTAL SUNDAYS

Domesticated hedonism — familiar, welcoming, tolerant, and benign — was what German taverns (and beer gardens) offered everyone (other than prostitutes) who stopped in for a drink and a little something to eat after work.

There was something else that German taverns offered as well: they were open on Sundays. Families could go to church in the morning, then spend the afternoon in a beer garden.

"Continental Sundays" became more and more common.

Temperance advocates — everyone from Carrie Nation to the Woman's Christian Temperance Union to the United Presbyterian

Church's General Assembly—considered alcohol to be "a covenant with Death, a link with Hell."[23] Temperance advocates—they called themselves "crusaders"—believed that drinking on Sundays was an egregious sin, a sin against God and man. They believed that a victory against those who profaned "God's day" with alcohol would lead to the greatest victory of all: prohibition.

Since German *lokales* and beer gardens offered beer and music and food—gaiety and frivolity instead of remorse and contrition—to people who wanted to *enjoy* themselves on the Sabbath, temperance crusaders organized against them.[24]

In 1901, the crusading temperance pastor of Brooklyn's James Methodist Episcopal Church, the Reverend Dr. Cuyer, made these remarks about German "Continental Sundays," as quoted in the *New York Times*: "The saloon is the menace to good government and the breeding place of vice, corruption, and anarchy . . . We must place ourselves on record against the Continental Sunday with its beer gardens and wine rooms in full operation . . . The great army of foreign born who rave and rant about liberty should take into consideration that the American Sabbath will not be surrendered to unholy hands without a strong protest and determined opposition.

German-Americans didn't think of themselves as debauched or unholy—or as foreigners; 1683 was the date of the first, permanent, German settlement in the United States (founded by Francis Daniel Pastorius in Pennsylvania).

In the fall of 1909 five thousand members of New York's National United German Societies of America gathered to celebrate the 250th anniversary of Pastorius's first settlement. They ate, drank, and watched performances of gymnasts from local *Turnvereinen*.

At the end of the day members listened to a speech by their president. "America is a Land of Extremes," he declared. "One of these extremes, the present Prohibition craze, is the most recent example. It is entirely beyond the province of the Government to interfere with what we eat and drink . . . The way to stop excessive drinking is: To educate children to be moderate; to take an occasional drink without subterfuge or hypocrisy; to encourage the drinking of milder beverages like beer and wine; to forbid drinking in the standing position in front of bars and to permit it only when sociably seated; to punish drunkards for degrading themselves; to do away with the senseless American habit of treating[25]; to abolish Prohibition laws, and, above all, to frown on the unreasoning and exaggerated denunciation of women."[26]

Lowry's Egyptian Cigarettes for Sale here

See Price-List on last page.

Café Boulevard

156 Second Avenue.

I. H. ROSENFELD

PROPRIETOR.

Table Celery 25, Mixed Fruit 25
Celery Root Salad 20

SPECIALTIES OF THE HOUSE.

Wiener Schnitzel	40
Natur Schnitzel	50
Schnitzel á la Boulevard	50
Wiener Rostbraten mit Zwiebeln	55
Knobel Rostbraten	55
½ Wiener Backhuhn	50
½ Paprika Spring Chicken	60
Spring Chicken Sauté (Hungarian style)	50
Chicken Liver with Onions on Toast	40
Chicken Liver á la Boulevard	50
" " Sauté with Mushrooms	55
Hungarian Gulash, to Order	35
" " á la Boulevard	50
Kalbspörkott	35
" with Nockerl	50
Reinbraten with Lyonaise potatoes	45
Whole Potted Spring Chicken en Casserole	1.25

Reed Birds, en brochette 75
Engl. Mutton Chop, baked Potatoes ... 50
Phila. Squab, broiled or Potted 75
Mallard Duck, en casserole ... ½ ... 75
Whole Teal Duck, broiled on toast ...
Lamb Kidneys, en brochette 50
Boston Duck, baked Apples 75
Shrimps à la Newburgh 50, in chafing dish 65
Pommerische Gänsebrust w. Salad ... 50
Frog Legs, breaded, Tomato sce, or à la Poulette ... 60
Boston Goose, stuffed w. Apples, Chestnuts Purée 75
Frische Gänseleber w. Onions 75, w. Trüffel
Fresh Mushrooms broiled 50, en casserole ... 60

Depot for M. Stachelberg & Co. Havana Cigars.

Daily menu, Café Boulevard, New York, 1900

Despite the efforts of temperance advocates,[27] Continental Sundays became more common, and their enjoyment more widespread. Outdoor beer gardens in Buffalo, Louisville, Cincinnati, Chicago, Milwaukee, St. Louis, and San Francisco grew larger and more elaborate.

Brewers bought land, then built music pavilions with picnic areas, concert halls, and vaudeville stages. The more ambitious park owners added merry-go-rounds and roller coasters. For example, in Milwaukee, Schlitz Park had a five-thousand-seat concert hall, a menagerie, and a pagoda. Pabst Park had a 1,500-foot roller coaster and a Katzenjammer Fun Palace.[28] Owners charged admission (ticket prices ranged from ten to twenty-five cents) as a way to keep out troublemakers. Concession stands sold cold beer to those who wanted it; they also sold soda, lemonade, hot dogs, sandwiches, ice cream, and candy. Trolley lines brought thousands and thousands of people — families with children, young couples, groups of young women, and groups of young men — to these parks on weekends during the summer.[29]

"On a warm summer Sunday in Chicago, after the first days of July and before the frost has come upon the pumpkin, 300,000 men, women, and children will enter Summer Gardens between the hours of 10 o'clock in the morning and 10 o'clock in the evening. There is a question as to how many people in those days will go to church from which the pastors are away on vacations, but as to the Summer Garden population, it is perennial and ever increasing."[30]

EATING BOHEMIAN

In 1906 the *New York Times* published an obituary for the city's French Quarter: "In the streets . . . north of 23rd, where once little [French] shoemakers and tobacco shops were most numerous, where the real French restaurant throve and dispensed really good *tables d'hote* at a modest price . . . where there were genuine *garcons* and really plump *dames du comptoirs*, where there were curious and somber little French wine shops — there now remains practically none."

The French Quarter and its table d'hôte restaurants had prospered because, by the 1880s, New York had "begun to go bohemia mad." Diners didn't mind if "restaurants provided poor dinners . . . none too clean tablecloths, [and] indifferent wines . . . if only they had a bohemian stamp on them."

South of Washington Square — in neighborhoods the French left behind as they moved north, past Twenty-third Street — cheap Italian restaurants began serving customers who weren't Italian. These customers described themselves as "bohemians."

The social satire *Bohemia Invaded and Other Stories* placed the patrons of such restaurants in the following occupational categories: "Art, plastic, pictorial and illustration, 25 percent; letters, poetry, prosody, typewriting and journalism, 25 percent; the stage, lyric, protean, and classic, 20 percent; Arctic explorers, tropical travelers, and illustrious exiles, 10 percent; ladies, bound by marital or other fragile ties to and usually escorted by atoms of the ingredients already named, 20 percent."[31]

It was the minestrone, spaghetti, and risotto, the roast chicken and chianti (called "red ink" by the writers who drank it) served by these places — combined with their low prices — that attracted their first bohemian customers. But it was the raffish glamour, the unpredictability and unconventionality of these bohemians, that attracted the next wave of customers — respectable people with steady jobs and steady incomes who came to be entertained by the scene.[32]

"It is a curious fact," a reporter wrote in the *Times* in 1885, describing the way middle-class people began to outnumber bohemians in Italian restaurants, "that as the quality of the guests . . . improves, the national dishes disappear and the Italian cook shows a stronger inclination to a hybrid cuisine than to the unadulterated and savory dishes of his motherland."

As the menus of such restaurants became more American, and their prices went up, many of their bohemian customers moved on.

No matter, the restaurants kept their reputation as picturesque places where *interesting* people dined. The restaurants prospered. The reporter continued, "The patronage of these places . . . is drawn from all classes of society. In the poorest establishments one [still] meets chorus singers, ballet dancers, foreign artisans, and rising professional men. In restaurants of the higher grade, the company is less distinctly foreign and considerably more stylish. In the best [Italian] restaurants, every element of society is represented. Professional men are to be seen everywhere and actresses abound, with an occasional representative of that portion of society more correctly described as the demi-monde . . . Nor is there any lack of quieter people: young couples, who dwell in furnished rooms and have no cook and no servant visit these restaurants constantly. People who have [visiting] country cousins [take them there] as a 'treat.'"

Gonfarone's was one of the best known of these atmospheric places. The restaurant had begun, authentically enough, as the dining room of an immigrants' boardinghouse.[33] By the first decade of the new century businessmen began to eat their lunch there. In the evening, college students, clerks, young lawyers, and young salesmen came to have their dinner.

The daughter of one of Gonfarone's owners wrote a memoir about the place. The restaurant, she said, was "not essentially an artists' and writers' hang-out. It had none of the trappings of pseudo-bohemian retreats and was completely devoid of artistic trappings."[34]

What Gonfarone's did have — other than an enormous and enormously cheap bill of fare[35] — was a staff that "acted" Italian.

There was a chef who muttered and waved a knife, a waiter who juggled plates and glasses, and a busboy who played the harmonica.[36] Everybody was friendly; everyone acted as if they were happy. The food, the wine, the smiles, and the accents "helped propagate among Americans a simple, Latinate variety of hedonism. [Gonfarone's] opened up new approaches to sensual and spiritual pleasures . . . [It] brought new tastes, new sounds, new scents, new forms, new colors, but above all new feelings to America . . . life was not all hard and earnest . . . [it] was an adventure to be enjoyed."[37]

WALKING ON THE WILD SIDE

Other Italian restaurants offered a different sort of "adventure" to their non-Italian guests. Instead of serving the Mediterranean equivalent of *Gemütlichkeit* with their food, these places offered a hint of criminal violence, a telltale scent of hidden danger, of Black Hand or Mafia activity. The young, middle-class couples who chose to eat dinner at these places came not to savor their sunny laughter but to sit, warily and excitedly, near the edge of something darker.[38]

The origins of such dining adventures can be traced to a criminal murder case — known as the "Barrel Murder" — that kept appearing and reappearing in the news from 1903 until 1909.

The brutal facts of that murder, the elaborate, Mafia conspiracy that prompted it, the relentless pursuit of the conspirators by New York detectives, special investigators, and Secret Service agents, along with the case's final, very public resolution — all this reinforced the perception that New York's Italian neighborhoods — their stores, saloons, and restaurants — were patronized by thieves, killers, and criminal gangs.[39]

HOTEL COLOMBO

RESTAURANT

Luigi Tirelli, Prop.

149 Bleecker St., New York.

BILL OF FARE.

30c TABLE D'HÔTE LUNCH
From 12 A. M. to 2.30 P. M.

40c TABLE D'HÔTE DINNER
From 6 P. M. to 9 P. M.

Pint Bottle of Claret included with Lunch & Dinner.

SPECIALTY
WEEKLY DISHES.

Monday	Polpettine di Vitello alla Fiorentina	10c
Tuesday	Tagliarini al Sugo	10c
Wednesday	Beef à la mode, with maccaroni	15c
Thursday	Codeghini e lenticchie	10c
Friday	Polenta e Bacalà	10c
Saturday	Cazzola alla milanese	10c
Sunday	Ravioli alla Genovese	15c
"	Trippa alla Crèole	10c

THESE DISHES ALWAYS READY AT MEAL HOURS.
DISHES TO ORDER ON NEXT PAGE.

Estimates for Private Lunch & Dinner parties can be obtained at the
Office on application.

NOTICE. Meals served in Rooms will be charged 25c. extra, for service.

Frugone & Balletto, Printers and Translators. 178 Park Row, New York.

Bill of fare, Colombo Hotel, New York, 1900

One month after police detectives and federal agents arrested the men charged with the Barrel Murder[40] a feature article entitled "The Mystery of the Table d'Hote and What It Brought About, Being a Tale of an Italian Restaurant with a History of Greenwich Village" appeared in the *New York Times*.

It was a darkly funny tale in which a young couple gossiped about the (thrilling!) possibility that a Mafia murder had happened in the basement of the restaurant where they ate and drank.

"Not so many years ago," the article began, "it was necessary to make various and sundry signs in order to gain admission [to this restaurant]. Within, a certain sense of danger to the limb added zest to the steady and continuous flow of the pink ink."

When it was observed that the [owner's] pretty, black-haired, young wife [who always sat at the front desk to make sure] that the two Italian waiters made no mistakes in serving their guests . . . was mysteriously missing from the desk . . . rumors ran riot: some, in deep, dark, and blood-curdling whispers suggested foul play.

There was whispered talk of the Black Hand and [the] Mafia . . . Black looks were shot at the . . . dark-eyed, nervous husband who sat high and dry in the chair [his wife] had occupied . . .

At length, unable to endure the suspense, a man and a woman who frequented the restaurant braced-up, [and] on their way out past the desk, made inquiries of the . . . husband,

"Where is she?" they demanded . . . looking hard to see if there was blood on his hands.

He shrugged his shoulders significantly, then with an explanatory finger and a rolling eye that might have meant most anything, pointed below.

The couple vaulted back. He had killed her, and buried her in the cellar.

Seeing the terror depicted in their orbs, [the owner] explained more lucidly, though in few words, his English being a trifle scarce, and not of the best variety:

"In the kitchen, cooking . . . I give her fifteen dollar to cook . . ."

A week passed.

The couple returned to the restaurant.

The owner's wife sat at the desk where her husband had been. The man was nowhere to be seen.

Once more supposition ran riot in the dining room . . .

"If she had sent the Mafia on her husband and accomplished his demise," reasoned the woman, "she is perfectly justified. Any man who can have the heart to make a chef of his pretty, black-haired wife in this day and generation deserves death at the stake. Fifteen dollars a week!!"

The man worked up his courage and asked the waiter what had happened to the husband.

The waiter shrugged and frowned and jerked his thumb in the direction of the dark-haired wife.

"Not murdered?" queried the man, bloodcurdlingly.

With a significant forefinger, the waited pointed below.

"Buried?" cried the man.

"Oh, no," said he. "In the kitchen. Chef."

The woman laid down her knife and fork with a smile.

"Good!" she exclaimed. "It was a hard fight. You can see it by her eyes, but her mouth proclaims victory. There's one thing I'll wager though: she gives him more than $15 a week to do the cooking."[41]

Other Pleasures

The coffeehouses on Washington Street,[42] in the "Little Syria" section of lower Manhattan, offered other amusements to visitors, especially if those visitors were adventuresome — and fashionable — uptown ladies.

"It is at night, when the lamps are lit that the . . . cafes [of Little Syria] are seen to the best advantage. Around the tables will be found dark-eyed, olive-skinned men who, in face and figure might well serve as models for an artist's masterpiece. They chat, argue, play chess, bezique, and a game resembling dominoes, and unconsciously fall into picturesque poses . . .

"Syrian women do not visit the coffee houses unless they run in for a minute to buy pastry. Their husbands and other male relatives would object strenuously if they lingered around these public places . . . but feminist sightseers of American and European nationality are free to enter and are treated with the utmost courtesy. They usually come in parties, but if for any reason an American woman elects to enter alone, the men are particularly careful not to embarrass her by staring, and, when she is about to leave, the door is opened for her with Chesterfieldian politeness . . .

"Many society women have found their way to these coffee houses, and the literary and journalistic world—or the portion of it prone to indulge in journalistic excursions—regards them as a happy hunting ground."[43]

Unfortunately, soon after this appeared, those happy hunting grounds became war zones.

At the time there were some six thousand Lebanese immigrants living in the seven-block neighborhood of Little Syria.[44] Most of them were Christians, either Eastern Orthodox or Maronites; some were Roman Catholics; others were Druse. All carried with them a historical memory of sectarian violence, clan wars, and blood feuds.

Late in the summer of 1905, the editors of one of the newspapers published in "the colony" wrote something that the colony's Eastern Orthodox bishop considered offensive. The bishop, as quoted in the *Times*, "called upon the younger members of his congregation to defend him with sword and dagger." Gangs of Roman Catholics and Eastern Orthodox men attacked each other. Skirmishes went on for months. One day, an Eastern Orthodox and a Roman Catholic got into a violent argument in front of a café. Friends tried to separate them. The Roman Catholic shouted, "I want to step on the beard of your bishop!" One month later, the brother of the monsignor who presided over the colony's Roman Catholics was stabbed and garroted while having dinner in a restaurant on Washington Street.

After the assassination, a police magistrate spoke with a reporter.

"The Syrian colony in lower Washington Street . . . is now . . . in a really alarming state . . . The rival Tongs in Chinatown are not more bitterly opposed to one another, nor are their members ready to go to greater lengths to gratify their enmity than are the adherents of the warring clans in Little Syria . . . There has been a reign of terror in the colony for months past . . . fights are constantly breaking out . . . Outsiders are as likely to get the worst of it as are the participants."

Well-to-do Lebanese businessmen and importers moved their offices, their warehouses, and their families to Brooklyn. Fashionable ladies and literary gentlemen stopped visiting the colony's cafés.

EATING CHINESE

The first Americans to visit the Chinatowns of San Francisco and New York were working-class white men who didn't go there for the food. From the 1850s until the 1920s, Chinatowns were places to gamble, buy sex, and use drugs.

In spring of 1910 the *New York Times* reported, "The Chinese inhabit . . . streets in some of the worst tenements in the city. The colony would soon die out were it not for the profitableness of the American trade . . . Such places as . . . Chinatown's City Hall, gambling [dens] . . . a Joss house [the shrine of a god, or demigod], with a few curio shops, tea houses, [and] a dingy Chinese theater . . . seem to furnish enough for hundreds to nightly visit Chinatown."

Since most of the white men who went to Chinatown to play faro or poker or to buy ten minutes with a prostitute also believed that the little

Chinese restaurant, 1905, Byron Company

Oriental Restaurant

樓芳萬約紐

Mann Fang Lowe Co.

3 PELL STREET,   NEW YORK.

April 19, 1904

Oriental dinner menu, Mann Fang Lowe Co., New York, 1904

pieces of meat that the Chinese ate with their rice had once been dogs or cats or rats they avoided Chinese restaurants. If, late at night, such men were still in a Chinatown and were hungry, they went to cheap quick lunches run by Chinese or Irishmen that served bread and beans and beef and coffee.

As to what ordinary Chinese workingmen ate: the powerful Chinese import and export syndicates — the Six Companies — that, as labor agents, brought men from the Pearl River delta region of Guangdong Province to work, before and after the Civil War, in the mines of California and Colorado and to lay track for the Central Pacific also imported their food, utensils, condiments, tea, herbs, and medicines.

Every twelve- or twenty-man crew of the fifteen thousand[45] Chinese laborers employed by the Central Pacific had, according to contract, its own cook. The supply trains that followed these crews and cooks had commissary cars.[46]

"Here is a list of the food kept and sold to the Chinese workmen [laying track for a line through the San Joaquin Valley in 1872]: dried oysters, dried cuttlefish, dried fish, sweet rice, crackers, Chinese sugar [sugar made from sorghum], four kinds of dried fruits, five kinds of desiccated vegetables, vermicelli, dried sea weed, Chinese bacon, cut up into small cutlets, dried meat of the [abalone], peanut oil, dried mushroom, tea, and rice . . . At this railroad store, they also sold paper bowls, chopsticks, large, shallow, cast iron bowls for cooling rice, lamps, Joss paper [for prayers], Chinese writing paper, pencils . . . India ink, Chinese shoes and clothing . . . Also scales . . . and Chinese tobacco."[47]

Braziers and woks, jars of soy sauce, dried lily stalks, packets of star anise, cloves, cassia (Chinese cinnamon), fennel seeds, fresh ginger and garlic, different kinds of pickles and candies may also have been available — but the sharks' fins and birds' nests, the thousand-year-old eggs and sea cucumbers that literate, nineteenth- and early-twentieth-century Americans considered the most exotic and unpalatable — and repulsive — Chinese foods were eaten not by workers gathered around

MENU

CHOP SOOY, with white Mushrooms............25c
PLAIN CHOP SOOY.............................15c
GUY GANG (Chicken Soup)...................30c
VEGETABLE SOUP, WITH MEAT.................25c
GUYSUE MEIN (Noodle Soup with Chicken)..25c
YET QUO MEIN (Noodle Soup with Pork).....10c
ONE HONE (Boiled Chicken and Dumpling)...25c

FRIED

CHOW MEIN (Fried Noodle with Boneless
 Chicken) large........................75c
CHOW MEIN (Fried Noodle with Boneless
 Chicken) small........................40c
BOR LOW GUY PAN (Boneless Chicken
 with Pineapple).......................75c
LYCHEE GUY PAN (Boneless Chicken
 with Lychee)..........................75c
GUY FOU YONG DUN (Chicken Omelet).........75c
FOU YONG GUY PAN (Chicken with
 Scrambled Eggs).....................$1.25
JAR JEE GUY (Boneless Chicken fried in
 Crackerdust)........................$1.00
MOO GOO GUY PAN (Boneless Chicken
 with White Mushrooms).................75c
FOU YONG DUN (Omelet with Ham)............50c
FOU YONG DUN (Plain Omelet)...............35c
FOU YONG HA (Omelet with Lobster).........75c
CHOW SANG HA (Fried Live Lobster).........75c
MOU GOO BOCK GOB (Fried Squab with
 White Mushrooms).....................75c
YOU JOR BOCK GOB (Fried Squab Whole)....50c
DEN NOON GUY (Fried Spring Chicken)
 Whole $1.00, Half....................60c

Oriental dinner menu, Mann Fang Lowe Co., New York, 1904

cook tents but by merchants and traders seated at their own tables in San Francisco and New York. *Fai cai*—a serving of rice eaten with a small portion of vegetables, meat, or fish—was the common meal of all but the poorest or the richest Chinese.[48] Bowls of rice, garnished with a scattering of other ingredients and washed down with tea, were what Chinese laborers ate before they went back to work.

At best, this work was difficult and dangerous; at its worst, it was barely tolerable. Isolation and exhaustion, combined with a fear of xenophobic/racist violence—violence committed by the same Americans who used Chinatowns to indulge their appetites—drove young Chinese men to the same vice districts as the Americans who despised them.

By 1882[49] an estimated 20 percent of Chinese living in the United States[50] smoked opium occasionally. ("Occasionally" was defined as during feast days and holidays or during binges lasting no more than fourteen days.[51]) An additional 15 percent of Chinese in the United States were estimated to smoke opium daily.[52] In San Francisco, the number of "occasional" Chinese smokers was 10 percent to 20 percent higher than the national estimate.[53]

A much smaller percentage of American whites smoked opium regularly and addictively during this era. Marginally employed clerks and messengers, petty thieves, gamblers, low-end pimps, and prostitutes were the first to become addicted, but by the late 1880s "merchants, actors, leisured gentlemen, sportsmen, telegraph operators, mechanics, ladies of good families, actresses, . . . married women, and single women"[54] began to smoke regularly as well.

Unlike the middle-class use of morphine, self-injected in private, opium smoking was a convivial habit. A pipe would be prepared, passed around, and shared in a drawing room or an apartment with other people. Unlike the workingmen who'd binge (and smoke) in a nearby Chinatown but would no more eat Chinese food than they would rotten meat,[55] the American opium smokers of this era—particularly the inhabitants of the demimonde—ate Chinese food as part of their sophisticated way of life. In this, they were joined by bohemians—the same sorts of people who expressed their contempt for good manners and proper conduct by crowding around the tables of immigrant restaurants. Though alcohol, not opium, was the bohemians' drug of choice,[56] the allure of the demimonde, the outcast otherness of the Chinese themselves, and the cheapness of their food drew them to Chinese restaurants.[57]

Reports about these new patrons appeared in big-city newspapers around the country.

In Chicago, in 1898, three Chinese restaurants opened almost next door to one another on Clark Street. Only "the one that stayed in the real Chinatown prospered."

"First and foremost, its patrons were those who had to live much at night. Actors and actresses made up much of the patronage. After the theater, they got in the habit of dropping in for a tiny cup of Chinese tea or a bowl of chop suey, which has been called 'Chinese Irish stew.' Then there were the cabmen. They like the Chinese fare. Policemen got the taste, and night reporters."[58]

In Los Angeles, after a Chinese gambler named Hu Hong struck it rich playing fan tan, he celebrated by holding a banquet at Tsoy Far Low's, a restaurant on Alameda known as "the Delmonico's of Los Angeles."

"Along toward midnight there is invariably a most picturesque gathering in this most strange restaurant . . . a place that has fallen over the edge of the world and is no longer in touch . . . with anything real. It is a gaudy, forgotten, cosmopolitan crowd that gathers there for midnight supper . . . There are painted white women, painted Chinese women, men of the lower part of the city—human night hawks—sitting with their hats pulled over their eyes, eating strange things from bowls with chopstick."[59]

Other, less glamorous, less well appointed—and less expensive— Chinese restaurants served an even more mixed group of customers.

A Chinese restaurant in Washington, D.C., that became a gathering place for bohemians had only three, barren rooms: "The back was a kitchen, the middle, a general eating room, and the front, one for people who were called—by courtesy—'ladies.' There was not even a pretense of Chinese . . . color—no hangings of gaudy red and gold, no attendants in gay robes . . . A rather decent looking boy waited on people. Now and then, the cook, who was also the proprietor, a thin, cold man with pinched nostrils, would come out of the kitchen and change money or clear off tables . . . There were several women in the front room, painted, soggy creatures in loud clothes. In the middle room, sat three Johnnies, out for 'a devil of a time.' They were very much frightened and cast apprehensive glances at the men around them. No wonder: The cream of the lower, submerged tenth was there—men who looked like convicts and wharf rats, rough animals who spoke in grunts and ate with their paws . . . Most of [these] animals fed on noodle soup and chop suey. If you want to see a sight . . . watch one of them get a hold of a six-foot noodle and commence to consume it. The 'chop suey' was a nasty smelling dish, fairly bathed in grease. The place was bathed in various awful odors — human and vegetable."[60]

Back in Los Angeles, another Chinese restaurant — this one, attached to a brothel — was visited by a beautiful and well- bred young woman, who came there, every night, to eat noodles and, perhaps, buy opium from the restaurant's cook.[61]

> She is pretty — oh, amazingly pretty; dresses handsomely, conducts herself like a patrician, but alas! Frequents a dirty chop suey joint [whose] chief patrons are outcast negroes and white damsels of no reputation . . . In the main room were three, blear-eyed hobos, sitting around a table, dulled with drink and "dope" . . . From an inner room came the sound of a negro girl begging "Babe" to buy her "so mo suey." He wouldn't do it . . . Then she wanted to smoke opium . . . "Nit," said Babe. "Ah don' pay fo' no smokes . . ." Into that atmosphere swept "My Lady of the Noodles" . . . She had a white opera cloak and wore a flower in her corsage. The white of her shoulders beamed through a thin, silk [shirt] waist [a silk blouse] . . . She swept a look around that took in every object and every person . . . "Pigs! All of you. Pigs!" [she said]. She threw her opera cloak over one of the Chinese high backed chairs . . . and glided out of the room. You could hear her speak . . . to the cook at the kitchen entrance . . . Presently she came back to her seat . . . Two dreadful females with imitation gold and cigarettes sailed by her with alarming picture hats. One of them stopped to stare at her rudely. My Lady of the Noodles looked up coldly and gave her a glance one might have cast at a brick wall. The girl passed on in a frozen daze . . . [Her food was brought to her.] This dainty young woman consumed three bowls, one after the other . . . It should be known that one life-sized bowl of noodles would satisfy a hippopotamus . . . Yet her table manners were exquisite.[62]

SLUMMING

Chuck Connors, a politically well-connected Irish crook who — with other Irish crooks — owned shares in gambling halls in New York's Chinatown,[63] supplemented his income (and did favors for his Chinese friends) by offering his services as a guide to wealthy tourists who, having read about the district's violence and depravity, wanted to see it — safely — for themselves. Connors would shepherd his well-to-do clients past innocent-looking storefronts, all the while cautioning them not to look too closely, lest they provoke an attack by lookouts. To the left, he'd say, behind that curio shop and down a flight of stairs, was an opium den; to the right, through that alley and up two flights of stairs, was a gambling hall; behind that grocery store across the street was a brothel where Chinese men had their way with white girls who had become their opium-addicted sex slaves.

As the tourists would look and gasp or clench their teeth, Connors would caution them to keep their heads down and stay close together. Eventually they'd reach a point where Connors — unbeknownst to them — had arranged a little show. Suddenly, there would be a terrifying shriek, then a Chinese man, dressed in chain mail, would dash past them, running for his life, chased by another man, also dressed in chain mail, waving a sword and screaming for revenge. The two crooks — whose tongs Connors had paid for their services — would disappear around a corner. Chinese pedestrians — who'd seen the performance many times before — would continue as if nothing had happened. Connors's clients would gasp and shudder, amazed and appalled by their close call — and by the unnerving indifference of the Chinese around them. Connors would explain sotto voce that it was probably a fight over a slave girl.

Once Connors's flock had regained its composure, he would suggest lunch at a nearby restaurant — whose surprisingly palatable, English-language bill of fare[64] had been arranged by Connors and the proprietors to accommodate everyone involved.[65]

As the *Chicago Tribune* explained: "Slumming parties paid better than anybody else. Waiters could charge them what they pleased . . . and when a screen was put around their table that meant a tip. Tips were introduced to . . . Chinese restaurants by the slummers."

"Slumming" was what the prosperous people who indulged in it called their Oriental adventures.[66] Sometimes these slummers were New York or San Francisco suburbanites; sometimes they were wealthy tourists from cities such as Cleveland or Minneapolis or Dallas. Sometimes they were European aristocrats.

In November 1904 two German princes, Prince Friedrich Karl and Prince Johann von Hohenlohe-Oehringen — accompanied by a New York police inspector who served as their escort — narrowly missed being caught in a shoot-out between two heavily armed gangs of rival tongs.

Five minutes after the princes passed a house at 10½ Bowery, Hip Sing and On Leong tong members, some wearing chain mail, some carrying "big revolvers of the best type," opened fire on one another. Two white workingmen, who had been visiting Chinatown for the usual reasons, were wounded. One of them, a man from Brooklyn, died at the scene.

One month before this happened "two sightseeing automobiles piled with men and women from the Waldorf-Astoria Hotel" went to Chinatown to attend the opening of a new restaurant. The hotel's maître d', the famous Oscar Tschirky, had arranged the expedition. He and the hotel's steward, a man named von Arinin, escorted the adventurers. Among them was a U.S. senator from Texas.

"It was about 9 o'clock when the autos reached Chinatown . . . instead of going directly to the restaurant, the party was taken over the Chinese theater." Unfortunately, the senator found the play not to his liking, so he left the theater to conduct a tour of his own. He came back drunk.

The senator was "about to make himself comfortable when he saw a Chinese villain in the act of stabbing the hero of the play. The [senator] scared the villain away by roaring, 'Git back thar or I'll clip your wing, you scoundrel!' . . . This started an uproar in the theater and gave nervous folk a chill, but [Oscar and von Arinin] quickly came to the rescue and the Texas Senator strolled into the street."

Oscar and von Arinin led their guests to a joss house on Mott Street. There, the senator got into a conversation about politics with "the guard of the sacred altar." He bought some joss sticks to take back to Texas with him to light fireworks. Then he noticed a big drum by the altar. He was in a jovial mood so he began to bang it. He didn't know it was sacred. The guard became alarmed and shouted at him. One of the senator's entourage rushed the man with his fists up. "Don't you call the Senator that or I'll sacrifice you right on that altar!" he yelled. Oscar and von Arinin intervened. They poured money into the temple's offering box and rushed their guests to the restaurant.[67]

TONG WARS

Such comedies of manners and misunderstandings might have continued for years. Opium-smoking members of the demimonde, antisocial bohemians, and little groups of well-to-do voyeurs might have continued to visit their respective Chinatowns—some to meet their connections, some to eat dinner and see their friends, others to gaze into the lower depths—and then return to their white worlds. Back home, safe and sound, they'd entertain their friends with droll or shocking stories about the curious things they'd seen and heard.

Unfortunately, the same sort of problem that stopped fashionable New York ladies and literary gentlemen from visiting the cafés in Little Syria put an end to white expeditions to Chinatowns throughout the country. In New York's Chinatown and in the Chinatowns of San Francisco, Los Angeles, Chicago, and Philadelphia as well organized criminal violence between armed groups of rival tongs—the Hip Sing versus the On Leong versus the Four Brothers (modern name: Lung Kong Tin Yee) versus the Bing Kong—turned Chinatown streets into shooting galleries where no one, whether Chinese civilians, white slummers, artistic opium smokers, or police patrolmen, was safe.

In August 1905 after an unusually bloody encounter between gangs of Hip Sing and On Leong, the New York police department stationed patrolmen on street corners throughout Chinatown. "Two years ago, the patrolman [standing watch on he corner of Doyers Street] said he would have summed up the whole situation [with] the words, 'Just Chinks,' but yesterday, he was obviously wondering what kind of people those were who, on a Sunday night, ablaze with fury, hacking, hewing, shooting, and stabbing as if possessed by . . . devils . . . were now sitting on the curbstones . . . as if nothing had happened, as if nothing could ever happen . . . 'Yes,' said the policeman at the corner, 'they look innocent enough, but . . . Wait 'til after dark.'"

A New York State judge helped negotiate a peace treaty that divided the district's gambling, drug, and prostitution concessions between the two major tongs, but it broke down in 1909 when the Four Brothers tong from San Francisco shot its way into the On Leong's New York territory.[68]

Because the tongs did business in cities across the country, a tong killing in Boston would be avenged by a killing in Philadelphia; a tong ambush in Chicago would be answered with an ambush in Los Angeles. Tongs from one city would send hit men to kill rivals in another city.

Sometimes the shootings were wild street killings, furious and indiscriminate. Sometimes they were assassinations—during a meal in a particular restaurant or during a lull, outside, behind a particular gambling hall. The year 1909 may have been the bloodiest year of the tong wars (350 tong members died in New York alone) but it was the persistence of the violence—attacks and counterattacks that continued, intermittently and unpredictably, from 1900 until 1928[69]—that changed the way white people ate Chinese food, and how Chinese restaurants served it.

Chop Suey

Because it was impossible for Chinese merchants (even members of the Six Companies) to dislodge the gambling, prostitution, and drug networks based in the Chinatowns of America's biggest cities, and also because restaurant and laundry work were virtually the only jobs available to ordinary Chinese workers in this era,[70] Chinese entrepreneurs began to open restaurants outside of their cities' Chinatowns.

In 1903, in Chicago, five years after two of the Chinese restaurants on Clark Street had failed almost as soon as they'd opened their doors, the *Tribune* reported, "If the signs of the time are not misleading, Chicago's appetite, like the nation itself, is expanding far towards the East . . . Just now on Clark Street there is being fitted up a Chinese restaurant that will occupy three floors of a corner building while on either side of it are other restaurants which have made small fortunes for the [Chinese] who are operating them . . . But not [only] on Clark Street are the Chinese catering . . . to Chicago's citizens. On Randolph Street there is a well patronized Chinese restaurant . . . North Clark Street and other thoroughfares have their quota of places where the mysterious chop suey is served . . . They have a chop suey to suit every purse, and he who does not care to eat the more popular mystery can find plenty of other things on the bill of fare to excite his curiosity."[71]

In that same year, in New York, a beautifully decorated Chinese restaurant opened near (what is now) Times Square: "There, under the light of multicolored lanterns and amid the silk and bamboo decorations that are quite luxurious from the Oriental point of view, chop suey is served to the midnight supper club. This resort, like many others of its kind that thrive within ten blocks of it . . . is not open in the daytime. . . . It is the men and women who like to eat after everyone else is abed [who] pour shekels into the coffer of the man who knows how to make chop suey."[72]

Back in Chicago chains of Chinese restaurants began to open throughout the city. "The Joy Let Yo Company has six. The Suey Hung Lo Company has three . . . Nor are the cafés confined to the Levee [the city's vice district]. On Randolph Street alone, there are four . . . One

New Year's, Chinatown, Port Arthur Chinese restaurant, New York, 1909

in the block that holds the Powers Theater [a well-regarded, legitimate theater] and three in the square from Dearborn to State Street. Along Clark Street there are several. North of Adams Street and south of Van Buren they are too common to attract attention. Harrison Street has three, and State Street is crowded with them. Down there, they have driven out some of the American lunch-rooms. The sort that used to advertise coffee and rolls for 10 cents and in some economical cases for 5 [cents] have given place to Chinese emporiums."[73]

At the opposite end of the scale were such places as Joy Hing Lo's—a sixty-eight-seat restaurant located at the corner of State and Adams Streets: "Its walls are of Chinese green and Chinese yellow, intermingled, and are paneled alternately with richly colored silk, heavily embroidered, and mirrors that reflect the light of thousands of incandescent lamps concealed beneath softly shaded lamps and swinging lanterns. At intervals, the [dining room] is divided by gilded columns serpentined by gilded dragons, richly carved by native workers . . . To lend an additional Oriental touch . . . a Chinese orchestra [furnishes] the music three nights each week, using the quaint musical instruments of China."[74]

By 1907 there were nearly two hundred Chinese restaurants in Chicago.[75] Unfortunately, the number of white customers didn't grow with the number of restaurants. "If it wasn't for the American dishes that we now serve," complained one restaurant owner to the *Chicago Tribune*, "there wouldn't be a Chinese shop suey place left in Chicago. How long has it been since any [restaurant has] received an order for bird's nest soup—six months? Yes, more than a year. All we serve nowadays is the plain chop suey for 30 cents and egg foo yung . . . There isn't much money in those dishes [especially when you serve rice and tea with an order] . . . Chicago [used to be] the best chop suey town in America. The business here [once] amounted to $2 million [equivalent to $48 million] per year."

Back in New York cheap Chinese restaurants began to open, one near the other, on Third Avenue, north of Rivington Street, then on Seventh Avenue, starting at Thirty-fourth Street.

"It was necessary to move chop suey quarters uptown when slumming ceased to be popular with New Yorkers . . . In San Francisco and other cities which have large Chinese colonies, a large number of persons have learned to like chop suey. Once or twice a week or even oftener they have a 'hankering' for it. But they dislike to come all the way to Chinatown after theater hours to get it . . . The result has been the establishment, within a few months, of one hundred or more chop suey places between 45th Street and 48th Street, and from the Bowery to 8th Avenue. A large number of these are in the Tenderloin.[76] Many persons who have seen this new crop of chop suey establishments have jumped to the conclusion that opium smoking and kindred vices associated with Chinamen have been going on there with the tacit consent of the police. . . .

" 'Nothing of the kind,' said Police Captain Burfriend . . . 'I know from experience that these chop suey "joints" as they are called are among the most orderly places in New York . . . There are many in which a man might take his wife or daughter without the slightest fear, provided she . . . did not object to being waited upon by a Chinese servant . . . Most of these chop suey places have no liquor licenses . . . Tea is the only beverage served. This itself is a great feature in keeping order. As to opium or other dope—that is absurd. Cigarettes are smoked, as they are in other restaurants—and smoked by women as well as men . . . But that is the fault of the patrons and not of the Chinamen.' "[77]

No matter what Captain Burfriend said, many of the chop suey restaurants that opened beyond the reach of the tong wars in America's big cities during this decade were located in or adjacent to vice and/or entertainment districts. As the *New York Times* reported, "Sunlight and the chop suey consumer are as far apart as the poles."

Just as the rumored presence of bohemians attracted middle-class New Yorkers to picturesque carefree kinds of Italian restaurants—or as rumored Mafia connections attracted other, more adventuresome customers to edgier sorts of places—so chop suey's reputation as a food eaten by opium-smoking actresses, gentlemen of leisure, and iconoclastic bohemians added to its allure. By the end of the decade the very act of going out for chop suey made middle-class Americans feel pleasantly naughty. If not "guilt by association," then "*touché* by association" added spice—if not to the food, then to the people who ate it. Chop suey may have been nothing more than a steaming pile of chopped meat and vegetables, covered with brown sauce, accompanied by a bowl of rice, but its fabled history as the preferred food of glamorous decadents, artistes, and rebels made the nice people who ordered it feel more adventuresome than they really were.

THE WHOLE WORLD IN ONE PLACE

Perhaps the best example of the way (some) Americans began to adapt other people's food and drink to their own pursuit of happiness was the 1904 opening of the Hotel Astor on Broadway, just north of Times Square.

William Waldorf Astor, the man who built the hotel, was the great-grandson of John Jacob Astor, a penniless German immigrant from the village of Waldorf. When John Jacob's grandson died in 1890, *his* son, William Waldorf, inherited $100 million—equivalent today to about $2.4 billion. Almost as soon as William came into his inheritance he began to build grand hotels and magnificent apartment buildings.

The first hotel William built (in 1893) was on Fifth Avenue, on the site of his father's house. William named the hotel after his family's ancestral village. The Waldorf's twelve stories (topped with domes and spires) housed a sumptuous Palm Court, a glittering Peacock Alley, and a magnificent ballroom. It was in that ballroom, in 1905, that Theodore Roosevelt gave his Lincoln's Day address to a gathering of the nation's rich, wellborn, and able.

The next hotel William built — the Astor, on Broadway — appeared, from the outside, to be less exuberant than the Waldorf. The Astor's Beaux-Arts facade and its massive size (a ten-story, block-long, behemoth of limestone and redbrick, topped by a gigantic, mansard roof) were grand but sedate.

Inside, however, the Astor had public rooms that replicated half a dozen countries and more than a dozen eras.

If an adventuresome man walking through San Francisco (after the 1906 earthquake, of course) had only to step across a street to travel — as if by magic carpet — from America to Japan to China to France to Italy to Greece,[78] then a guest at the Astor had only to walk (or take an elevator) from one public room to the next to travel from one country — or century — to another.

At street level the Astor appeared to function in a predictable, women-separate-from-men, American sort of way.

"Dining, reception, and reading rooms for women are on the main floor, with entrances on 45th Street and Broadway, while, to the left, on the 44th Street side, are the men's café and restaurant, [and] the billiard room for men."

After that, time and place, history and geography became less predictable. "On the mezzanine floor are the Spanish Renaissance [lounge] and the Chinese [tea] room." Both rooms were decorated with statuary, wall hangings, paintings, porcelains, rugs, and furniture appropriate to their countries and eras.

"The men's dining room, in the German Renaissance, 16th century style, is in oak, with wainscoting sixteen feet night . . . The walls and ceiling are adorned with hunting scenes and trophies of the hunt . . .

"The billiard room is in the Pompeian style . . .

"The bar is in [the] Flemish [style] . . .

"Then there is the *Orangerie* — a reproduction of an Italian garden. This room is 104 by 75 feet . . . encircled by a gallery . . . The rear recalls the famous terrace at Versailles. A fountain is built against the terrace, surmounted by a marble [statuary] group. Orange trees and palms are about the tables; the walls are latticed; the ceiling is done in a sky effect, and from the back wall, a moon, electrically lighted, sheds a soft light.

"Between the mezzanine and the ninth floor are the sleeping rooms, 500 in number . . . These rooms are decorated and furnished in various styles, with state chambers in Louis XIV . . . and suites in Colonial, Art Nouveau, Empire, Francis, Marie Antoinette, Madam de Maintenon,

Spanish Renaissance, Dutch Renaissance, German Renaissance, Florentine, and Elizabethan."[79]

Thirty feet below ground a new era in another country began.

Down long flights of stairs, through wrought-iron gates, men — but only men — could enter vaults that were replicas of one of the great monastic wine cellars of medieval Germany — the cellars of Eberbach-on-the-Rhine.[80]

Double sets of huge, oak doors swung open on forged, iron hinges. Life-size, wooden statues of monks (one, *Bruder Kellermeister*, carried a huge tankard and keys; the other, *Bruder Kuchenmeister*, carried a basket of fruits and vegetables)[81] guarded the entrance to a stark, white, vaulted, high-ceiling room whose oak refectory tables could seat four hundred guests.

Carved oak barrels, each as tall as a man, lined the room. Other rooms, with twenty-foot ceilings, ran parallel to it. Some rooms had alcoves where other barrels stood; some were lined with rows of smaller barrels; and some were stacked, ceiling high, with cases and cases of wine.

Banquets (for men only) were held in these rooms.

"The waiters were garbed like the cellar men of Europe, with blue jumpers and huge leather aprons, while behind [them], a reproduction of the famous Heidelberg Tun [a massive cask, said to have been made from the wood of more than a hundred oak trees, capable of holding fifty thousand gallons of wine] concealed [a small] orchestra."[82]

From its Chinese tearoom to its German rathskellar the Astor embodied how Americans, living in (or visiting) this country's big cities, began to participate in the ways foreigners pursued happiness. Old world open-heartedness, German *Gemütlichkeit*, bohemian nonconformity, Italian hedonism, Sicilian ruthlessness, Levantine sensuality, Oriental decadence — all were ways of being and behaving that Americans tried to experience, no matter how briefly or superficially, by eating immigrant food in immigrant restaurants. The food they ate wasn't a magic potion — it didn't transport or transform them — but it was the experience of eating it, the sights and sounds of the restaurants, the people in them and the neighborhoods around them, that gave immigrant food the power to make the people who ate it feel more differently alive.

—ML

SPLENDID FOOD

BEGINNINGS

On a sunny morning in May 1883 Oscar Tschirky stepped off a ship's gangplank and into New York City. He was sixteen. Oscar had traveled with his mother by train from Switzerland to France, and then by steamer to New York. Oscar's father had stayed behind in Switzerland to settle their affairs, but he planned to join them in the fall. They'd all been summoned to America by Oscar's older brother, Brutus, who'd gone to New York to seek his fortune some months earlier. Brutus had found a good job in a high-end Manhattan restaurant kitchen; he urged his family to come share in his success.

The Manhattan that greeted Oscar and his mother was a jumble of people, carriages, and telegraph wires — all noise and motion. Oscar was amazed. Brutus, who'd hired a hansom cab for them, was nonchalant.

Brutus's brownstone on East Twenty-second Street would be their home. Peering out his bedroom window at the buildings across the street, Oscar's eyes fell on an enormous poster of Lillian Russell, the era's premier musical actress. Lillian would reign as the queen of New York café society until the passage of time, combined with too many big restaurant dinners and the emergence of a more delicate feminine ideal, dethroned her. Her decline was yet to come; in 1883, Lillian Russell was twenty-two, creamy and voluptuous. Oscar stared and stared.

Brutus interrupted Oscar's daydream. "Come on, I have plans for you. We need to go downtown to file your citizenship papers, and then there's someone I want you to see about a job."

Sherry's head waiter, 1902, Byron Company

That someone was a Monsieur Pusse, an acquaintance of Brutus and the maître d'hôtel of the Hoffman House. Located at Twenty-fourth Street and Broadway, west of Oscar's new home, the Hoffman was one of the leading New York hotels of the era. Its velvet-draped, mahogany-paneled public rooms welcomed visiting dignitaries and the city's dealmakers. Senators and lobbyists, reporters and robber barons, gambling men and rakes all gathered around the hotel's distinctive square bar, the first of its kind in New York. Huge oil paintings of peachy nudes, including Bouguereau's life-sized *Nymphs and Satyr*, kept the atmosphere festive.[1] So did the bartenders, who invented cocktails as their customers wagered on horses and plotted corporate mergers.[2]

Oscar spoke little English, but his compact, muscular frame (he had been a champion wrestler in Switzerland) radiated energy. Impressed by his vigor and willingness to start work on his first day in America, Pusse hired him as a busboy. The pay — $18 a month, or about $360 now — wasn't much, Pusse admitted, but there would be chances for advancement and, who knew, maybe Oscar would end up as a maître d' himself one day.

Oscar resolved to make himself indispensable. In the back of his mind was an idea that maybe someday he could be a headwaiter and oversee dinners for the glorious Miss Russell.

Months of work passed for Oscar without so much as a glimpse of the actress. The poster of Lillian across from his bedroom window disappeared, replaced by a giant advertisement for Cream of Wheat. But Oscar's hard work began to pay off. His busboy exertions caught the eye of Ned Stokes, the Hoffman's owner.[3]

Stokes promoted Oscar to room service waiter, then asked him to work Sundays as the steward on his yacht. There, Oscar plied the players at Stokes's all-night poker parties with steaks and whiskey and cigars. With Stokes's permission, Oscar was allowed to keep whatever was left on the poker table once the guests had retired.

The first Sunday night, Oscar found $49 and change — equivalent to nearly $1,000 today — still on the poker table. Shocked, he asked Stokes if there had been some mistake. "No, Oscar, they know the rule," Stokes said.[4]

Working Sundays on the yacht gave Oscar a very comfortable salary — and the chance to meet the men who ran the city. His weekday job at the Hoffman helped too. By winter he was tending bar alongside the nymphs and satyr, drinking in the gossip and earning the goodwill of businessmen and politicians.

Not once did he see Lillian Russell; the Hoffman House bar was a men's club. Even in the private dining rooms of the Hoffman, Miss Russell and her actress friends never made an appearance.

Four years passed. One evening, Oscar was headed home from work at the Hoffman, crossing Madison Square where Fifth Avenue and Broadway meet at Twenty-sixth Street. Delmonico's restaurant was located at that intersection. Oscar had heard of Delmonico's, of course. Everyone had—it was the first and best European-style fine-dining restaurant in New York, probably in the entire country—but Oscar hadn't thought much about the place. He was happy with his work at the Hoffman House. Happy, that is, until he saw the Delmonico's doorman step to the curb and call out, "Miss Russell's carriage, please!"

Suddenly, there she was.

"I remember the smooth flow of her blue gown, the exotic effect of her golden hair, but most of all the banked-down fire that smoldered in her beautiful face. She was the loveliest woman I had ever seen, lovelier than the picture on the poster I had stared at those first few days I spent in New York. I could hear but a few snatched words, uttered in a clear, musical voice. Then her friends closed around her as she stepped into the carriage."[5]

The next day, Oscar paid a visit to Philippe, Delmonico's headwaiter. As soon as a position opened there, Oscar gave Ned Stokes a week's notice and then began waiting tables at Delmonico's. All Oscar thought about was the opportunity to serve the magnificent Miss Russell. What he didn't know was that he was stepping into the start of something even more grand.

Aristocratic Food for American Aristocrats

At Delmonico's, Oscar worked his way up from grillroom waiter to manager of the private dining rooms, a job that involved planning menus and overseeing service for many parties, small and large. He supervised birthday dinners and three-day poker marathons, corporate banquets and bachelor parties, weddings and society debuts. He even organized the lavish dinner parties that "Diamond" Jim Brady threw for the beautiful Lillian and her pretty friends.

Old money—New York's Four Hundred—felt comfortable at Delmonico's. Beginning in the mid-1800s, the restaurant had secured a reputation as the city's temple of gastronomy—and as the one place outside their private homes where New York society families could throw a socially acceptable affair.[6]

The Swiss brothers who founded Delmonico's in 1829 had started out as wine merchants, pastry chefs, and confectioners to New York's society ladies. Once they moved into the restaurant business, they understood the importance of appealing to both masculine and feminine tastes. They opened their restaurant downtown, in the Financial District, and served the businessmen of the neighborhood. Society families began building mansions farther north, where there was still room to build on a grand scale. Delmonico's followed them, moving to Fifth Avenue and Twenty-sixth Street in 1876, and then, in 1897, to Fifth Avenue at Forty-fourth. As the restaurant moved northward, it kept the business of society families by providing an atmosphere of gentility and restraint. A writer of the period reported, "The dining room upstairs and the café downstairs were comfortable but plain, and the [private dining] rooms upstairs were commodious, but not ornate. There was an absolute air of simple elegance about the place."[7] Its decor—soothing, calm—comforted society patrons.

The Delmonicos sought to reassure their clients in other ways. During the early nineteenth century, restaurants' private dining rooms had gained a reputation in both Europe and the United States as places where wealthy men took mistresses or prostitutes for something more than dinner.[8] To attract New York's most respectable families, the Delmonico brothers imposed strict rules to prevent any chance of scandal. Early on, Charles Delmonico decreed that all couples, married or not, had to keep the doors to their dining rooms open at all times. This ruffled the feathers of more than one upscale patron, but it also meant that even the most proper young lady could dine with a male escort in one of Delmonico's private rooms without fearing for her reputation.[9] Writing in 1904 for *Town and Country*, Walter Germain Robinson noted that "New York, until the eighties, had only one restaurant to which it was considered absolutely proper for unmarried women, with or without escorts, to go, and even not risky for married couples, without being classed as Bohemian—and that was Delmonico's."[10]

The Delmonico family hired a succession of French-born and -trained chefs through the decades. The greatest of these chefs—the one who made Delmonico's reputation on both sides of the Atlantic—was Charles Ranhofer. As the son of a restaurateur in St. Denis, a suburb north of

Paris, Ranhofer grew up in the business. In the mid-1840s, when he was barely in his teens, Ranhofer's father sent him to Paris to apprentice with a succession of the city's leading pâtissiers. Ranhofer rose quickly and was hired straight out of his apprenticeship into the kitchens of Prince Hénin of Alsace. He was named chef to the prince before his seventeenth birthday.[11]

Ranhofer had been schooled in the French *haute cuisine* that had emerged in France's noble houses before the revolution and had been codified in the early nineteenth century by the great French chef Antonin Carême. Like Ranhofer, Carême had trained as a pâtissier; he understood pastry making and confectionery to be branches of architecture. Carême emphasized elaborately composed dishes, both sweet and savory: great truffled towers of poultry and fish in aspic, elaborately molded ice cream bombes and mousses, and, most dramatically, *pièces montées*.[12] These imposing sculptures were edible in name only, but they dazzled with their artistry and detail. Under Carême's watchful eye, a half dozen or more skilled artisans would turn sugar, egg white, and vegetable gums into sailing ships, Greek temples, figures from classical mythology, and all manner of flora and fauna.[13]

Ranhofer was one of a small handful of French, Alsatian, and Swiss chefs who brought Carême's ideas — and the secrets of *pièce montée* — to the United States in the mid-nineteenth century.[14] He also brought a dictatorial leadership style.

Lorenzo Delmonico recalled his first meeting with Ranhofer, in 1861: "He was perfect in dress and manner, and his attitude was such as to make me feel that he was doing me a great favor by coming into my employment . . . He gave me plainly to understand that he would be 'chef' indeed. 'You are the proprietor', he said. 'Furnish the room and the provision, tell me the number of guests and what they want, and I will do the rest.' That was the way it was."[15]

For more than three decades Ranhofer ruled the kitchens and pantries of Delmonico's with an iron hand. A crew of more than fifty cooks and pantry men, sauciers and grill men, sugar sculptors and bakers obeyed his every word. A hand gesture or a glare was enough to send them scurrying.

From his experiences catering to the French aristocracy, Ranhofer knew how to please an American elite that took its cues — in architecture, dress, and food — from Europe. He had developed a keen sense of the grand meal as a work of art, one meant to delight all the senses. New York society received his art with enthusiasm. The old-money members of the Four Hundred — and the new-money millionaires who were beginning to nip at their heels — made Del's the fashionable place to hold a formal dinner in the 1870s and '80s.

As the pace of city life quickened and elite New Yorkers became both more hurried and more sophisticated in their tastes, Ranhofer began to shape Delmonico's menus to suit them. By the 1880s he had begun shifting the service for formal dinners away from the French style that had been prevalent in the nineteenth century (imagine a dinner in an Edith Wharton novel, with gloved servers bringing several dishes at once, uncovering them in unison, and then circling the table to serve each guest in turn) to what became known as "Russian" and later as American service. In the new style, individual portions of food were whisked from the kitchen and placed before each guest as quickly and quietly as possible, one course at a time. The *Chicago Daily Tribune* estimated that a typical eleven-course society dinner served "à la russe" might take two hours instead of three or four.

The *Tribune* described the impact this had on the kitchen and waitstaff. "When these 120 minutes have been cut into eleven minute sections, the chef and the corps of waiters and attendants necessarily have to keep wide awake; for six minutes for the laying of a course and the removal of the soiled dishes after a guest has dined may be considered about as rapid work for the servitors as is possible without imposing the spirit of haste upon the guest. Even at six minutes for this serving and removing of a course a good many of the quickened actions of waiters must be executed in the regions beyond the dining room doors."[16]

Even though so-called American service required a small army of waiters, and precise choreography from kitchen to table, it had two big advantages: it allowed food to be served at its ideal temperature, whether piping hot or ice cold, and it highlighted the chef's artistry, one course at a time.

Ranhofer innovated in other ways. Because he'd spent time cooking in restaurants in New Orleans before coming to New York, he introduced Creole seasonings and dishes such as gumbo to Delmonico's patrons. He also made use of Indian curry and Hungarian paprika. Soon after samples of the "alligator pear"—the avocado—were brought to New York from Caracas in 1895, Ranhofer added them to Delmonico's bill of fare.[17] Even though he admired and made use of local and seasonal ingredients, Ranhofer also made out-of-season produce (grown in hothouses or shipped from Florida or California in refrigerated railcars) a symbol of luxury.

THE SPREAD OF SPLENDOR

By the early 1890s New York City's Four Hundred were joining their nouveau riche counterparts in hosting banquets and balls in public venues. The venue of choice for many remained Delmonico's, but hosts could also hold their parties at such private clubs as the University Club and the Knickerbocker, at freestanding restaurants such as Martin's on University Place, and at such luxury hotels as the Fifth Avenue Hotel.

These new places catered not only to society folk concerned with "correctness" but to celebrities and newly minted big spenders—people who were less interested in striking just the right tone than they were in opportunities to show off their wealth. The newcomers embraced some of the trappings of bohemianism that Delmonico's core clientele had carefully avoided — at a time when being "bohemian" began to sound more exciting than scandalous.

The greatest among Delmonico's new rivals was Sherry's. In 1889 Louis Sherry, another society confectioner turned restaurateur, opened his first New York City restaurant in a converted mansion on Fifth Avenue at Thirty-seventh Street. He later moved up Fifth Avenue to a Stanford White–designed building just opposite Delmonico's, sharpening the competition. While Delmonico's had aimed for quiet, even staid elegance in its decor, Sherry's model was Versailles: mirrored ballrooms, coffered ceilings, gilt moldings on pastel walls. Sherry's rooms were palatial in scale; his menu was every bit as elaborate — and expensive — as Delmonico's.

Sherry's chefs at luncheon, 1902, Byron Company

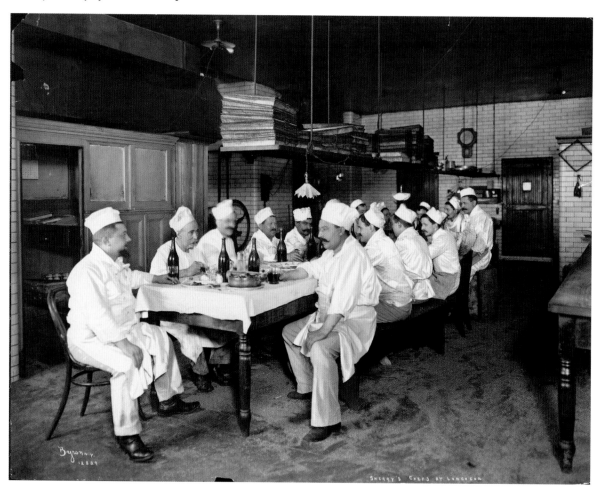

Through the 1890s and early 1900s society columns listed wedding and birthday dinners, anniversary parties, and benefits for hospitals and children's aid societies, all hosted by Sherry's. Sorosis, one of the earliest clubs for professional women, held its meetings at Sherry's, at least until a bachelor party displaced a Sorosis meeting and the membership decamped in a huff to the new Hotel Savoy. While the "Patriarchs" of New York's oldest families still sponsored their annual dress balls at Delmonico's,

Hotel Astor, 1904, Byron Company

their wives, the "Matriarchs," held their spring cotillions at Sherry's.[18]

From the outset, Sherry's was a less buttoned up sort of place than Delmonico's. Residents of the blocks around the restaurant filed repeated civil complaints about late-night noise, traffic congestion from the parked carriages of patrons, and the early-morning racket of professional "criers," who summoned the patrons' carriages as their parties let out.[19]

The restaurant also hosted "stag dinners" for young men. Held on Saturday nights, such dinners featured lavish food, free-flowing liquor, and risqué entertainment. One of the most infamous, the "Awful Seeley Dinner," was held at Sherry's in December 1896. Herbert Barnum Seeley, the twenty-five-year-old nephew of P. T. Barnum, and his friends, known to Louis Sherry as "gentlemen . . . of the highest standing," booked one of Sherry's private rooms. Seeley and his friends then asked an entertainment agent to provide "sensational dancers" for an after-dinner show.[20] The agent secured some chorus girls and an exotic dancer named Little Egypt, who had earned renown for her "danse du ventre" performances in Sol Bloom's Egyptian Village at the 1893 Chicago world's fair.[21]

A rival entertainment agent whose girls hadn't been hired for the event tipped off police. A plainclothes officer interrupted young Seeley's party. The officer described a chaotic scene in which inebriated guests cavorted with showgirls and a partially dressed Little Egypt. After months of conflicting testimony, and after both Sherry and Seeley threatened to sue the police, the indictments were dropped.[22]

In an earlier era, a private dinner that ended in a vice raid might have been disastrous for a restaurant serving respectable society types.[23] But far from hurting business, the Seeley dinner scandal helped confirm what wealthy New Yorkers already knew: Sherry's had become the favored site for a younger, "smart" society crowd.

The *New York Herald* summed it up: "Looking over the program [for the social season], it seems that the very young buds are to blossom in Sherry's pink-and-gold room. The full-blown roses will, as usual, fill the Madison Square Garden assembly rooms with their perfume; while the wall flowers, the old timers, the patricians, will cling to their old walls at Delmonico's. It seems a fit and proper arrangement."[24]

Sherry's wasn't the only rival to Delmonico's. Each year between 1893 and 1910 new luxury hotels, such as the Waldorf, the Hotel Astor, and the Knickerbocker, opened their doors to tourists and their dining rooms to upper-class locals. In addition to Sherry's, such freestanding restaurants as Rector's vied for wealthy patrons' attention.

Ranhofer remained the acknowledged chef of chefs, but as Delmonico's bloom faded Ranhofer's own health declined.[25] In response, he decided to create a book that would preserve his legacy. The result was a ten-pound, 1,200-page illustrated compendium of everything Ranhofer had learned about making and serving *haute cuisine*. Ranhofer called the book *The Epicurean*.

In its pages, there was advice about table service, with diagrams showing proper place settings. There was advice for procuring and storing produce, meat, and game, including how to keep turtles alive in a kitchen cellar until they were needed for soup. There was a directory of the wines of the world and which foods they might best accompany.

At the book's core, there was a staggering selection of menus reproducing the more than three decades of dinners and banquets that Ranhofer had created for Delmonico's.

And, finally, there were recipes—3,715 of them, numbered for easy reference. Collectively, *The Epicurean*'s recipes and instructions unlocked the secrets of fine cuisine for anyone in America with enough kitchen experience to understand them.

A typical Ranhofer recipe was as intricate as a Russian nesting doll. It incorporated a series of components that required advance preparation by a sizable kitchen crew. In an era before most electric kitchen equipment (other than the rotisserie) was available, pureeing a sauce or soup meant forcing it through a series of successively finer mesh sieves; making ice cream meant hand cranking the custard in a barrel-sized vat surrounded by ice and rock salt. In the Delmonico's kitchen, half a dozen men would have made the components of a recipe such as the one that follows.

(1978) PULLET A LA NANTUA (POULARDE A LA NANTUA)
Split down the back of a singed and very clean pullet; bone the breast and legs, leaving on the wing bones; season the inside meats and fill the empty space with quenelle forcemeat (No. 89) combined with crawfish butter (No. 573) and prepared red pepper (No. 168) also the crawfish tails cut lengthwise in two. Sew up the pullet, truss and have the breast well-rounded, then cover over with slices of fat pork and lay it in a narrow saucepan, cover three-quarters of its height with skimmed stock (No. 194a), adding aromatic herbs and mushroom peelings; cook it in this alone for one hour; it should really only be poached; then drain off the pullet, untie and dress it on a thin layer of forcemeat poached on a dish covered lightly with veloute sauce (No. 415) reduced with a part of the stock and finished with red butter (No. 580). Serve with small timbales of fat rice made in timbale molds (No. 6) letting it be quite white; serve with the remainder of the sauce in a sauce-boat.[26]

Dinner, Hotel Knickerbocker, New York, 1907

The publication of *The Epicurean* earned Ranhofer a reputation as the "American Escoffier." Ironically, the book enabled Delmonico's growing list of competitors, both in New York and in other American cities, to copy Delmonico's signature dishes with ease, and to use Ranhofer's recipes to invent specialties of their own.

The publication of *The Epicurean* also sealed Delmonico's fate as a star in slow descent. Leopold Rimmer, who had worked as a dining room manager at the height of Delmonico's prestige, called the book "the greatest mistake ever made against the interest of the Delmonicos'

FRUITS

Bananas	20	Pear (1)	20
Orange (1)	15	Bar-le-Duc Jelly	40
Orange Marmalade	20	Baked Apples	25 15
Grape Fruit (half)	30	Hothouse Grapes	1 00
Apples (1)	15	Stewed Prunes	25
Domestic Grapes	50 30		

COFFEE, TEA, Etc., with Cream, Rolls and Butter 25

Tea, per pot	25	Coffee, with cream	20 per pot with cream 35
Chocolate, cup	20	Milk, bottled special	20
Cocoa per cup, with cream	20	Broma, per cup	20

CEREALS, with Cream 25

Oatmeal	20	Wheatena	20
Standard Cereals (to order)	20	Indian Meal Mush	20
Hominy	20		

French Rolls	10	Corn Muffin	10
Milk Toast	20	Boston Brown Bread	10
Dry Toast	10	Graham Bread	10
Corn Bread	10	Griddle Cakes	25
English Muffin	10	Dipped and Buttered Toast	15

EGGS

Boiled (1)	10	Omelette with Tomatoes	40
Scrambled, plain	35	with shrimp	60
Shirred	30	with kidneys	50
Omelette, plain	35	with chicken livers	60
fried with bacon or ham	50	Spanish	60
Oeufs Bénédict	50	with fines herbes	40

CLAMS AND OYSTERS

Little Necks, steamed	50	Oysters, steamed	50
Fried	50	Fried	50
Soft Clams à l'Ancienne	60	Broiled	50

FISH

Fried Filet of English Sole	1 00 69	Fried Scallops, sauce tartare	75 40	Pan Fish with bacon	60 35
Salmon, Meunière	75 40	Salt Codfish with cream	50 30	Salt Mackerel	50 30
Broiled Bluefish	60 35	Fried Eels, sauce ravigote	60 35	Bloaters (1)	40
Sea Bass with fines herbes	60 35	Finnan Haddock	40	Fried Scrod	50 30

STEAKS AND CHOPS

Small Tenderloin	60	Small Steak	75	English Mutton Chop	75
Tenderloin	90	Sirloin Steak	1 25	Lamb Kidney, maitre d'hôtel	35
Vienna Steak	50	Lamb Chops	75 40	Calf's Liver and bacon	60 35
Veal Chops, fines herbes	50	Tartare Steak	90	Chicken Liver au Marsala	80 45
Corned Beef Hash	40 25	Veal Kidney, Bercy	50	Squab Chicken	1 25
Fried Scrapple	40	Smoked Beef in cream	40	Squab	90
Broiled Ham	40		Bacon	30
Deerfoot Sausages	50 30		Country Sausages	40 25

POTATOES

Fried	25	Julienne	30	Baked	20
Sauté	25	Lyonnaise	25	Hashed browned	25
Maitre d'hôtel	25	à la crème	25	Sweet, fried or grilled	35

Guests are requested to pay waiters only on presentation of a check   6. Jan. 1907   1–6–07

Breakfast, Hotel Knickerbocker, New York, 1907

LUNCH

Caviar d'Astrakhan, special importation, per person......75

Buzzard's Bay.....................30	Cape Cod.........................30
Little Neck Clams.................25	Blue Point.......................25
	Cotuits.......................30	

HORS D'OEUVRE

Supreme of Grape Fruit...............75

Mackerel in oil....................40	Celery........................50 30
Norwegian Sardines................25	Westphalian Ham..............60
Herrings à la Hollandaise, p. p.....25	Grape Fruit, half.............30
Stuffed Egg à la Venitienne (1)......20	Stuffed Olives à la Cannoise......30
Tomato, Knickerbocker (1)..........30	Lyons Sausage.................40
Mushrooms à la Tyrolienne.........30	Anchovy Salad................40
Smoked Salmon in slices...........50	Shrimps à la Parisienne, p. p......30

POTAGES (per person)

Consommé aux perles du Japon............25	Gumbo à la Créole.................35
Consommé Brunoise au riz.................25	Cream of Asparagus...............30
	Cream Santé..................25	

POISSONS

Bass a l'Arlesienne..................80 45	Salmon, meunière.................80 45
Kingfish, Bercy....................80 45	Scallops, Florentine (1)...........60
Broiled Smelts, maitre d'hôtel..........75 40	Fried Whitebait................75 40

PLATS DU JOUR

Tripe a la Mode de Caen, p. p................40	Oeufs, Georgette (1)...................30
Chicken Pie with fresh mushrooms (1)...........65	Veal and Ham Pie, p. p. (cold)............50
Mutton Chops à la Lyonnaise (1)...............50	Chicken Salad, Olivier, p. p..............45
Braised Boston Duck, peas à l'etuvée, p. p......65	Vermont Turkey, cranberry sauce....90 50
Scallops of Veal, Milanaise................60	Roast Beef, (1 slice)...................50
Oeufs, Byron.......................50	Roast Lamb, mint sauce............75 40

COLD DISHES

Egg in Jelly á la Valencienne (1)........20	Virginia Ham.................75 40
Egg in Tarragon Jelly (1)..............20	Pâté of Game St. Hubert, p. p.......45
Suprême of Chicken, Toquette (1).......75	Assorted Meat.........75 with Chicken....90
Galantine of Capon, truffled...........50	Chicken.........1 75 90 Roast Beef.....50
Terrine de Foie-gras.......1 00 1 50 2 00	Pâté de Foie-gras, p. p...............75
	Boned Squab á la Rossini.........1 50	

SALADS

Chicory..............50 30	Lettuce...........50 30	Potato..............40 25
Escarole..............50 30	Macédoine...........60 35	Ecossaise...........60 35
Romaine..............50 30	Tomato..............60 35	Russian..........1 00 60
Field Salad...........50 30	Knickerbocker.......90 50	Victoria............90 50
	Florida.............60 35	

ROTIS

Boston Duck.................2 75		
Milk-fed Guinea Chicken.......2 25	Squab Chicken.........1 25	Squab Guinea Chicken........1 50
Squab....................1 00	Jumbo Squab..........1 25	Chicken Casserole, bonne femme..2 25
	Chicken Casserole, Woodmansten..................2 50	

GAME

Canvas-back Duck................4 50	Mallard Duck.................2 25
Red-head Duck..................3 50	Ruddy Duck..................1 75

VEGETABLES

Hot House Asparagus...................1 75

	Artichokes......................60	
Asparagus, Argenteuil.....1 50 80	Spinach with cream..........50 30	Rice en Pilaff............40 25
Oyster Bay Asparagus.......75 40	Spinach à l'Anglaise.........50 30	Endive Flamande.......60 35
Celery braisé à la moëlle......60 35	Spaghetti au gratin..........50 30	Stuffed Tomatoes........60 35
Green Peas...........50 30	Stuffed Sweet Pepper........50 30	Bermuda Onion, cream sauce (1)...20
String Beans...........50 30	Parsnips à la poulette........50 30	Cauliflower...........70 40
Potatoes, Sautés...25 Lyonnaise..30	Persillées..25 Dauphine..25	Brussels Sprouts.........50 30

ENTREMETS

Knickerbocker Ice Cream Souvenir...................75

Pêche Melba, (1).............60	Macédoine de Fruits, p. p......60	Gateau pont neuf............10
Cold Rice Pudding and cream.....20	Stewed Prunes and Pear, p. p....30	Compote of fresh fruits, p. p......50
Marrons Glacés.............50	German Apple Tart............25	Patisserie, Parisienne (2).........15
Pea Pie...................20		

GLACES

Café Parfait.........30	Vanilla............30	Nesselrode Pudding......40	Chocolate..........30
Coupe St. Jacques......60	Lemon............25	Tutti Frutti..........35	Caramel..........25
Biscuit Tortoni........30	Orange...........25	Strawberry.........25	Sorbet Cherry Brandy....35

CHEESE, special importation (20 per person)

Port du Salut...........	English Cheddar...........	Gervais...........25	Pont l'Evêque...........
Roquefort........ Gruyere........	Gorgonzola....	Confiture de Bar-le-Duc...40	Coulommiers........

FRUITS AND COFFEE

Grapes: Malaga 50	**Fresh Strawberries......1 00**	Pear (1) 20	Apples 25
Demi-tasse.......15	Turkish...........20	Spécial.............25	Pot of Coffee with cream...35

Lunch, Hotel Knickerbocker, New York, 1907

Luncheon

HOTEL KNICKERBOCKER

Caviar d'Astrakhan, special importation, 75 per person

Blue Points	.25	Cape Cod	.30
Cotuits	.30	Little Neck Clams	.25
	Buzzard's Bay	.30	

HORS D'OEUVRE

Norwegian Sardines	.25	Westphalian Ham	.60
Herrings à la Hollandaise, p. p	.25	Grape Fruit, half	.30
Stuffed Egg à la Venitienne (1)	.20	Stuffed Olives à la Cannoise	.30
Tomato, Knickerbocker (1)	.30	Lyons Sausages	.40
Mushrooms à la Tyrolienne	.30	Anchovy Salad	.40
Smoked Salmon in slices	.50	Shrimps à la Parisienne, p. p	.30
Royans	.40	Carciofini	.30
Mackerel in oil	.40	Celery	.50

POTAGES (per person)

Consommé aux oeufs pochés	.30	Gumbo à la Créole	.35
Consommé Julienne	.25	St. Germain	.25
	Cream, bonne femme	.25	

POISSONS

Koulibiac de Saumon, Moscovite(1)	1 00	Frogs' Legs, fines herbes	.90
Filet of Shad meunière with egg plant	.90	Sea Bass à l'Anglaise	.75
Halibut Steak, Horly	.80	Fried Scallops, sauce tartare	.80

PLATS DU JOUR (Ready Dishes)

Pieds de Mouton, Poulette, p. p.	.50	Oeufs a la Reine (1)	.30
Stewed Beef, Napolitaine, p. p.	.40	Veal and Ham Pie, p. p. (cold)	.50
Chicken Pie with fresh mushrooms (1)	.65	Chicken Salad, Olivier, p. p.	.45
Brochette of Sweetbread, vert-pré (1)	.45	Vermont Turkey, cranberry sauce	.90
Lamb Chops with string beans	.80	Roast Beef (1 slice)	.50
Scrambled Egg, McDonald	.50	Roast Lamb, mint sauce	.75

COLD DISHES

Egg in Jelly à la Valenciennes (1)	.20	Virginia Ham	.75
Egg in Tarragon Jelly (1)	.20	Pâté of Game St. Hubert, p. p.	.45
Suprême of Chicken, Jeannette (1)	.75	Assorted Meat......75 with Chicken	.90
Galantine of Capon, truffled, p. p	.50	Chicken......1 75 90 Roast Beef	.50
Terrine de Foie-gras......1 00 1 50 2 00		Pâté de Foie-gras, p. p.	.75
	Boned Squab à la Rossini	1 50	

SALADS

Chicory	.50	Lettuce	.50	Potato	.40
Escarole	.50	Macédoine	.60	Ecossaise	.60
Romaine	.50	Tomato	.60	Russian	1 00
Victoria	.90	Knickerbocker	.90	Field Salad	.50
		Florida	.60		

ROTIS

Squab Guinea Chicken	1 50	Squab	1 00	Chicken en casserole, bonne femme	2 25
Milk-fed Guinea Chicken	2 25	Jumbo Squab	1 25	Squab Chicken	1 25
	Chicken Casserole, Woodmansten	2 50			

GAME

English Snipe	.90	Woodcock	1 25	Red-head Duck	3 50
Grouse....3 50 broiled..3 50	1 75	Large Golden Plover	1 00	Mallard Duck	2 25
Partridge...3 50 broiled..3 50	1 75	Canvas-back Duck	3 50	Ruddy Duck	1 75
Quails	1 00			Virginia Sora	.90

LEGUMES

Hot House Asparagus 1 75

		Brussels Sprouts	.30		
Asparagus Argenteuil	1 50	Spinach with cream	.30	Rice en pilaff	.40
Oyster Bay Asparagus	.75	Spinach à l'Anglaise	.50	Endive Flamande	.60
Celery braisé à la moëlle	.60	Spaghetti au gratin	.50	Stuffed Tomatoes	.60
Green Peas	.50	Stuffed Sweet Pepper	.50	Bermuda Onion, cream sauce (1)	.20
String Beans	.50	Parsnips à la poulette	.50	Cauliflower	.70
Potatoes: Sautés...25 Lyonnaise...30 Persillées...25				Dauphiné	.25

ENTREMETS

Deviled Ice Cream Souvenir	.75	Parisian Basket Ice Cream Souvenir			.75
Peach Melba (1)	.60	Macédoine de Fruits, p. p	.60	Tarte aux cerises	.30
Cold Rice Pudding and cream	.20	Stewed Prunes and Pear, p. p	.30	Patisserie, Parisienne (1)	.10
Mince Pie	.20	Cream Caramel	.25	Compote of fresh fruits, p. p	.50

GLACES

Café Parfait	.30	Biscuit Tortoni	.30	Orange	.25
Tutti Frutti	.35	Vanilla	.30	Lemon	.25
Caramel	.25	Strawberry	.25	Chocolate	.30
Nesselrode Pudding	.40	Coupe, St. Jacques	.60	Sorbet Cherry Brandy	.35

CHEESE special importation, (20 per person)

Port du Salut	English Cheddar	Gruyere	Gorgonzola	Pont l'Evêque	Roquefort Coulommiers
	Gervais 25		Confiture de Bar-le-Duc 40		

FRUITS

Grapes: Malaga 50	Fresh Strawberries 1 00	Pear [1] 20	Apples 25

COFFEE

Demi Tasse........15	Turkish........20	Special........25	Pot of Coffee with cream....35

Guests are requested to pay waiters only on presentation of a check. c New York, Saturday, December 22, 1906

Daily menu, luncheon, Hotel Knickerbocker, New York, 1906

Après le Théâtre

Supper—Grill Room

Caviar d'Astrakhan, special importation, per person 75

Oysters—Blue Point 25   Buzzard's Bay 30   Cotuit 30   Cape Cod 30
Little Neck Clams 25

BROTHS (hot or cold)

Chicken Gumbo, in cup	.30	Consommé au Marsala	.25
Clam Broth	.25	Chicken Consommé	.30

Consommé au fumet de celeri 30

READY DISHES

Terrapin a la Maryland	**3 50**	**Turtle Fins a l'Americaine**	**1 00**
Frogs' Legs, Provençale	.80	Sliced Chicken à la King	1 50
Crab Flakes, Kossuth	1 25	Deviled Lamb Kidneys, p. p.	.40
Crab Flakes, Newburg	1 25	Broiled Squab Chicken, Virginia	1 50
Deviled Crabs, each	.45	Welsh Rarebit	.40
Broiled Lobster	1 25	Scotch Woodcock	.50
Lobster à la Knickerbocker	1 25	Canapé Lorenzo	.60
Broiled Quail à la vert-pre	1 00	Brochettes of Chicken Liver (1)	.50
Cassolette of Sweetbread au paprika	.75	Scallops à la Waleska	.80

OPEN GRILL

Broiled Squab à la diable	1 00	Grilled Sardines	.50
Deviled Bones	.60	Filet Mignon Béarnaise (1)	.50
Broiled Pig's Feet, St. Menehould	.40	Deviled Lamb Kidneys (2)	.40

Club Sandwich 35

POULTRY AND GAME

Jumbo Squab	1 25	Squab Chicken	1 25
Large Golden Plover	1 00	English Snipe	.90
Grouse	3 50 1 75	Woodcock	2 25
Partridge	3 50 1 75	Virginia Sora (2)	.90
Quail	1 00	Broiled Squab Guinea Hen	1 50

COLD

Pâté de Foie-gras, p. p.	.75	Boned Squab à la Rossini	1 50
Terrine de Foie-gras truffé	1 00 1 50 2 00	Roast Beef	.50
Galantine of Pullet, p. p.	.50	Chicken	2 00 1 00
Suprême de Volaille à l'estragon (1)	.75	Beefsteak, tartare	.60
Virginia Ham	.75	Raw Beef Sandwich	.30

SALADS

Green	.50	Crab Meat	1 00
Lettuce and Tomato	.60	Lobster	1 00
Chicken	1 00	Victoria	.90
Knickerbocker	.90	Chiffonnade	.75

Hot House Asparagus, Vinaigrette 1 25

ENTREMETS — ICES

Fresh Strawberries	**1 00**	**Parisian Doll Ice Cream—Souvenir**	**.50**
Macédoine of Fruits with kirsch, p. p.	.60	Nesselrode Pudding	.40
Peach, Melba (1)	.60	Tutti Frutti	.35
Coupe aux Marrons	.60	Café Parfait	.30
Pear, Ranavolo (1)	.40	Iced Biscuit	.35
Vanilla	.30	Chocolate	.30
Coffee	.30	Lemon	.25

Orange 25

Demi-tasse 15   Turkish 20   Special 25   Pot of Coffee with Cream 35

Daily menu, supper, Hotel Knickerbocker, New York, 1906

business," claiming that Ranhofer's magnum opus "gave away all the secrets of the house, and every Tom, Dick, and Harry who calls himself a cook, and has learned his trade in Delmonico's kitchen, can make up the finest dinners with that book, which tells him everything he doesn't know."[27]

Soon after *The Epicurean* appeared in 1893, the Chicago Hotel Monthly Press distributed the book nationally and began issuing its own line of handbooks for American chefs and restaurant staff. Many were inexpensive pocket guides, with such as titles as *The Vest Pocket Vegetable Guide, The Vest Pocket Pastry Book*, and Charles Fellows's *The Chef's Reminder* (1896), a cheat sheet for cooks that listed the components of hundreds of classic sauces, soups, and entrées.[28] For American-born kitchen crews, Fellows included a glossary of French culinary terms, along with their pronunciations. *The Practical Hotel Steward* (first published in 1900) used sample menus from big-city hotels, among them many in the South, Midwest, and West—including the Willard in Washington, D.C., the Oriental in Dallas, and the Hotel Statler in Cleveland—to teach hotel restaurant managers how to oversee purchasing and service, plan banquets and special dinners, and develop bills of fare.[29]

Three Banquets for Prince Henry

The Epicurean and the guides that followed it not only dealt a blow to Delmonico's,[30] they also broke New York's monopoly on American fine dining. New York would remain the city with the most developed restaurant scene for decades to come, but by the early 1900s other cities had their own European chefs, elaborate dishes, and elegant dining rooms. Boston had the Locke-Ober, with its Franco-German menu; Chicago, the College Inn and the Blackstone Hotel; Atlanta, the Kimball House and the Aragon; San Francisco, the Hotel St. Francis, its kitchens helmed by a fez-wearing Alsatian, Victor Hirtzler, the West Coast's first celebrity chef.

The culinary ambitions of cities such as San Francisco and Chicago mirrored other ambitions. In early 1902, when Prince Henry of Prussia announced a visit to the United States, Chicago's German-American community and businessmen bid successfully to host the prince in the Second City.[31] Tall, blond, and dashing in his naval uniform, Henry was the first member of the German royal family to visit the United States. His visit provoked frenzied excitement—and fierce competition to host him—in U.S. cities with sizable German populations. In Chicago, German singing societies and veterans of the Franco-Prussian War lobbied the German consulate. An overnight stop in Chicago was added to a crowded itinerary that centered on a ceremony to launch Kaiser Wilhelm's yacht *The Meteor* at Shooter's Island in New York.

The *Chicago Daily News* and *Daily Tribune* chronicled plans for the welcome dinner, ballroom decorations, and entertainment. The prince would stay at the Auditorium, a massive complex that had been designed in the late 1880s by Dankmar Adler and Louis Sullivan as an opera house to rival—or surpass—New York's Metropolitan. Attached to the Auditorium was a four-hundred-room hotel with enormous art nouveau public spaces. The German-American civic leaders on Prince Henry's reception committee ordered that the hotel's banquet room and ballroom be decorated in a manner "more elaborate than any kind every attempted in Chicago." As reported in the *Chicago* press, "The hall was a blaze of color and the tables were arranged so that all could have full view of the Prince. The table of honor was of triangular form, with the Prince seated in the center of its base . . .

"The table of honor had a fountain for its center, and in the water were many goldfish. Surrounding the edge of the pool were wreaths of Easter lilies and highly colored foliage. The base between that point and the inner edge of the table was covered with ferns and bright leaves, surmounted by three set pieces representing the German and American flags and the American eagle. These were made of carnations, violets, and daffodils."[32]

When the prince's private train pulled into Chicago's Union Station shortly after 6:30 p.m. on March 3, a police escort cut through rush-hour traffic to deliver him the Auditorium. He had ten minutes to settle into his hotel suite before being escorted to dinner. From dinner, he was escorted to a concert of German songs and orchestral music at the Chicago Armory, and from there he was driven back to the Auditorium for a ball.

9758-Dining-room, Fairmount Hotel, S. F.,—only building on Nob Hill that withstood the fire. Copyright 1907 by Underwood & Underwood, U-103838

Dining room, Fairmont Hotel, San Francisco—only building on Nob Hill that withstood the fire. June 4, 1907

The two hundred guests at Prince Henry's welcome dinner were men from Chicago's political and business elite — among them Mayor Harrison, J. Ogden Armour, Marshall Field, and Honore and Potter Palmer II. They paid $50 (equivalent to $1,000) each for the privilege of dining with the prince.[33] The menu they were served that evening was a textbook fin de siècle banquet that could have been pulled directly from the pages of *The Epicurean*:

Hors d'oeuvres variés

Consommé Impériale

Huîtres sur coquilles • Johnnisberger Cabinet '93

Mousseline de Foie Gras Perigordine

Aiguillettes de Pompano, Moderne

Salade de Concombres

Filets de Chapon Chevalière • Moët et Chandon Cuvée Brut

Pointes d'Asperges Nouvelles

Terrapène a la Maryland

Sorbet Abricotine

Canvasback Duck Rôti • Chambertin

Salade de Grape Fruit

Glaces en Surprise

Fraises • Petits Fours

Camembert • Port de Salut

Liquors • Apollinaris

Café

The dinner was a display of money-is-no-object luxury. After the assorted hors d'oeuvres (an old-fashioned touch, absent from most menus after 1890), oysters, and consommé came a succession of ingredients that conveyed expense, by being out of season, imported, or endangered or all three: foie gras, truffles, and liqueurs and cheeses had been imported from France; pompano, grapefruit, and strawberries had been sent by refrigerated railcar from Florida; terrapin and canvasback duck were the rarest of rare game, delicacies that commanded astonishingly high prices.[34]

A daintier buffet supper, designed to appeal to the ladies, was served at the ball that followed the dinner and choral performance.

CHAUD:

Small Patties à la Reine

Lobster à la Newburg

FROID:

Boned Capon à la Gelée

Chicken Salad

Assorted Sandwiches

Cornets Chantilly

Mixed Ices

Cakes

Coffee

Moët et Chandon White Seal[35]

The *Tribune* observed that the prince did not touch any of the buffet's oysters, but "fears of a delicate appetite were dispelled by the hearty way in which he attacked the other viands. He ate as a hungry sailor should, and managed throughout the meal to keep up a running conversation with Mayor Harrison and Mr. Eddy."[36]

Two formal banquets bookended Prince Henry's arrival and departure from New York. Both were planned and overseen by none other than Oscar Tschirky. By then Oscar had abandoned his last name—no one in America could spell it, anyway—and had left Delmonico's to oversee the dining rooms of the Waldorf-Astoria. Both of the Waldorf-Astoria's Prince Henry dinners were huge affairs, with more than a thousand dinner guests. By Oscar's command, the ballrooms were festooned with tens of thousands of

American Beauty roses and twinkling electric lights. A light display in the shape of the German eagle presided over the table of honor. The eagle was wired to glow more brightly as the prince entered the room.

The *New Yorker Staats-Zeitung* sponsored the prince's arrival dinner. The menu was as old school as the one Henry would later have in Chicago, but it had an even greater quantity and variety of meat courses. In addition to canvasback duck, terrapin, and fish, there was green turtle soup, a ham mousse, sweetbreads, and delicately sauced chicken breast. Oscar paired an aged Riesling from the Rhine with the oysters and a Mosel Riesling with the ham.

Even though the banquet was held on February 26, a Lenten fast day for the city's Catholics, New York's Archbishop Corrigan—who was among the invited—issued a special dispensation for Catholic guests: they could eat fish or meat at the dinner, but not both. This was fortunate for both the archbishop and his flock. With the exception of the lettuce salad, the asparagus accompanying the ham, and the desserts, every dish on the menu contained meat or fish. The four hundred "magnificently dressed" ladies who watched the banquet from the ballroom's galleries did not have to choose. They were served a "collation" of "bouillon, chicken salad, assorted ices, claret punch, and wines."[37]

After a whistle stop tour by private train of the mid-Atlantic, South, and Midwest, interrupted by his dinner in Chicago and at least nine other formal breakfasts, luncheons, and dinners, the prince returned to the Waldorf-Astoria for a farewell banquet. This one was given by the German Society of New York. There were 1,720 guests, counting four hundred ladies in the galleries and the prince's 120-person entourage.

Beef fillet replaced terrapin on the menu; rare red-headed ducks replaced canvasbacks. Otherwise, the bill of fare obeyed the rules: course after course of luxury dishes, marching in close succession, from oysters to desserts, *pièces montées,* liqueurs, and petits fours.

The *New York Times* reported that the prince seemed pale and "very tired." After ten days of feasting, giving speeches, and making witty conversation in his excellent, lightly accented English, he spoke German throughout this dinner.

The *Times* published a vivid description of Oscar as he deployed his troops to serve the prince, his entourage, and his guests.

By the time six o'clock has come, everything is ready, and a squad of men—cooks or waiters—are in their places near the ovens, all on the alert for the signal that means they are to transfer the food to a special elevator and send it upstairs to Oscar. The grand ballroom is on the second floor, the kitchens in the basement.

It is announced to the chef that the guests are ready to sit down. Through a tube [Oscar] transfers the information downstairs. Then he rings a bell, and in two minutes the oysters are on the tables, having been prepared at the carving tables. The waiters stand like statues, each at his post. The guests file into the imitation fairyland . . . and then proceed to make way with the first course. Meanwhile, the "wine men" have placed on each table the beverage prescribed for this stage of the feast, and the diners find their glasses filled before they have had time to unfold their napkins.

The bell that Oscar rings is just outside the door between the hall of carving tables and the ballroom. He himself never goes into the dining room. He walks up and down the long, canvas-covered tables, and every time he gets to the end nearest the ballroom he pokes his head about two inches inside the door to see how far the eating of the course has advanced. At the right moment, when all or a majority of the diners seem to have finished their oysters, he touches an electric button. The bell rings — so loudly that everybody on the floor can already hear it. On the instant the waiters begin to take away the oyster plates, and the "wine men" replace the first wine with the second.

. . . In this way the dinner proceeds. Each course is brought from the kitchen just in time, then heated until the diners are ready to consume it. There is no colliding of waiters — except very rarely. They march in regular lines. Each one knows where his place is, and who is the one he must follow in and out of the ballroom.[38]

SPLENDID COMPETITION

Conspicuous consumption of valuable goods is a means of reputability to the gentleman of leisure. As wealth accumulates on his hands, his own unaided effort will not avail to sufficiently put his opulence in evidence by this method. The aid of friends and competitors is therefore brought in by resorting to the giving of valuable presents and expensive feasts and entertainments.

—THORSTEIN VEBLEN,
THE THEORY OF THE LEISURE CLASS, 1899

"Extravagant? Why certainly, society is getting to be more extravagant every minute. Entertainments which my wife thought very elegant ten years ago, she turns her nose up at now. Her dinners alone now cost ten times as much as they did then."

— A MILLIONAIRE, *WASHINGTON POST*, 1906

Banquets like the Prince Henry dinners allowed business leaders and politicians to show the world that American cities could hold their own when compared to the capitals of Europe. Sumptuous dinners also gave American aristocrats — plutocrats and oligarchs alike — a public way to display their wealth.

Wealthy hosts and hostesses sponsored the modern equivalent of potlatches, which, though private, were so spectacular as to be reported as news. The newspaper accounts helped hosts put their peers, predecessors, and competitors to shame.

Such competition began in the 1880s but came into full public view with the Bradley Martin ball, held at the Waldorf-Astoria in 1897.[39] With Oscar's help, Mrs. Cornelia Martin held a costume ball at the Waldorf and deliberately scheduled it to compete with the main society entertainment for that week: a performance at the Metropolitan Opera of the popular opera *Martha*, featuring the soprano Madame Nordica. Mrs. Martin invited everyone who was anyone, without distinguishing between old money and new, to skip the opera in favor of her ball.

Between seven hundred and nine hundred prominent New Yorkers accepted the invitation and came, dressed, according to Mrs. Martin's requirements, in costumes of the sixteenth, seventeenth, or eighteenth centuries. The buffet supper was simply an inventory of everything *luxe*: caviar, oysters, terrapin, truffled foie gras in aspic.[40]

Coming directly on the heels of one of the most brutal depressions the United States had experienced since the end of the Civil War, Mrs. Martin's ball shocked the public, incensed social reformers, and accomplished something else: Cornelia Martin launched a nationwide competition among America's wealthiest people to throw the most lavish banquet or ball.

For nine years, between 1899 and 1908, one potlatch followed another. There was the "Chanler dinner" at the Waldorf, sponsored by clients of Tammany Hall boss Richard Croker and inspired by the novel *Quo Vadis*. Croker's "friends" turned the hotel's Myrtle Room into an ancient Roman arbor with a bronze fountain, a trellis covered with bunches of edible grapes (in February), and cages of nightingales.[41] Then, in Pittsburgh, a corporation sponsored a dinner that featured a giant fish tank, custommade for the event, in which swam a young woman clad only in spangles and golden fish scales. There was even a rumor that a mining company president "in the west" had celebrated a lucky strike by holding a banquet inside the mine; the waiters had worn tuxedos and headlamps.[42]

LET THEM EAT CAKE

To go into details would be to describe an affair as elaborate as was ever given at a French court.

— *WASHINGTON POST*, 1905

Such conspicuous consumption may have peaked at a ball given by James Hazen Hyde at Sherry's on January 31, 1905. Hyde was the twenty-eight-year-old son of the Equitable Insurance Society's founder, Henry Hyde. Hyde's father had made James the company's first vice president. Over six feet tall, with slicked-back dark hair, a tidy goatee, and piercing brown eyes, James Hyde cut a swath through New York society. A *Chicago Daily Tribune* profile of "the seven most eligible bachelors in the United States" began with a description of him. Young Mr. Hyde was an avid horseman who favored coach racing, the most expensive of equestrian pastimes. His clothes were all custom-made for him in Paris: "His coats run to one or the other extreme: either they reach to his ankles or they end near his waist line. His 'cutaways' are marvels of the extreme kind, and his tie usually is a vivid scarlet or royal purple."

Though he'd grown up in the United States and attended Harvard, Hyde played the part of a prince in exile, affecting a "low, cultivated voice that approaches effeminacy, and his accent is known as 'Continental,' being neither English nor French, and least of all American."[43]

Whatever his accent, Hyde was an ardent Francophile. While still a student at Harvard, he'd endowed an exchange program for French and American professors at his alma

James Hazen Hyde, 1905, Byron Company

left: Madame Réjane (French actress) at Hyde Ball, 1905, Byron Company

right: Mr. and Mrs. Arthur Iselin, Hyde Ball, 1905

mater. For this he'd been honored with the Légion d'honneur. After graduation, he spent part of every year at a residence he'd bought in Paris.

In late 1904, during one of his stays in Paris, Hyde decided to throw a costume ball in New York, inspired by the palace of Versailles. Though the architect and decorator Stanford White had designed Sherry's pastel pink and blue ballrooms to resemble the palace's reception rooms, the resemblance was not quite enough for Hyde. Instead, he hired Whitney Warren, another prominent architect, to transform one of Sherry's ballrooms into a replica of a garden the great French architect Le Nôtre had designed. Hyde wanted a French palace garden. At Sherry's. In New York. In January.

Not only did the decor have to be perfect, so did the entertainment. Hyde scheduled the ball for a night when the Metropolitan Opera would not be performing — not to spare his guests the choice Cornelia Martin had forced on hers, but because he wanted the Metropolitan's orchestra and its conductor Nathan Franko to provide the music.

He asked the Opera Ballet to perform and to choreograph an eighteenth-century "contra dance" to be performed by some of the guests. He hired the Met's makeup artists and costumers to transform Sherry's waiters into wigged footmen. And he secured the services of Byron, the society photographer, to take pictures of the guests as they arrived in costume.

As a final touch, Hyde asked his good friend Gabrielle Réjane, the leading French comedic actress of the day, to perform a short play. Hyde and Réjane scoured eighteenth-century texts for something suitable. When they failed to find anything they liked, Hyde commissioned a one-act play from the Italian dramatist Dario Niccodemi. Hyde ordered a stage set and costumes for the play to be made in Paris and rushed to New York.[44]

The ball met Hyde's expectations and astonished his guests. They walked across a turf-covered floor into a ballroom redolent with roses, wisteria, and heather, past eighteenth-century sculptures that had been shipped from France. The debutantes, doll-like, with rouged cheeks and taffeta gowns that showed their ankles, performed their contra dance, escorted by men in black-and-white Pierrot costumes. The Opera Ballet danced a minuet and a gavotte. Réjane was carried in on a sedan chair for her performance.

Miss Elizabeth Marbur (dramatist's agent), 1905, Byron Company

The midnight supper that followed was a testament to Hyde's refinement and taste. No oysters or terrapin—Hyde was a famously picky eater—but Pol Roger 1889 champagne to accompany the lobster medallions. Pheasant, salad, ham *en gelée*. And for dessert, sculpted ice cream bombes and an assortment of bonbons, petits fours, and hothouse fruits. Carême—and Ranhofer—would have approved.

The *New York Times* and the *New York Herald* published multipage accounts of the ball, complete with illustrations of the ballroom and Madame Réjane's dramatic entrance, photos of some of the more illustrious guests, and lengthy descriptions of the setting and costumes. The newspaper headlines trumpeted their admiration: SOCIETY ENJOYS A "LOUIS XVI FETE" IN 1905 / MR. JAMES HYDE'S SPLENDID 18TH CENTURY COSTUME PARTY AT SHERRY'S AND A MOST VARIED AND ORIGINAL ENTERTAINMENT.[45]

Hyde Ball at Sherry's Restaurant, 1905, Byron Company

Unfortunately for Hyde not everyone was an admirer. A war had been brewing between Hyde and the Equitable's president, James W. Alexander, for control of the company.[46] The Hyde ball touched off a battle between Alexander and his allies on one side and Hyde and his supporters on the other.

The major papers in New York, Boston, and Chicago were only too happy to cover the conflict. Their reports detailed accusations and counteraccusations on an almost daily basis between February and June 1905. Arguments about how to manage the business turned personal, and Alexander insinuated that Hyde might have used Equitable assets to bankroll some of his more lavish entertainments. Someone started a rumor that the Hyde Ball had cost $200,000 ($4 million), though later reports and Hyde's 1959 obituary in the *Times* suggest that it probably cost closer to $75,000.[47]

Hyde's net worth in 1905 was estimated at $20 million ($400 million), so he had ample personal resources to pay for his ball, whatever its true cost. No matter: even the suggestion that Hyde had been dipping into company accounts—and the revelation that he and Alexander were each paid $100,000 a year, double the salary of President Roosevelt—infuriated policyholders and alarmed Equitable agents across the country, who feared for their livelihoods if the company failed. What had begun as an internecine war for control of the Equitable company metastasized into a series of investigations, ending with an inquiry by the New York State Legislature into business practices at all the major insurance companies operating in New York.[48]

Worse yet, the newspapers lost their admiration, using the scandal to point out an even greater scandal. The *New York Herald* juxtaposed a sidebar containing Hyde's portrait and a description of the ball and his spending habits with another story, about a fourteen-year-old newsboy who'd starved to death while trying to support his widowed mother and baby brother.[49]

. . . And Jolly, Too

No matter how large a dinner may be, or how small, the giver, first of all, wants it jolly.

— New York Sun, 1905

Hyde's troubles didn't stop the potlatch. The rich continued to throw huge banquets and "intimate" luncheons and dinners for twenty or thirty guests. European visitors to the United States were struck by the extravagance of the events—and by how often they took place. The British Lady Blank, quoted in the *Sun* in 1905, declared that in England such dinners were "really only given to royalty."[50]

As the competition to spend and eat more lavishly continued, the ways in which the rich displayed their money when they ate began to change. Delicacies from the Gilded Age that had become luxury standards, served at nearly every high-end banquet—sea turtle, terrapin, canvasback duck—had been hunted ruthlessly throughout the 1890s. As a result, they were in very short supply.

The Lacey Act of 1900, designed to protect endangered waterfowl and other game by banning out-of-season, interstate transport, was hampered by spotty enforcement. Restaurants routinely bought American game on the black market, then claimed it had been imported from Europe. Society hosts caught serving game out of season simply paid off inspectors.[51]

Even with the corruption, high-profile sting operations throughout the decade — against game wholesalers in Los Angeles and against cold-storage facilities in Boston and several New York counties — began to put a damper on the illicit trade.[52] Cheaper alternatives — calf's head instead of turtle for soup, teal or mallard for canvasback duck — were being substituted, often on the sly, for the genuine items. Outside of the fall and winter game season, some law-abiding restaurateurs changed the "game course" — the last of several meat courses in a multicourse formal dinner and the centerpiece of many after-theater suppers — by offering farm-raised chicken and turkey. Squab (also known as pigeon) became the new canvasback.

With the most expensive, exotic game no longer readily available, hosts discovered they could no longer spend impressively on food alone: "As explained by the banquet manager of the St. Regis, about $20 per plate is all it would ever be possible to expend on food, unless very exceptional and extraordinary dishes are ordered out of season or from foreign countries. However, even birds' nests, for birds' nest soup — à la the heathen Chinese — are now to be obtained at comparatively reasonable figures in no more distant quarter than Mott Street."

Hosts seeking to spend — and to let everyone know they'd spent — $50 or $75 per plate turned more and more frequently to "elaborate decorations and the entertainment furnished by singers or dancers or numbers from current theatrical attractions. . . . Acting on this principle, a man or woman might entertain three friends at a cost of many thousands."[53]

A favorite entertainment that was costly and allowed for guest participation was the tableau vivant. After dinner, society ladies would change into custom-made costumes and, with appropriate musical accompaniment, pose against ornate backdrops, mimicking the subjects of famous paintings. One such event, thrown in 1909 by Mrs. William K. Vanderbilt as a benefit for the Lisa Day Nursery, included, "The most gorgeous tableau of all . . . the 'Vision Fugitive,' preceded by an aria from 'Herodiade,' posed by Mrs. Harry Payne Whitney. With a peacock standing as high as herself on her right, Mrs. Whitney posed straight as an arrow, in full yellow silk Turkish trousers and a flowing yellow silk jacket covered with gold spangled net. On her head was an enormous Turkish turban of yellow silk, and rising from the center was a superb cluster of white feathers caught with gorgeous gems. Strings of pearls and other jewels glittered around her neck. A long golden scepter was held like a stave in her right hand."[54]

The food began to take a back seat to the spectacle at "smart" dinners. The new entertainments included a treasure hunt dinner, with a rare black pearl hidden in one of each guest's oysters. Animals were a popular attraction. There were horseback dinners, in which the guests' saddles were fitted with trays and champagne buckets; barnyard dinners, with geese and swine parading in banquet rooms; and monkey and dog dinners, at which the nonhuman "guests of honor" were presented with diamond collars while their human hosts made champagne toasts.[55]

Mrs. Stuyvesant Fish, wife of the president of the Illinois Central Railroad, was one of the most enthusiastic sponsors, in New York and Newport, of what became known as the "freak dinner." At her dinners, service of the food was permitted to take no more than fifty minutes, in order to accommodate musicales, animal tricks, and practical jokes.[56] Other society hostesses shortened their dinners, too, even if the entertainment they offered was as tame as a vocal recital or a bridge tournament.

Some old-money aristocrats rebelled against the "freak fêtes."

In 1908, a group of Chicago society women, including Mrs. Ogden Armour of the meatpacking Armours, boycotted a "monkey dinner" planned as a benefit for a Chicago hospital. Sniffed Mrs. Armour, "I certainly shall have nothing to do with it. I am not interested in the debut of monkeys."[57]

That same year, having endured a few too many costume parties and animal guests during recent Newport summer seasons, a group of New York's oldest families, led by the Vanderbilts and Astors, gave the *Times* to understand that the older generation would be resuming control of the 1908 summer social calendar, in order to restore some dignity to the proceedings.[58] Said *the* Mrs. Astor, "I hope my influence will be felt in one thing, and that is in discountenancing the undignified methods employed by certain New York women to attract a following. They have given entertainments that belonged under a circus tent rather than in a gentlewoman's home . . . Women of this stamp are few in New York, but alas! They are so appallingly active!"[59]

Shorter dinners were becoming popular for other reasons. Women were still lacing themselves into corsets that made consuming a twelve-course dinner painful, if not impossible. There was added pressure from changes in fashion.

In the 1880s plumpness had signaled prosperity for both men and women, but by the early 1900s the feminine ideal was uncompromisingly slender. Bodices became more form-fitting; skirts became narrower. It became harder to hide a fleshy figure. Women were suddenly dieting. "Don't Be Fat" admonished a 1905 Kellogg's advertisement for "obesity food," a mail-order precursor to Special K. The ad displayed the "before" and "after" photographs of a matron in a summer tea gown and pearls.

Women had already been excused from full participation in formal banquets: either they were served a light "collation" (as at the Prince Henry dinner) or they were permitted to skip courses or nibble a few bites from their favorite dishes. A 1903 article in *Pictorial Review* let women know that "A menu at luncheon, as well as at dinner, would be rather formidable to some women if compelled to go through it from start to finish, but they are at liberty to please themselves in this matter, to refuse every course if they feel inclined."[60]

Men could still be corpulent, but gout and dyspepsia drove many toward moderation. Russell Chittenden, director of Yale University's Sheffield Scientific Center, blamed men's digestive troubles on the four meals per day—breakfast, lunch, dinner, and a late-night supper—that upper-class men commonly ate. Chittenden noted that those four meals could contain four thousand or more calories, far beyond the twenty-five hundred recommended for a sedentary man's daily intake. Rich sauces and heavy consumption of wine and cocktails added insult to injury.

William Muschenheim, the proprietor of the five-star Hotel Astor, agreed: "The average dinner-out congests himself—and frequently herself—with far too many dishes for his or her own good. Personally, it is my opinion that too much meat is consumed by most persons of sedentary occupation. Meat in moderate quantities is perhaps necessary in this latitude as a means of imparting strength. But meat once a day is quite sufficient for the average person, man or woman, who takes no special exercise between meals."[61]

Some nutrition experts—the Kellogg brothers among them—went further, advocating vegetarian and grain-based diets.[62] Meat substitutes such as the Kelloggs' infamous Nuttolene and Protose were the butt of many jokes, but some of the best-known industrialists and bankers of the day embraced simplicity. J. P. Morgan was famous for a plain, even spartan daily food regimen; corned beef and cabbage with black coffee was a regular evening meal.[63] John D. Rockefeller hosted dinners as elaborate as those of any of his peers but ate mutton chops while his

Hotel Astor, December 7, 1904,
Byron Company

guests made their way through the full banquet menu. Newspapers ran stories about judges and politicians who skipped multicourse "businessmen's lunches" in favor of graham crackers and milk.[64]

A growing gourmet movement stressed the *quality* of food; meals based on massive arrays of dishes chosen mostly for their expense were beginning to be replaced by simpler, more refined menus. *Town and Country* published the thoughts of an English epicure, Lieutenant Colonel Newnham-Davis, quoting him as saying; "A gourmet is an amateur of all that is delicate and artistic in the pleasure of the table; a gourmand is simply a greedy fellow with the means to gratify his greediness." A gourmet dinner, said the lieutenant colonel, should have only "five dishes at the most." As an example, he suggested a light soup followed by sole, pressed duck with a seasonal salad, artichoke bottoms in a delicate sauce, an ice cream bombe, and petits fours.[65]

FINE DINING TAKES HOLD

Even if middle- and upper-middle-class people couldn't keep up with the sumptuous competition of the wealthy, they could rub elbows with the rich and famous by taking meals in the dining rooms of fine restaurants.

Dining out — not just attending private banquets but appearing for a meal in the public dining rooms of a high-end restaurant or hotel — became a way to participate in the upper-class lifestyle. In 1907 an article in *Health* magazine noted Louis Sherry's estimate that "between three hundred and fifty to four hundred thousand wealthy New Yorkers dine in public every evening, the number of such diners out [is] steadily increasing."[66]

As restaurant dining in general, and fine dining in particular, expanded, newspapers ran stories about every aspect of the restaurant business. The stories ranged from reports about which New York and Chicago places were the most fashionable to behind-the-scenes visits to restaurant kitchens.

No one benefited from this attention more than Oscar Tschirky. As "Oscar of the Waldorf," he became first a New York institution, then a national one. A Tin Pan Alley song of the era featured him in its chorus.

At the Waldorf "Hyphen" Astoria,
No matter who or what you are,
Be sure to nod at Oscar as you enter;
Just to speak to him by name
And for "ten" he'll do the same
That's the proper thing for the Waldorf "Hyphen" Astoria.[67]

"Meet me at the hyphen" became a one-liner on the vaudeville circuit. Tourists from all over the United States flocked to the Waldorf-Astoria for a glimpse of its celebrated clientele and the chance to see Oscar.

The Waldorf turned out to be an ideal place for seeing and being seen. The high-ceilinged Palm Court that joined the two hotels — a favorite for ladies' lunches and afternoon tea — was a particularly rewarding spot for gawkers. A red-carpeted hallway that banquetgoers had to cross to reach the hotels' ballrooms became known as "Peacock Alley" for the opportunity it gave men and women to strut their finery. The Waldorf's innovation was so popular that Peacock Alleys were included in the designs for other luxury hotels, including the Willard in Washington, D.C.

Tourists from the hinterland were joined at the Waldorf-Astoria by ordinary New Yorkers, eager to celebrity-watch. In the evenings, after the theaters let out, the crush of would-be patrons and onlookers hoping to see Vanderbilts and Whitneys or their favorite actors and actresses eating supper became so unmanageable that Oscar invented a solution: a velvet rope that separated the chosen from everyone else.

"No hotel had attempted to do such a thing before, and it took New York some time to accept the idea," Oscar wrote. "At the beginning we were met with dark frowns—but it wasn't long before other hotels had their plush ropes, if they needed them. I found out that when the rope was up more people than usual wanted to gain admittance. It seemed that when people learned they were being held out they were all the more insistent upon getting in."[68]

LOBSTER PALACE SOCIETY

Tables, tables, tables; people, people, people; known and unknown; pretty and plain, the seers and the seen. Festive parties; family parties; parties not of the Tenderloin—merely visiting as if they might visit Chinatown; fashionables and would-be fashionables; Americans and New Yorkers.[69]

By the mid-1900s the Waldorf-Astoria was just one—albeit the most famous—of a series of luxury hotels along Fifth Avenue. All had their own elegant dining rooms, palm courts, grillrooms—and wealthy patrons.

A different sort of neighborhood, in another part of Manhattan, attracted a different set of well-to-do diners. What had begun as a vice district known as the Tenderloin slowly changed, beginning around 1899, into a glittering entertainment zone known as the Great White Way. Theaters and cabarets opened in the streets around Times Square.[70] With them came restaurants that served theatergoers as well as performers.

The biggest and most fashionable of these Broadway restaurants were known as "lobster palaces"—the name a fair summary of their cuisine and decor. Among the lobster palaces, Rector's was the archetype, and not just because it was the first of its kind to open in the neighborhood.

Charles Rector and his son, George, Chicago restaurateurs, had made the original Chicago Rector's a loud and lively headquarters for that city's new money.[71] Charles had guessed—correctly—that Chicagoans would be eager to spend at a restaurant where fresh seafood, rushed by train from East Coast markets, was served in luxurious surroundings. As he sized up his chances for success in New York in 1899, Rector had another spot-on hunch: that New York's theater district, then located in the mid-Thirties, would be moving uptown. He anticipated the move and was there to serve the crowds when they arrived.

The journalist and bon vivant Julian Street described the scene: "Rector's remains open later than most of the 'gilt-edged' Lobster Lairs;

Daily menu, Rector's, New York, 1900

it is gayer; life is higher. You're apt to see Broadway celebrities; musical comedy favourites, actors, actresses, show girls, women of not in the least 'doubtful character,' and the invariable sprinkling of onlookers."

All that celebrity on display was irresistible to two kinds of people: wealthy men with—or in search of—actress girlfriends, and the tourists and local New Yorkers who wanted to watch them. The atmosphere was intoxicating: big, columned dining rooms, laid out to focus diners' attention on entry foyers or sweeping entry staircases; the constant popping of champagne corks; the drama of choosing a live lobster from a big glass tank and then watching it arrive soon after, cooked and borne in on a silver platter. At the hotel restaurants, wealthy diners had had to import the entertainment. At the lobster palaces, whether in New York or in Chicago where they originated, the restaurant and the other diners *were* the entertainment.

A reporter in Chicago wrote of these places, "They go to see the gowns and the hats and to watch the people come and go and laugh and eat and drink; they go to hear the music and to get into the rhythm with the life of Saturday night in bohemia. And in getting into rhythm with it they become a part of it. They go to see others and the others go to see them. Incidentally, usually they eat because they cannot see if they do not eat, any more than the plebeian at the horse show can see society without paying to see the horses."[72]

Broadway lobster palaces quickly multiplied, each distinguished by special decor or entertainment. There was the Café de Beaux Arts, which stood out for its musical offerings: "There is a Neapolitan string quartette, an orchestra, and a corps of several vocal soloists, all good. They go from room to room, so that you get variety, with neither too much nor too little music."

There was Murray's Roman Gardens: "Inside, it is quasi-Pompeiian, with plashing fountains, mirrors, pergolas, and landscapes set into the walls so cleverly that a man who once sat there from seven P.M. until two A.M. is reported to have imagined himself traveling abroad."[73]

Topping them all for visual splendor was the Café de L'Opera: "The colour scheme is blue and gold, with black marble columns surmounted by golden capitals representing bulls' heads—or are they calves of gold? There is a black marble stairway that is quite the most magnificently heathen-looking thing in town. At the bottom of it stands a gigantic winged lion, with a man's head, in bas relief. The broad stair-landing, visible from the main dining room, would be a fine place to make burnt offerings to barbaric gods, while vestals tripped about, a la Isidora [sic] Duncan and Maud Allan."[74]

Not that the lobster palaces ignored the food. Charles and George Rector had decided that their kitchen should rival that of Delmonico's and Sherry's; George had trained at two famous restaurants in Paris to ensure this.[75] Rector's set the standard for the district.

Prices for such luxury items as terrapin and Chateaubriand were high, but the extensive menus of both New York and Chicago lobster palaces could also accommodate smaller budgets.

"Broiled live lobsters and champagne, Munchner and Camembert, no matter which it is, there is music and clinking glasses, laughter and nodding ostrich feathers, and shaded candles setting cheeks aflame, bare arms and shoulders all aglow and glistening teeth set in smiles, and in the early morning—songs! It's the millionaire's Saturday night in the millionaire's bohemia—at the Annex, at Rector's, at the College Inn. It may cost $2 or $202—that night! It may be beer and Camembert for two, 25 cents for the waiter and a cab home; or it may be lobster and champagne for 30, opera buses and automobiles.

"No matter which it is, there is the music and the laughter, the clinking glasses and the song, the animated faces and the ceaseless hum of voices."[76]

The lobster palaces drew their largest crowds after the theaters let out. The late-night meal of choice was a light supper—perhaps oysters or crab canapés, game birds and salad, and some sort of ice cream. And champagne, plenty of champagne—or a reasonable substitute. It was

OVERLEAF: *Daily menu, Rector's, New York, 1900*

RELISHES

Anchovies on toast..................40
Caviar on toast....................35
Tomato, Surprise..................40
Celery.............................40
Olives.............................25
Stuffed olives....................35
Stuffed mangoes...................35
Radishes..........................20
Gherkins..........................15
Dill pickles......................15
Chow chow.........................20
Pickled walnuts...................25
Pickled beets.....................20
Small onions......................20
Sardines..........................40
Bar-le-Duc........................40

OYSTERS

Blue Point cocktail...............30
Blue Points.......................25
Cotuits...........................25
Rockaways.........................30
Shrewsburys.......................30
Cape Cods.........................25
Lynnhaven Bays....................30
Shell roast................doz..70; half..35
Pepper roast...............doz..70; half..35
Fancy or Pan roast.........doz..70; half..35
Steamed, in shell..........doz..70; half..35
Steamed, Washington style, doz..70; half..35
Broiled, butter or cream sauce, doz..70; half.35
Escalloped, in shell.......doz..1 00; half.50
Box stew...................doz..70; half.35
Cream stew......50 Dry stew.............35
Fried oysters..............doz..60; half..35
Fried oysters in butter, tomato s'ce.80; half.40
Rector's combination fry..................50
Oyster patty..............................50
Oysters à la Newburg.............doz...75
Oysters en brochette.............doz....75
Oysters au gratin................doz....75
Oysters Algonquin................doz....80

CLAMS

Clam cocktail.....................30
Little Necks, on shell............25
Large clams, on shell.............25
Steamed Little Necks........doz..50
Stewed Little Necks.........doz..50
Shell roast, Little Necks...doz..50
Fancy or Pan Roast, Little Necks......50
Steamed soft shell clams, Boston style.....60
Fried soft shell clams....................60
Stewed soft shell clams...................50
Shell roasted soft shell clams............60
Fancy or Pan roasted soft shell clams......60
Soft shell clams en brochette.............75
Minced clams..............................60
Clam fritters.............................50

SOUPS

Chicken consommé..................50
Chicken orka......................60
Strained okra in cup..............35
Mock turtle.......40 Tomato......40
Croûte-au-pot.....40 Consommé....40
Consommé in cup...................25
Consommé jelly in cup.............30
Chicken consommé jelly in cup......35
Split pea........40 Mongole.......40
Consommé Julienne.................40
Strained okra jelly in cup........35
Clear green turtle soup...........75
Clear green turtle in cup.........40
Clam chowder......35 Clam broth, in cup.....25

SHELL FISH, ETC.

Broiled live lobster, Chili sauce...80; half.40
Broiled live lobster, stuffed......1 00; half.50
Steamed live lobster, parsley sauce.90; half.50
Cold boiled lobster................80; half.40
Deviled lobster...................1 00; half.50
Lobster à la Williams...............1 00
Lobster, Bordelaise.................1 00
Lobster à l'Américaine..............1 00
Lobster à la Newburg...............1 00
Lobster à la Française..............90
Curry of lobster....................90
Lobster à la Créole.................90
Escalloped lobster..................90
Lobster croquettes, shrimp sauce....90
Lobster cutlets.....................90
Stewed lobster......................90
Deviled crab........................40
Crab ravigote.......................60
Stuffed crab........................75
Hard shell crabs....................40
Escalloped crabmeat................1 00
Crabmeat à la Maryland.............1 00
Oyster crabs à la Newburg..........1 50
Oyster crabs sautés................1 50
Stewed oyster crabs................1 50
Fried scallops......................50
Terrapin...........................2 50
Stewed snapper......................90
Frogs legs, fried...........75 Poulette...75

FISH

Bluefish............................50
Halibut.............................60
Fresh mackerel......................60
Perch...............................50
Sea bass............................65
Striped bass........................65
Black bass..........................65
Flounders...........................50
Filet of sole.......................60
Filet of bass à la Marguerie........75
Pompano.............................50
Fish cakes (2)......................40
Kippered herring....................35
Shad, broiled.............75
Shad planked, whole....2 50 half...1 25
Smelts..............................60
Salmon broiled......................80
Salmon boiled, Hollandaise..........90
Salmon cold, sauce tartare..........80
Spanish mackerel....................65
Whitebait...........................60
Kingfish............................65
Sheepshead..........................65
Whitefish, broiled..................60
Whitefish, planked, whole.2 00 half.1 00
Finnan haddie, steamed..............60
Finnan haddie à la Rector...........75

GAME

Canvas back duck...................4 00
Red head duck......................3 00
Mallard duck.......................1 50
Teal duck...........................90
Ruddy duck.........................1 50
Reed birds..........................85
Squab...............................75
English snipe.......................
Plover..............................
Rail birds..........................75
English Pheasant 2 50

SALADS

Lobster......75	Escarole......40
Shrimp......75	Potato.......35
Crab.........75	A la Russe...75
Chicken......80	Macédoine...60
Celery........50	Chiffonade...60
Sweetbread.1 00	Tomato.....50
Lettuce......40	Cucumber...40
Chicory......40	Watercress..30
Romaine.....40	Cold slaw...30

STEAKS, CHOPS, ETC

Small steak...................60
Small steak with onions................70
Small steak with mushrooms..........85
Sirloin steak...................90
Sirloin steak, Béarnaise............1 15
Sirloin steak, Bordelaise............1 15
Extra sirloin steak.............1 75
Club steak.............3 00
Tenderloin steak..................90
Châteaubriand..................1 75
Porterhouse steak............2 00
Extra porterhouse steak...........3 00
Hamburg steak......................60
Lamb chops.........................60
Mutton chops......................60
English mutton chop...............50
Lamb fries.............................65
Ham, broiled........................40
Bacon, broiled....................40
Pork chops.........................50
Veal cutlet, broiled..............60
Veal cutlet breaded, tomato sauce......70
Vienna schnitzel....................75
Sweetbreads, broiled................80
Sweetbread sauté au jus............85
Sweetbreads with peas...............1 00
Sweetbread patties..................85
Sweetbreads stewed in cream........1 00
Sweetbread cutlet...................90
Sweetbread en coquille..............75
Calf's head à l'Huîle................75
Calf's head en tortue................85
Calf's head, Poulette...................85
Country sausage.....................40
Marrow bones.......................60
Calf's brains au beurre noir........50
Kidneys broiled.....................50
Calf's brains fried, tomato sauce........60
Calf's liver.............................50
Chicken broiled..........1 50 half....75
Chicken, deviled, half..............85
Chicken croquette...................75
Chicken cutlet.......................75
Chicken patties.....................75
Chicken fricassée....................90
Chicken curry with rice.................90
Chicken sauté, Marengo................90
Chicken à la Terrapin.................1 00
Chicken à la Maryland.................90
Chicken roasted..........1 50 half....75
Chicken hash.........................75
Chicken hash with green peppers.......85
Chicken liver sauté..................65
Chicken liver en brochette...........75
Tripe, Special, en casserole..........1 00
Tripe and oysters...................75
Pigs feet, broiled..................60
Pigs feet, pickled..................50
Boston baked beans..................50
Welsh rarebit.......................40
Golden buck.........................50
Scotch woodcock.....................50

COLD MEATS AND GAME

Boned capon...................80
Pâté de foie-gras.................1 00
Roast beef....................60
Chicken....................1 50 75
Ham....................40
Virginia ham.................75
Westphalia ham................75
Tongue....................50
Game pâté.................1 00
Squab....................75
Chicken sandwich..................30
Club sandwich....................35
Tongue sandwich..................20
Swiss cheese sandwich............20
Beef sandwich....30   Ham sandwich.....15

VEGETABLES

POTATOES	POTATOES
Baked..........20	French fried....20
Special baked...25	Sautées.........25
Lyonnaise.......25	Parisienne......25
Saratoga........25	Stewed in cream.20
Croquettes......25	Julienne........25
Au gratin.....25	Hashed browned.25

Bermuda potatoes.......25
Sweet potatoes, fried or baked..........25
French peas. 35 French string beans..35
American asparagus....................60
French asparagus.....................1 00
Artichokes.........................60
Celery au jus.....................50
Cauliflower, Hollandaise.50 Au gratin.50
Spanish peppers sautés.................60
Green peppers farcis..............50
Stewed tomatoes................25
Baked tomatoes...................40
Stuffed tomatoes......................50
Brussels sprouts....................40
Egg plant............30 Corn........30
Macaroni with cream...30 Au gratin...40
Spaghetti, Italienne....30 Au gratin...40
Spinach................................40
Beets.............................25
Lima beans........................35
Boiled rice........................20
Fresh mushrooms broiled.1 00 Sautés.1 00
Fresh mushrooms sautés, under glass.1 25

ICE CREAM AND DESSERT

Vanilla ice cream...25	Orange ice......25
Chocolate ice cream.25	Lemon ice......25
Nesselrode pudding.35	Café parfait.....30
Roman punch......30	Baked Alaska...60
Bisquit Bellevue...30	Charlotte Russe..25
Fruit tarts.......35	Crème Bavaroise.25
Chocolate éclair...20	Vanilla éclair.....20
Wine jelly........25	Bouche de Dame..30
Meringue à la crème.25	Baked apples with cream.25

CHEESE

American........20	Cream...........25
Neufchâtel.......25	Swiss.........25
Gorgonzola.......30	Roquefort.......30
Camembert.......30	Brie............30
Edam............30	Stilton..........30

COFFEE, ETC, ETC.

Coffee, per cup.......................10
Coffee, per pot.......20 with cream......30
Demi-tasse.........................10
Café Special, per cup..................25
Tea, per pot.........................25
Chocolate or Cocoa with whipped cream...25
Milk, per glass......10 Cream, per glass..20

13 Mov. 1900

possible to order modestly: Welsh rarebit (40 cents at Rector's) and its many variants (golden buck, royal buck, scotch woodcock) were little more than cheese sauce on toast, but served lobster palace style, in a silver chafing dish, they blended right in.

An average lobster palace supper might run two or three dollars (equivalent to $40 to $60) for a couple, within reach for a growing number of urbanites as an occasional treat. Besides, the music and people watching that accompanied the lobster palace supper made it a complete entertainment, whether or not the restaurantgoers had actually been to the theater. Late in the decade, many of the lobster palaces and hotels added dance floors, which only added to their nighttime appeal. By 1913, Julian Street observed, "Starting at the Café des Beaux Arts and rapidly passing on to George Rector's, Murray's, and Bustanoby's, the mania for restaurant dancing has spread until, to-day, you may see people rise from supper in some of the hotels, to trip the light, and exceedingly fantastic, rag-time toe."[77]

The Social Mixture

Restaurant life also has done much to make New York extremely informal. People meet constantly at restaurant dinners and luncheons who might never by any possibility come together in the more formal manner of social entertainment at home . . . This is true to such an extent that numerous people in town live their entire social life in the various restaurants where they meet new acquaintances and entertain and are entertained without anybody's ever knowing their place of residence.

— New York Sun, 1903

People of position have taken to frequenting the restaurants where dancing is the attraction — restaurants which are, in effect, merely public dance halls of a more expensive kind than those run for the working classes. Practically any well-dressed person who is reasonably sober and will purchase supper and champagne for two, may enter. This creates a social mixture as was never dreamed of in this country — a hodge-podge of people in which respectable young married and unmarried women, and even debutantes, dance, not only under the same roof, but in the same room with women of the town.

— Julian Street,
Welcome to Our City

A growing middle and upper-middle class found new ways and new places to emulate the dining habits of the wealthy. City dwellers with some discretionary income could order a supper after an evening at the theater. They could take tea or luncheon or cocktails in a hotel palm court. They could manage a Sunday dinner with family in one of the good hotels as a monthly, or even weekly, splurge.

The restaurants, including some of the most exclusive, were ready for them. As it became clear that more people were dining out, and more frequently, restaurateurs and hoteliers rushed to meet the demand by building ever more palatial places to eat. Smaller establishments, feeling the pressure, expanded.

The result was intense competition among high-end restaurants for patrons.[78] Some of the grand hotels that had opened after 1900 made a point of stressing their accessibility to middle-class guests. The St. Regis Hotel, built in 1904 by John Jacob Astor IV, declared in 1906 that its prices were "no higher than that of any other high class hotel, dining room or restaurant. As a matter of fact, it is possible to dine at the St. Regis economically as well as sumptuously."[79] At the gala opening dinner of the New York Ritz-Carlton in 1910, the manager made it plain that he sought a much bigger and broader clientele than the Four Hundred: "William Harris said . . . that the object of the management was to cater to the good, average American citizen. They [the Ritz-Carlton company] had not come to cater to millionaires, he said, because there were not sufficient to go around."[80]

The need to fill tables posed a dilemma for Sherry's and the Waldorf-Astoria, for instance, which had staked their reputations on exclusivity back when elite diners had fewer choices. They had to find a way to accommodate less affluent diners while still assuring their wealthy regulars that not just anyone could secure a table.

As early as 1901 Oscar had shared a telling anecdote with reporters.

A number of well-known men and women were lunching in the palm garden at the Waldorf the other day when an incident occurred that revealed the methods employed to preserve the social atmosphere of this resort of the modish world . . . Habitués of the garden know that to obtain a table they must either give their names in advance or apply to the head waiter for an unoccupied table, and then remain in the corridors outside or in the adjacent parlors until notified that their table is ready for them. On this day, however, two large and overdressed women appeared in the doorway, and, catching sight of the unoccupied table, started rapidly toward it. One of them, although it was barely two o'clock, was in a demi-toilette. She also wore a large picture hat and a rope of artificial pearls that was literally a rope, and which extended from her throat below her knees. The head waiter appeared to be absent, and without hindrance and with a sort of dancing gait they reached their goal, and were about to seat themselves. Suddenly Oscar, the maitre d'hotel, appeared at the entrance to the upper garden, and gliding quietly but rapidly to the table, remarked to them in a very polite but firm tone: "Ladies, this table is reserved." The women looked at him a moment, and then, without a word, turned and retraced their steps.[81]

Oscar's story let his society patrons know that coarseness and bad manners would not be tolerated at the Waldorf-Astoria. For everyone else, it explained exactly what good manners were — and what it took to earn a place at a Palm Court table.

Giving the appearance of exclusivity became a popular tactic for increasing business. Julian Street wrote that "The head waiter at an hotel, the restaurant of which is crowded every night, told a friend of mine that but few people came there when they opened. And how do you suppose he got them to coming? Simply by humming and hawing when some one telephoned for a table reservation; by mumbling vaguely the names of fashionable people, and saying, 'I'm not sure you can have a table for to-night, but if you'll call up later, I will see.' The minute that person thought he might not be able to get in, he was obsessed with a mad desire to do so. He went up to see about it, and when, at last, he was promised a table, a great elation filled his bosom. Such tactics started people coming, and, once started, the movement soon became an avalanche."[82]

Newspapers ran articles in their Sunday magazines aimed at educating those who were new to fine dining. Some of the articles decoded the puzzling Franglais of high-end restaurant menus[83]; others tried to reassure middle-class patrons that they could order a meal in one of the fancy places without bankrupting themselves. The *New York Times* sent a reporter to ask the managers and proprietors of many of the city's best-known restaurants whether two people could have supper in various well-known restaurants for $5 — and whether such a $5 menu would include wine. The Bustanoby brothers, French proprietors of the Café des Beaux Arts, cheerfully obliged with a generous menu.

Coupe de Grapefruit, Beaux Arts

Celery Carciofini Olives

Chicken Gumbo in Cup

Lobster a l'Americaine

Quail Flambe, Henri IV

Salade Canaille

Peche Voilee Marcelle

Petits Fours

Friandises Pieces Montees

Moka des Princes

When the reporter asked Louis Bustanoby to include a pint of sparkling Burgundy, Louis confessed that the menu would have to be trimmed. Still, with wine included, he managed to offer a supper of oysters, consommé, pigeon en casserole, a mixed salad, and, alongside the dessert of biscuit tortoni and petits fours, the house's signature after-dinner drink: Liqueur Forbidden Fruit.[84]

At the Waldorf-Astoria, Oscar answered the reporter with a peevish sniff, before telling his secretary in a flat, world-weary voice, "Take this down:

Croquille of Crab, Gadski

Broiled Quail, Waldorf Salad

Neapolitan Parfait

Coffee

"See if that can be got up for five dollars. It it can't, let me know. I'll be in the barber shop." (It could.)

Louis Sherry declined to offer any menu, noting that his patrons "now simply order what they want" at supper — perhaps a club sandwich, perhaps an omelet.[85] In fact, the sort of light meal he described could be had, at Sherry's, for no more than three or four dollars for a couple, including tip.

Meanwhile, owners of more modest restaurants upgraded their cuisine and decor. An example of this was I. H. Rosenfeld's Café Boulevard on Second Avenue.[86] The Boulevard had been a sturdy, central European family restaurant for years, where a four-course Sunday dinner, from soup to strudel, might cost 40 cents per person. Early in the decade the café's excellent food began attracting affluent diners from uptown who wanted to eat well while "slumming" on the Lower East Side.

Rosenfeld saw his opportunity. He built an enclosed courtyard off the dark-paneled dining room, added some potted palms, and hired a Hungarian Gypsy orchestra, starting a fad that quickly spread to other New York restaurants. *Town and Country* reported in 1904, "In a short time, the place became renowned. Society discovered it, and it was considered Bohemian to go to the Café Boulevarde, and that always makes half the success of a place . . . it has branched out. House after house has been taken. It has had a dado painted in the most approved nouveau art and gilding is everywhere. The waiters are dressed in Delmonico manner; the band, augmented by other players, discourses the last favorite ditties of Broadway; and the price of the dinner has gone up with the other improvements. It is now another large, modern restaurant."[87]

"I have never seen such crowds as we are now having for luncheon," the Waldorf-Astoria manager Barso told the *Times* in 1909. "We are compelled every day to fill the main foyer with tables, but even with this we are unable to accommodate the guests." Said assistant manager Fogg of the Hotel Belmont, "Night after night we are compelled to turn away people while our dining rooms are crowded to overflowing all day." Rector's and its neighbor Shanley's both expanded later that year, to better accommodate their after-theater crowds.[88]

In Chicago, a reporter observed that residents of that city were also dining out in increasing numbers; one article put the nightly number of diners in the restaurant district on Randolph Street at 27,000.[89] Chicagoans could choose from an array of high-end to moderately priced restaurants and hotel dining rooms just in that neighborhood.

The influx of middle-class diners accelerated changes that were already under way in fine dining: shorter menus, quicker service, less adherence to the rules of French haute cuisine.[90] The French classics that appeared on many menus now were joined by homier American fare. Café Martin, a downtown mainstay that was trying to make a new name for itself as dining out boomed, hired African-American cooks from the South to prepare chicken à la Maryland; James Regan of the Knickerbocker Hotel hired a woman from Georgia to bake Sally Lunn, an English sweet bread, as well as coconut cakes for afternoon teas. The Bustanoby brothers of Café Beaux Arts found a way to distinguish their restaurant by purchasing a farm and hiring a French gardener to grow all the restaurant's vegetables, a century before "farm-to-table" became an American fine-dining catchphrase.[91]

By then, Chef Ranhofer was a distant memory. The simpler, faster dinners of 1908 and 1910 might not have pleased him, but some of the trends that took hold—incorporating the flavors of American dishes, paying attention to the quality and freshness of ingredients—originated with him and his *Epicurean*, the cookbook that launched a restaurant revolution.

BACK TO THE FUTURE

In the mid-1970s a young American chef sat in a tatty motel room in Berkeley, California, weighing his options. He'd just returned from a few months' stay on the Île Saint-Louis in Paris, where he'd fled after a bad falling-out with a business partner, the founder of the restaurant where he had been working. One of their quarrels concerned the future of the restaurant, a Francophile place that had just gotten a strong review in *Gourmet*.

The restaurant's success had raised questions, and the questions had spawned disagreements. Should it be strictly formal, with white tablecloths and a prix fixe menu, or should it add a more casual bistro to accommodate growing crowds? How faithful did the restaurant need to be to the idea of "French" cooking?

And whose French cooking were they arguing about, anyway?

The restaurant's menus had veered, sometimes brilliantly, sometimes awkwardly, between homey provincial fare and more elaborate, haute cuisine classics. At the same moment the California restaurant was trying to strike the right balance, some of France's most honored chefs—Paul Bocuse, the Troisgros brothers, Michel Guérard—were pioneering a completely different approach, by jettisoning both the elaborate, multistep preparations of Carême and the *ragoûts* of *grand'mère* for lighter, plainer sauces, shorter cooking times, fewer courses, and an emphasis on local, seasonal ingredients. This *nouvelle cuisine* was centered on an idea as revolutionary as it was simple: to prepare elegant food that revealed the flavors hidden in the ingredients themselves.[92]

The California chef loved Paris. He loved the food, loved the artists and writers who were his companions, loved the intellectual conversations he'd missed in laid-back northern California. But throughout his stay in France, and then once he'd returned, an idea kept humming in his mind.

In his travels and conversations with illustrious chefs—household names such as James Beard, Richard Olney, Jean Troisgros—the same question kept bobbing, just below the surface: "What about an American restaurant?"

What if French techniques, both classical and *nouvelle*, could be used to bring out the best qualities of local, seasonal California ingredients?

Squinting in the dim light of his motel room, the chef reached for a massive cookbook he'd hauled with him to Paris and back again. He thumbed idly through the chapter on soups until his eyes fell on a title: Cream of Corn à la Mendocino ("Crème de maïs verte à la Mendocino").

That single recipe lit up the dingy room. The chef took out a pencil and began to sketch a week's worth of new menus for the place in Berkeley. California ingredients, accentuated through the use of French technique. All in the service of local flavors. A new way for a new era.

And then the chef put on his whites, left his motel room, and headed back to the restaurant he thought he'd left behind.

The year was 1976. The restaurant was Chez Panisse. The chef was Jeremiah Tower. And the cookbook that had answered his question was Ranhofer's *Epicurean*.[93]

—LS

AFTERWORD

Dining In at the Dawn
of the New American Century

Even though restaurant dining increased,[1] people still ate most meals at
home. What did they eat? Community cookbooks and recipes in newspapers
reveal that the sturdy, meat-and-potatoes cooking of nineteenth-century
rural America was alive and well, in all its regional variations: baked beans
and cod cakes in Boston, gumbo in Louisiana, barbecued pork in Tennessee,
Puget sound oysters and blackberry pie in Washington State, chili con carne
in California.

Even so, the forces that were reshaping dining out were also changing
what people cooked and ate at home. An energetic "domestic science"
movement sought to make American diets healthier; a growing food
industry took advantage of better transportation networks and novel
manufacturing processes. The movement of people from unfamiliar
regions and from distant countries guided Americans toward new ways of
eating and new foods.

Then, as now, trends in restaurant food trickled down and were
adopted in simpler forms by home cooks. These developments touched
every sort of meal, from breakfast to supper, from weekday family
dinners to special-occasion parties.

Eating to Live, Not Living to Eat

Domestic science (later known as "home economics") got its start in the
1880s, as more women began to complete high school and college, and as
scientists made discoveries about food chemistry, human digestion, and
nutrition. The earliest domestic scientists were educated women who'd
founded cooking schools or lobbied to organize new departments within
agricultural and women's colleges. Approaching cooking and home keeping
as if they were scientific endeavors seemed to these women the best way

"Dere aint go'n'er be no leavin's"

Make your boy's food tasty—Mother—for it has to do some big things. It has to make flesh, blood, bone and muscle and supply boundless Energy. **Remember, the boy of today is the man of tomorrow.**

Don't injure him physically and mentally with indigestible meats, pastries, rich puddings, etc., that act as a drain on his nervous energy.

But feed him plenty of

EGG·O·SEE 10¢

all there is in wheat—and he'll be your heart's joy—strong, healthy, bright, smart and quick at his studies.

You won't have to coax him to eat it either, Mother, for its delicious rich flavor when eaten with cream and sugar is just what he craves most for.

Egg-O-See keeps the blood cool and is the ideal summer food.

Give him some tomorrow—"there won't be no leavin's."

Prepared under conditions of scrupulous cleanliness.

Every grocer in the country sells EGG-O-SEE—the whole wheat cereal. If your grocer has not received his supply, mail us 10 cents and his name (15 cents west of the Rocky Mountains) and we will send you a package of EGG-O-SEE and a copy of the book, "-back to nature."

FREE "-back to nature" book

Our 32-page book, "-back to nature," outlines a plan of right living, including menus for 7 days and recipes for preparing the necessary dishes, based on a whole wheat diet, with suggestions for bathing, eating and exercise, illustrated from life, exceedingly simple and attractive. By following its precepts, abounding and vigorous health is sure to result.

Published to sell at 25 cents a copy, this handsomely illustrated book will be mailed FREE to anyone who writes, as long as this edition lasts. Address

EGG-O-SEE CEREAL COMPANY
472-522 Front Street   Quincy, Illinois

to modernize domestic life. In public lectures, at world's fairs and regional expositions, and in newspapers and magazines, domestic scientists found receptive audiences eager to learn about the latest in food and nutrition advice.

That advice was grounded in emerging research on the chemical composition of food and the digestion times required by different substances. In 1900 the importance of vitamins had yet to be understood, but through the experiments of the Wesleyan University chemistry professor Wilbur Atwater and others there was at least some understanding of the body's use of protein, carbohydrates, and fats. The number of calories required to sustain people of different ages and activity levels was known and publicized in newspaper articles and taught in college nutrition courses.[2]

The work of such scientists led home economists to issue recommendations: that food be treated as fuel, that diets be tailored to individual needs. An office worker or student, for instance, needed a far lighter, less caloric menu than a farm laborer. What's more, if office workers or students attempted to eat like farmhands, they would suffer the consequences: indigestion, gout, obesity, or worse. The less active the person, the more important it was for his or her food to be "digestible." Food that was difficult to digest — because it was too fatty, too sugary, too acidic — was the enemy of good health, responsible not just for dyspepsia but for everything from delinquency to epidemic disease to mental breakdown.

"The puny, weak, peevish, and badly behaved children, the lawless and ill-tempered, are always [the] badly fed," declared Sarah Tyson Rorer, the principal of the Philadelphia Cooking School.[3] Rorer, who was more famous in her day than her Boston Cooking School rival Fannie Farmer, wrote numerous cookbooks and gave sold-out lectures and cooking demonstrations around the country. People listened to her.

Home economists sought to reform the family table meal by meal. They started with the first meal of the day.

Nineteenth-century breakfasts could be nearly as heavy as dinners: fruit or cornmeal mush doused in cream, accompanied by several kinds of bread, waffles, or griddlecakes, served alongside bacon, grilled meat or creamed fish, and potatoes or grits. For people who had no time for such an elaborate meal, a wedge of pie (apple, mince, lemon meringue) washed down with coffee was the breakfast of choice.

The home economists disliked both kinds of breakfast. Although few of them fully embraced vegetarianism, most thought it sufficient to eat meat once or twice a day—and not in the morning. Pie came in for special attack because it contained a great deal of sugar, and also lard, then the most common fat for pie crust. Rorer shunned lard and most other pork products, saying that "life is too short to spend it in digesting pork."[4] She served her own family pie—perhaps made with Olive Butter, a commercial blend of suet and cottonseed oil that Rorer began endorsing in the 1890s—just once a year, at Thanksgiving.

The breakfasts home economists advocated were far more modest: rolls and coffee, a poached egg with toast and fruit, or one of the increasing number of instant breakfast cereals, topped with milk or cream. Cereal manufacturers advertised heavily in cookbooks, newspapers, and magazines, promising that their breakfasts would deliver digestibility, energy, and health. In the ads, rosy-cheeked children beamed over bowls of Grape-Nuts, Ralston Health Food, Granose Biscuit, Cream of Wheat, Elijah's Manna.

Lunch, Dinner, Supper, Tea

Lunch was a work in progress. In the more rural parts of the country, and in most homes on Sundays, the midday meal was still the largest, with a roast or some other substantial meat dish at the center, flanked by vegetables and potatoes. In the evenings, families would eat a much smaller, simpler meal—sliced cold meat left over from dinner, bread and butter, applesauce, and hot cocoa, for instance—that was known in different parts of the country as supper, lunch, or high tea.

As more and more workers commuted to offices and factories farther from their homes, and as the pace of work demanded shorter breaks for the midday meal, the biggest meal of the day for many shifted to the evening. "After a hard day's work is over let us dine," wrote Mrs. Rorer. "The pleasure of dinner is greatest because our leisure gives time for thorough mastication, which increases the enjoyment and pleasure of eating."[5] Lunch became a time for quicker, more portable, lighter foods.

The new "lunch hour" elevated the sandwich. What had been a teatime and picnic dainty of thin, crustless bread spread with butter and chopped watercress or currant jelly became more varied and substantial. Cookbooks listed dozens of sandwich fillings to lend variety to lunch boxes: finely chopped walnuts or olives with cream cheese; peanuts ground to a paste and moistened with whipped cream; leftover veal or sweetbreads minced with mayonnaise. The "club sandwich" began life in men's social clubs, then made its way to department stores, lunch counters, and finally to home tables. With its layers of toast, sliced chicken, bacon, lettuce, and tomato, the club sandwich became more than a light snack between meals.

Warm luncheon dishes for those still able to eat at home made use of repurposed ingredients from the previous night's meal. Home economists, for whom thrift was almost as important as nutrition, were full of suggestions. "Croquettes" and "patties" were staples of ladies' luncheons that cleverly transformed odds and ends of leftover seafood, roast chicken, or beef. Minced and bound with white sauce, rolled in bread crumbs, and fried in butter, even a small quantity of meat could yield a second meal.

Home economists such as Farmer, Rorer, Marion Harris Neil, and Marion Harland also championed salads as luncheon staples. Salads were both "dainty" and "refreshing" and so were ideal dishes for both office workers and ladies at home. The salads of choice included chicken, lobster, and shrimp. These were dressed with mayonnaise or "cream dressing," a concoction of vinegar, sugar, eggs, and butter that was boiled together and sometimes thinned with whipped cream. Meat- or fish-based salads had been around for decades as picnic and late-night supper fare; in the 1900s they became noonday staples.

Lettuce salads were less common in homes than in restaurants, but this was something the home economists hoped to change. Rorer in particular argued for a green salad on the table at least once each day—but the "green salads" of the era were not casually tossed but meticulously arranged, sculptural affairs. Fannie Farmer's predecessor at the Boston Cooking School, a Mrs. Lincoln, gave instructions for arranging leaves of lettuce in the bowl to reconstruct the shape of the lettuce head, then using two forks to carefully coat each leaf with French dressing (vinaigrette) so as not to disturb the arrangement.[6]

The home economists' enthusiasm for salad included not just lobster and lettuce but also nearly any cooked vegetables, nuts, or fruits. A salad that appeared in many cookbooks involved a reengineered banana: the cook was instructed to cut a vertical slice from the skins of whole bananas, scoop the fruit from the banana skin shells, dice the flesh, mix it with chopped celery or walnuts and French dressing, then stuff the mixture back into the skins before serving the packages nestled on individual lettuce leaves.[7]

A 1906 recipe from the *Table Talk Illustrated Cook Book* for "Water Lily Salad" called for arranging slim wedges of egg white, dyed pink with beet juice, like flower petals on a "lily pad" of lettuce, then topping them with sieved egg yolk and a dot of mayonnaise in the center. Other popular salad variations began with a block of Neufchâtel cheese, mixed the cheese with chopped nuts, pimientos, or chutney, then formed the mixture into balls and served them in lettuce cups with French dressing.[8]

Even baked beans got the salad treatment, as in this 1903 recipe from a magazine feature on salad variations:

> Cold baked beans pressed tightly into small cups that have been rinsed in cold water may be unmolded and dressed with a French dressing and shredded lettuce, or surround the little mounds with chopped cooked beets, mixed with French dressing. Or make little cups of cooked beets, by scooping out the interior and fill with baked beans mixed with celery, cress, or lettuce shredded. The scooped-out portions can be chopped and mixed with bits of cauliflower for the next day's luncheon, or with equal parts of sliced or diced turnips and carrots.

Fussy presentations were commonplace, on the theory that visually attractive, "tidy" food would encourage family members to eat more healthfully. Unfortunately, few home economists had as much interest in how the food tasted. "There are still a few women who do elaborate cooking to please the palate and appetite, and the general habits of people," complained Mrs. Rorer in her 1902 *New Cook Book*. "They are still in the palate stage of existence. Strive to reach a higher plane of thought—eat to live."[9]

As they reached for that higher plane, Mrs. Rorer and many of her colleagues shunned most spices. Even though many spices—cinnamon, curry powder, bay leaves, mace, mustard, ginger, cayenne pepper, and paprika (whether these were genuine, adulterated, or artificial was an open question)—were available from grocers, home economists seldom called for them. Their recipes for meats and poultry used little seasoning other than salt and a "suspicion of pepper," with onions added in minute quantities, and garlic missing entirely. If leftover cooked meat or vegetables needed a little something extra on their second trip to the table, they might be served cloaked in a basic white sauce—just milk thickened with butter and flour, faintly seasoned.[10]

The fear of assertive seasoning seems to have reflected not so much concern about the purity of commercial spices as the Anglo-Saxon backgrounds of many of the leading cooking teachers and the "scientific" belief that highly spiced food irritated the mucous lining of the stomach. Mustard, pickled condiments, cayenne, and black pepper prompted special warnings. Tabasco sauce, oddly, was held to be the only "nonirritating" form of pepper.[11]

In an era when many people consumed fried foods and looked forward to sugary desserts each day, Mrs. Rorer considered both to be an abomination. (She was happy to bow to popular demand and demonstrate fritters and cakes in her public lectures, but she always presented the offending items with a stern, "These things all look so good, but they are so deadly.")[12] Lightly cooked foods were equally hazardous. Marion Harland, in her 1902 *Mother's Cook Book*, scolded that those who enjoyed rare meat were lucky rather than wise (perhaps not so off-base in an era of uneven refrigeration and questionable food handling). She added, "Vegetables, also half done, which is the state in which they are often sent to the table, are productive of great gastric derangement, often a predisposition to cholera."[13]

To play it safe, cooking authorities directed home cooks to boil spinach for forty minutes, asparagus for forty-five, canned sweet corn for twenty, and spaghetti for half an hour. Beets might need several hours.

Modern Conveniences

In no line of housekeeping progress has improvement been greater or results more satisfactory than in the canned good industry.[14]

As home economists preached their gospel of healthy home cooking, food retailers and manufacturers promoted convenience foods to an increasingly harried public. Big-city caterers opened takeout counters. Germans and central European Jews started delicatessens, which sold not only sliced meats and sandwiches but also prepared foods — chicken pie, sliced roast beef, soups, apple dumplings — that only needed to be reheated before serving.

Home economists questioned the expense and wholesomeness of such prepared foods. "Ready made foods are only an imitation," a Chicago cooking school instructor told the *Tribune* in 1906. "They look beautiful and appetizing on the outside, but did you ever eat anything in your life bought in this way that was not a disappointment? In too many cases they are made of materials that we would not employ in our homes."[15] Single office workers and the growing population of middle-class families with disposable income but no household servants didn't listen: take-out delicatessen food was a sure way to a hot meal at home.

Canned and bottled foods made convenience more affordable — and accessible to those living outside the big cities. Everything from baked beans to tomato soup to California peaches was available in cans. Sometimes the food was real; sometimes it only looked like what it was supposed to be. The Armour Company, on its way to becoming infamous for its "embalmed beef," canned all kinds of other meats — sweetbreads, lambs' tongues, tripe, stewed kidneys — as well as such mysterious preparations as "hash" and "potted sandwich spreads." The hurried cook could buy Steero stock cubes for soup, Underwood deviled ham for canapés, Alpha New England Salad Cream ("Contains no oil! Never spoils!") for the salad course, Wonderland pudding tablets to make junket (rennet) pudding for dessert. Food manufacturers advertised heavily in newspapers and magazines — and they sold or gave away glossy, illustrated recipe pamphlets featuring their products. Armour had perhaps the most ambitious pamphlet program; fourteen separate booklets, published in 1905, listed recipes for school lunches, winter suggestions, summer pickups, bachelor "stein suppers," and ladies' card parties. Typical Armour recipes always began, "Dice contents of one can..."

Despite a steady stream of news reports about the appalling quality of canned foods, home economists readily endorsed new food products.

The Boston Cooking School approved and exclusively used Knox granulated gelatin. Mrs. Simon Kander and Mrs. Henry Schoenfeld, the Milwaukee cooking teachers who wrote the 1903 *Settlement Cook Book*, endorsed Dr. Sherman's Cream Tartar Baking Powder. Mrs. Rorer was the biggest endorser of them all, adding her name and compliments to Olive Butter, the lard substitute, as well as cocoa, baking powder, gas stoves, cookware, and a shelf-stable processed cheese called MacLaren's Imperial Cheese. The MacLaren's recipe booklet contained over a dozen recipes credited to Mrs. Rorer, including her very own

Spaghetti with Cheese
Boil a quarter of a pound of spaghetti in salted water for half an hour. Drain, cover with cold water for fifteen minutes, drain. Rub together two level teaspoonfuls of butter and two of flour and a cupful of milk (½-pint), stir until boiling, and add gradually a quarter of a pound of

MacLaren's Imperial Cheese, and teaspoonful of salt, and a dash of pepper. Add the spaghetti, reheat over hot water and serve, or turn it into a baking dish, cover the top with bread crumbs, dot with bits of butter and bake twenty minutes. Macaroni may be used in place of spaghetti.[16]

Alpha New England Salad Cream, 1903

Chicago Tribune writer Hugh Fullerton lampooned the popularity of the new convenience foods in a 1906 article, "Practical Cookery for Men: Short Course in Domestic Arts." He offered the following list of recipes to husbands whose wives were too tired to cook dinner after a day of social activities, or who only knew how to make chafing dish "rarebits and fudges":

Mulligatawny soup: Select the right can off the shelf at the grocery, pour into sauce pan, turn on gas, and serve.

Spaghetti a la creole: Buy cooked spaghetti (cold) at the nearest delicatessen, pour into pan, pour catsup over it, warm, sprinkle liberally with cayenne pepper, and serve.

Chicken en casserole: Buy potted chicken, scrape out of can into casserole, pour catsup over, put in green peppers, and sprinkle with cayenne, add a little Worcestershire to help hide the taste of the chicken, and serve hot . . .

Chicken salad: Buy double portion at nearest restaurant, carry home in oyster bucket, place on lettuce leaves, on the missus' best hand-painted china, and serve.

Philadelphia scrapple: Take all the pork chops, veal, beef, fish, chicken and potatoes left over during the last few days, chop together, simmer down on the stove, throw in some dead dough when nearly done, and serve.

Irish stew: Take the same materials and add large pieces of turnip and potato.

"When in doubt," Fullerton advised, "throw in a lot of cayenne pepper and call it 'Spanish style'—then no one can tell the difference."[17]

With convenience foods came convenience cooking methods. The chafing dish—a pan set into a stand over an alcohol lamp, permitting tabletop cooking—became wildly popular in the early 1900s. Cooks could sauté food directly in the pan, or "blazer," or they could fill the blazer with water and use a second, nesting pan as a double boiler to make sauces or custards or to reheat canned soup.

A chafing dish allowed a housewife to scramble eggs to order at the breakfast table—and to whip up lobster Newburg for a ladies' luncheon. College girls used chafing dishes in their dorm rooms to host "fudge parties." A *New York Times* article for young women about packing for college put a chafing dish and a matching set of long-handled cooking utensils at the top of a list of essentials.[18] Bachelors became known for their skill at making all manner of fancifully named, late-night chafing dish snacks: Welsh rarebit, Golden buck, scotch woodcock, English monkey.[19]

Armour's pamphlet *Chafing Dish Suppers* suggested that four friends, each with her or his own chafing dish, could together cook up an impressive, multicourse dinner party. Chafing dish recipes tended to feature thick, creamy sauces, low cooking temperatures, and little or no frying; long-handled spoons and forks allowed the cooking to happen at arm's length. As long as the hostess prepared all the ingredients in advance and brought them out in separate bowls, she and her friends could cook the meal in the dining room, dressed in their party silks, with no muss or fuss.[20]

Chafing dish cookery bridged the no-nonsense practicality of home economists and the stylish world of society entertainment. Nearly everyone used one or knew someone who did. Welsh rarebit was the universal chafing dish supper, loved by men about town and college girls, children and adults, city mice and country mice alike. The seasoning might vary, the sauce might be poured over toast or large crackers, church or temperance cookbooks might substitute cream or milk for beer, but the classic recipe, made with semisoft American or "new" cheese, ended up in cooking school and women's association cookbooks across the country.

"Just too sweet for anything. College girls making candy"

Welsh Rarebit, No. 2.
1 lb. cheese cut into dice,
½ c. stale ale,
1½ teaspoons butter,
¼ teaspoon dry mustard,
Salt and cayenne.

Put butter into the chafing dish; when melted, add cheese, mustard, salt and pepper, and gradually the ale or beer. Stir constantly. If desired, one teaspoon of Worcestershire sauce may be added.[21]

Elegant Entertaining at Home

When it came time to serve company, daintiness and elegance were the goals of the era's middle-class hostess. Cooking magazines like *Table Talk* were her guidebooks. *Table Talk* had been founded in the late 1880s by Mrs. Rorer as a monthly devoted to nutrition, "sanitary homekeeping," and instruction in basic cooking techniques. Gradually the magazine's publisher began allocating more and more space to articles about table decorations and party planning, with instructions on how to make pastel-tinted desserts and favors for a "Holly and Hearts Engagement Luncheon," a "Shamrock Dinner," or a "North Pole Party."

Mrs. Rorer disapproved. She believed that reliable family meals such as pork chops with applesauce and sweet potatoes or broiled chicken with cornbread and peas (dessert strongly discouraged) were sufficient to entertain the fanciest guests. In 1893 she stepped down from the helm of *Table Talk* to start a new publication, called *Household News*. For another decade she remained a regular contributor to *Table Talk*, offering advice about cooking methods and menu planning on a budget. By 1903, though, she had had enough of the theme-party frivolities that were corrupting the magazine. She severed all connections with *Table Talk* and went to work for *Ladies' Home Journal*, where she edited the Home Section.[22]

Meanwhile, *Table Talk*, under its new editor Marion Harris Neil, became the *Martha Stewart Living* of the era. Its editorial mix of everyday recipes and special-occasion foods and its investigations into exotic regional and ethnic cuisines made it popular and influential. Each issue offered a month of menus with recipes, articles on how to cook a single ingredient—rice, rabbit, rhubarb—in a dozen or more ways, and detailed plans for at least two different parties. The more formal dinner parties emphasized French or continental fare modeled on the cuisine served by expensive city restaurants. *Table Talk* even offered periodic advice from "our Paris Correspondent," Frances B. Sheafer, who taught readers how to serve such authentic hors d'oeuvres as celery root and radishes. Photo essays showing proper table settings appeared alongside articles describing how to deliver French-style service (with or without a servant).

Big-city Sunday papers provided other kinds of advice: entire pages of the "Women's" and "Society" sections described the most sumptuous parties thrown by society hostesses, complete with the menus, the place settings, the flowers, and the gowns and jewels worn by the guests. The city sections of the papers included recipes from chefs and maître d's of the best restaurants and their suggestions for seasonal menus.[23]

All the coverage of elite dining and entertaining upped the ante for middle- and upper-middle-class housewives, who tried to copy the social events of the wealthy on a more modest scale. A woman vying for position in her "set" would strive to ensure that everything—the food, the table, the favors and entertainments—at her ladies' luncheon, afternoon tea, or dinner party set the proper tone, as described by the papers.

Sometimes this meant scouring greengrocers for just the right expensive or exotic ingredient. In 1903—the year Mrs. Rorer quit—*Table Talk* reported:

> Recently among women of fashion the informal luncheon has given occasion for the introduction of certain novel fruits, some of which are natives of South America and have only been procurable in the large Eastern cities through the fact that they are now successfully grown in Mexico and southern California . . . One of these delicacies which has been a great favorite at ladies' luncheons during the past season is the chirimoya [*sic*], a fruit native to Peru, but now grown in Mexico.
>
> At a luncheon they are served as a separate course, just before the sweets . . . It reveals inside the thin tough rind a custard-like substance which is very sweet and at first sickish, but, as with the persimmon, the flavor grows upon one, and one taste encourages another until a real appetite is acquired for the foreign edible.[24]

If a hostess couldn't find "chirimoyas," she could still impress her guests with molded gelatins and frozen desserts, mainstays of every high-end restaurant and banquet menu. In a decade that adored anything creamy, pastel, and elaborately shaped, gelatins and ices displaced cakes, pies, and steamed puddings as the most fashionable way to end a fashionable meal.

Charles Knox's invention of powdered gelatin in 1896 allowed women without servants to prepare molded gelatins and aspics without the hours of arduous preparation that had been required before.[25] Knox developed the product after watching his wife, Rose, boil calves' feet for hours to make "jelly," and after receiving a letter from Mrs. Rorer asking for a consistent, easy-to-measure gelatine for use in cooking schools. Knox's "sparkling gelatine," in plain and lemon "acidulated" variations, was an immediate hit with consumers. A recipe pamphlet written by Rose, "Dainty Desserts for Dainty People," gave any housewife instructions for preparing foolproof, jewel-like tomato aspics, salmon mousses, and Bavarian creams for her guests.[26]

Even more likely to impress were frozen desserts: ice creams, sherbets, frozen puddings, and parfaits, flavored with vanilla, coffee, fruit, rum, and raisins. Not everyone owned an ice cream churn, but most of these desserts could be packed into molds—shaped like mountain peaks, crowns, or scalloped melons—and frozen under layers of rock salt and crushed ice. Canned pineapple (shipped from Hawaii and heavily promoted in women's magazines by the Dole Company from 1905 on) and Costa Rican or Jamaican bananas added exotic excitement.[27] This recipe, a $1 winner in a 1907 *Chicago Tribune* recipe contest, showcased both fruits:

White Mountain Frozen Pudding
One pint sweet cream, whipped to stiff froth; one cup granulated sugar, boiled until it threads; one cup mixed nuts chopped fine, two ounces candied cherries, one small can sliced pineapple, whites of four eggs beaten to a stiff froth. Pour the sirup over the beaten eggs, then add this to the whipped cream, also the fruit, cut in small pieces, and the nuts. Pack in ice and salt to ripen about eight or ten hours. It can be served with or without the following sauce: Yolks of two eggs, over which pour gradually the sirup made as above, with one cup granulated sugar, add juice and grated rind of one lemon; also three large bananas, mashed. Serve cold over the pudding.[28]

The Taste of Others

The love of exoticism that made Japanese tearooms so popular in the biggest cities and attracted urban diners to Italian and Chinese restaurants filtered out to middle America. Ladies who lived far from New York, Chicago, or San Francisco could still host Japanese-themed teas — dressed as geishas.

The invitations to a Japanese sociable should be written as the natives write, up and down, instead of across, and have a cherry blossom or a Japanese lady in watercolors in one corner of each.

The guests should be informed beforehand that each one is to tell something or read something about Japan, any little item of interest that may have been heard or read, a pretty poem or a little story. The hostess and whoever assists her in receiving should wear kimonos and have tiny fans in their hair...

Tea, of course, must be the beverage. Sandwiches made of thin slices of brown bread and cream cheese, little fancy cakes, and Japanese nuts will answer for refreshments.[29]

For a Japanese-themed dinner, the *Table Talk Illustrated Cook Book* offered an appealing, if telegraphic, recipe for "Japanese ice cream."

An egg custard is thickened with boiled rice puree, then flavored with strong green tea and vanilla. Serve in glass dishes with preserved ginger cubes.[30]

Small-town hostesses experimented with other exotic foods as well. Cookbooks from the north, south, and midwestern United States included recipes for a chutney-like condiment called India pickle, made with chopped tomatoes, apples, onions, and raisins and spiced with daring amounts of mustard seed, ginger, and "tumeric" ("This you have to get of the druggist," advised one contributor to a 1906 Winnetka, Illinois, church cookbook).[31] In a 1908 *Table Talk* feature on "Curries as They Should Be Made," Marion Harris Neil offered recipes for steamed rice, lentil *dal*, and spicy curries of rabbit, crab, and hardboiled eggs.[32]

Sometimes the "exotic foods" that middle-class hostesses served to impress their friends came from ethnic communities that were an established part of the American landscape. The *L.A. Times*'s 1906 cookbook — a compilation of winning recipes from its 1905 recipe contests — prominently featured "Seventy-nine Old-Time California, Spanish, and Mexican dishes," including refried beans, enchiladas, and *chiles relleños*. The *Times* cookbook included an early recipe for Tamale Pie, a fusion casserole that became a favorite throughout the Southwest.

No. 79 Tamale Pie. Mrs. S. B. Bagnall, Oxnard, Cal. — One pound round of beef, with a little fat; one pound pork, fat and lean, cut in small bits or chopped coarsely in meat chopper. Put together to boil, keeping well covered with water. Prepare from dried chiles one-half teacup of pulp. This is done by removing seeds and veins, boiling in water until soft, and then scraping with a knife. When meat has boiled one hour add the pulp, one and one-half dozen olives, one dozen raisins, three cloves garlic, salt to taste. To make crust, put in saucepan two-thirds cup fresh lard (home made if possible), one pint water. When boiling add one teaspoon salt, one large teacup cornmeal, stirring in slowly. When cool enough to handle spread this on bottom and side of shallow two-quart granite basin; thicken meat with one tablespoon cornmeal, boiling about five minutes. Pour the meat onto the crust. Having saved enough dough to make cover, work this into round, thin pats and place on top of meat. Bake in oven one-half to three-quarters of an hour. Better than tamales. Improves by warming over the second or third day.[33]

Creole and Southern cooking enjoyed widespread popularity in the North and West as well. While city restaurants were adding fried chicken, gumbos, and Southern pastries to their menus (and hiring African-American cooks to make them), home cooks in Kentucky, Connecticut, and Washington State were following recipes for Creole omelets, Chicken Maryland, and Sally Lunn bread. Sometimes there was confusion about the origins of these dishes; any food that featured hot peppers and onions might be called "Spanish."[34]

Because German and Scandinavian immigrants to the East and upper Midwest had earned reputations for baking, cookbooks of the era, including Farmer's *Boston Cooking School Cook Book*, tucked in a selection of *kuchens*, cardamom-laced coffee cakes, and ginger cookies from those countries. The 1903 *Settlement Cook Book*, originally written to help Jewish immigrants adjust to American life, quickly became a best seller in the Midwest. Its recipes for smoked goose, goulash, and poppyseed torte reflected the central European Jewish roots of its authors. Even the spice-averse Mrs. Rorer included an ethnic recipe section in her 1902 *New Cook Book*, with Jewish, Spanish, Creole, and Hawaiian dishes.[35] By the end of the decade community cookbooks from states as far apart as Indiana and Connecticut included recipes for "Virginia Corn Pudding," "Mexican Eggs," and "German Apples."

Looking at all the potted meats, prune jellies, and baked bean salads filling 1900s cookbooks, it is easy to understand how the food writer Amanda Hesser could declare the first decades of the twentieth century "a culinary abyss."[36] Certainly, the home economists' pursuit of a bland and starchy version of wholesomeness, coupled with the food industry's obsession with processed foods, led to some dismal cooking and eating—and to some culinary bad habits that persisted well into the 1960s.

No matter. Tucked among the era's cream sauce–choked entrées and overcooked vegetables were recipes for straightforward dishes that would not be out of place on twenty-first-century tables: barely sweetened blackberry pandowdy, assertively seasoned chili Colorado, cinnamon-scented "Beef a la Creole." Magazines such as *Table Talk* and cooking teachers such as Fannie Farmer talked not only about nutrition and digestibility but also about the pleasures of the table. They, and the home cooks who followed their advice, passed on to their children and their children's children the kind of simple, flavorful American cooking that endures.

—LS

Merry Christmas

Calendar 1901

Christmas dinner, Hotel Pabst, New York, 1900

WISHING YOU
A VERY HAPPY NEW YEAR

GARDEN CITY HOTEL
GARDEN CITY, L. I.
J. J. LANNIN CO.

Dinner held by Garden City Hotel, Garden City, Long Island, 1908

NOTES

INTRODUCTION

1. See http://digitalgallery.nypl.org/nypldigital/index
   .cfm.
2. Andrew Otroski, "Life in a College Town: Frank
   Made Her Mark," *Williamsport Sun-Gazette*, June 28,
   2007.
3. Allyson Ryley, "The Prime of Miss Frank Buttolph:
   Notes Toward a Menu History of New York City,"
   American Book Collector 7 (November 1986).
4. *New York Times*, May 22, 1904.
5. "Measuring Worth; Real GDP," http://www
   .measuringworth.com/datasets/usgdp/result.php.
6. Campbell Gibson, ed., "Population of the 100
   Largest U.S. Cities . . . 1790–1990" (U.S. Census
   Bureau, June 1998). See http://www.gov/
   population/www/documentation.
7. "Historical Statistics of the United States, Millennial
   Edition Online," Cambridge University Press. See
   http://hsus.cambridge.org/hsusweb; Campbell J.
   Gibson and Emily Lennon, eds., "Historical Statistics
   on the Foreign Born Population of the United States,
   1850–1990" (U.S. Census Bureau, February 1999).
   See http://www.census.gov/population/www_
   documentation; Page Smith, *America Enters the World*
   (New York: Penguin Books, 1985), 126–45.
8. "Statistical Abstract of the United States, 1910"
   (Washington, D.C.: U.S. Government Printing
   Office, 1911); "Statistical Abstract of the United
   States, 1920" (Washington, D.C.: U.S. Government
   Printing Office, 1921).
9. Smith, *America Enters the World*, 9–11.
10. Ibid.
11. See http://www.measuringworth.com/datasets/
    usgdp/result.php.
12. Smith, *America Enters the World*, 143–60.
13. "Statistical Abstracts of the United States," 1911, 1921.
14. "Yorkshire buck" was in the same family of foods
    as "Welsh rarebit": toasted bread or muffins were
    smothered with a mixture of cheese, eggs, butter,
    and—for Yorkshire buck—ale, whisked together,
    and melted in a double boiler or chafing dish. The
    toasted bread or muffin was topped with a poached
    egg and a piece of bacon, then covered with the
    melted cheese mixture from the double boiler.
15. Rebecca Freedman, "The Queen and Her Menus,"
    eBook Central, New York Public Library, April 28,
    2011.
16. Jeremiah Tower, *California Dish: What I Saw (and
    Cooked) at the American Culinary Revolution* (New York:
    Free Press, 2003), 55.

CHAPTER 1: PURE FOOD

1. Oscar E. Anderson Jr., *The Health of the Nation*
   (Chicago: University of Chicago Press, 1958), 135.
2. Carl Sandburg, *Always the Young Strangers* (New York:
   Harcourt, Brace, 1953), 417.
3. *New York Times*, March 26, 1899.
4. Graham A. Cosmas, *An Army for Empire* (Columbia:
   University of Missouri Press, 1971), 294.
5. *New York Times*, June 18, 1906; *Chicago Tribune*
   February 5, 1906.
6. Written and performed by Lew Dockstader's
   Minstrels, Washington, D.C., October 4, 1903.
7. James H. Young, *Pure Food* (Princeton, NJ: Princeton
   University Press, 1989), 155.
8. Testimony, First Session, 59th Congress, quoted in
   ibid.
9. In 1899 *McClure's* had the distinction of carrying more
   advertising than any magazine in the world (*Printer's
   Ink* 28 [August 1899]). By 1907—just before the
   financial panic and collapse of that year—*McClure's*
   circulation hit 500,000. Frank Luther Mott, *A
   History of American Magazines*, vol. 4 (Cambridge, MA:
   Harvard University Press, 1957), 599.
10. Anthony Arthur, *Radical Innocent* (New York:
    Random House, 2006), 11.
11. Ibid., 43.
12. *The Lancet* 165 (January 7, 14, 21, and 28, 1905).
13. Arthur, *Radical Innocent*, 66.
14. Source for European export figures: *Chicago Tribune*,
    May 29, 1907.
15. Arthur, *Radical Innocent*, 71.
16. Smith, *America Enters the World*, 78.
17. See Arthur and Lila Weinberg, eds., *The Muckrakers*
    (Urbana: University of Illinois Press, 2001).
18. Year-to-year export figures for 1906 published in the
    Chicago Tribune, July 13, 1906; year-to-year export
    figures for 1907 in *New York Times*, August 11, 1907.
19. Arthur, *Radical Innocent*, 76.
20. Ibid., 77.
21. *New York Times*, May 28, 1906.
22. *New York Times*, May 29, 1906.
23. *Chicago Tribune*, June 5, 1906.
24. *Chicago Tribune*, July 13, 1906; *New York Times*,
    August 11, 1907.
25. *New York Times*, June 1, 1907.

CHAPTER 2: QUICK FOOD

1. *Chicago Tribune*, July 15, 1903.
2. *Chicago Tribune*, July 25, 1909.
3. *Chicago Tribune*, February 21, 1901.

4. Joel Denker, *The World on a Plate* (Boulder, CO: Westview Press, 2003), 48–51.

5. Donna R. Crabaccia, *We Are What We Eat* (Cambridge, MA: Harvard University Press, 1998), 115–16.

6. One of those young Greeks who worked long hours and saved his money was named John Raklios. By 1919 Raklios owned a chain of nineteen quick lunches in Chicago. By then, Greeks in Chicago owned a third of the city's lunchrooms.

7. Jan Whittaker, "Quick Lunch," *Gastronomica* 4, no. 1 (Regents of the University of California, 2004): 61.

   The humble New York City ancestors of the Rotunda were two tiny, "beef-and-beans"/"ham-and-beans"/ "pork-and-beans," carved-to-order places that fed a variety of men and boys—laborers, reporters, newsboys, conductors, businessmen, even authors (Mark Twain and Bret Harte among them)—who had nothing in common but big appetites and a taste for plain, cheap food. Hitchcock's opened for business in 1857. Mr. Hitchcock himself carved the corned beef. During the Spanish-American War, Teddy Roosevelt was said to have promised his men, as they gagged on their "embalmed beef" rations, that he'd buy them a meal at Dolan's when they got home. William Grimes, *Appetite City* (New York: North Point Press, 2009), 82–83.

8. *Munsey's Magazine* 14 (March 1901). A 1911 Rotunda menu offered an entrée of "spicy lamb with asparagus tips" for $1.00 (equal to about $23 now) and a dessert of "Monte Carlo pudding with cognac sauce" for 15 cents (Monte Carlo pudding was made with cream, sugar, and candied violets). Whittaker, "Quick Lunch," 70.

9. Women office workers and sales clerks not fed and sheltered by their employers organized "lunch clubs" that were open to any woman who understood that a place calling itself a lunch club was a place that was (1) free of men (2) served fifteen-cent, three-course meals (in 1909, a second-floor women's cafeteria in Chicago offered a choice of "tomato soup, Hungarian goulash, Irish stew, roast beef, stewed tomatoes, mashed potatoes, fried potatoes, apple pie, cherry pie, coffee or tea"), and (3) had restroom lounges furnished with upholstered chairs and sofas.

   Schrafft's began in Boston as a sweetshop operated by a candy seller named William Shattuck, then turned into a restaurant (and then a restaurant chain, managed by Shattuck's sister and an all-woman staff trained in "domestic science") that catered to women office workers and women shoppers. See

Jan Whittaker, "Domesticating the Restaurant: Marketing the Anglo-American Home," in *From Betty Crocker to Feminist Food Studies* (Amherst: University of Massachusetts Press, 2005), 96.

   Mary Elizabeth's was another chain that catered to women. Like Schrafft's, Mary Elizabeth's began as a candy seller. In Mary Elizabeth's case, the candy was made at home by Mary Elizabeth Evans and her two sisters. Starting with a little stand in an office building in Syracuse, New York, Evans opened shops in New York City in the best and busiest neighborhoods. Candy led to scones, scones led to dainty sandwiches, dainty sandwiches led to nice salads. (Grimes, *Appetite City,* 208; Jan Whittaker, "Restaurant-ing Through History," September 11, 2008, at: http://victualling. wordpress.com).

10. *Chicago Tribune*, February 10, 1900.

11. They included the Trocadero, the Throgmorton (described as "the Delmonico's of London's financial district"), and the Popular, a café where London's most fashionable people refreshed themselves after shopping.

12. *Chicago Tribune*, July 21, 1907.

13. *New York Times*, October 13, 1907.

14. *New York Times*, April 4, 1908.

15. *Chicago Tribune*, July 25, 1905.

16. *New York Times*, November 17, 1909.

17. One dollar in 1903 could buy what almost $26 can buy now. In 1909 a "street laborer" could earn $1.50 per day (equal to about $37 today). Doing that kind of shovel work in a steel mill, in front of a blast furnace, or in a rolling mill was more dangerous, so it paid more: $1.75 per day (equivalent, in 1909, to about $43 today). Single men—immigrants or native born—who lived together in back-alley tenements or basements might be able to survive on $8 to $10 per week, but married men with families had to rely on their wives to take in boarders. Skilled workers—men who knew how to use tools other than picks and shovels (or butcher knives in the case of the packinghouse workers who went on strike in Chicago in 1904 because the owners refused to pay them more than $5.50 per week)—earned as much as $15 per week (*Chicago Tribune*, April 18, 1909).

18. *Chicago Tribune*, March 2, 1905.

19. *New York Times*, June 2, 1905.

20. *Chicago Tribune*, February 3, 1907.

21. Restaurant and hotel waiters formed their first national unions in 1891. In 1893 waiters at the Holland House Hotel on New York's Fifth Avenue walked out just before dinner. From the Holland House, the strike spread to Delmonico's (where it ended almost as soon as it began); from there, it spread to a big, popular

place called Degnan's (where the shock of the place's ninety waiters walking out killed the owner). By May the strike had spread to luxury hotels in Philadelphia and Chicago. None of the strikes lasted long or ended well for the waiters: 1893 was the start of one of the most severe and long-lasting depressions the country had suffered since the end of the Civil War. There were more men looking for work than there were jobs. Any waiter who went out on strike was easily replaced. (*New York Times*, April 30, May 3, 1893; Grimes, *Appetite City*, 162–63).

22. One of Kohlsaat's waiters—known only as "Rastus"—had a smile so big and bright that a local account executive from the J. Walter Thompson Agency noticed it one day at lunch. He offered Rastus fifty cents to pose for an advertising photograph for Cream of Wheat cereal. The agency pasted Rastus's smiling face on a drawing of a black man dressed in white, holding a sauce pan in one hand and a steaming bowl of cereal in the other. "Rastus," the Kohlsaat waiter, became an advertising icon, the hot cereal equivalent of pancake mix's Aunt Jemima (who was a former slave named "Nancy Green" who'd moved to Chicago). For an account of Rastus and Cream of Wheat, see "The Truth About John Lee Mahin and the Darky," *Printer's Ink* (November 3, 1921): 64.

23. *Chicago Tribune*, May 6, 1903.
24. *Chicago Tribune*, May 12, 1903.
25. *Chicago Tribune*, May 27, 1903.
26. *Chicago Tribune*, June 6, 1903.
27. *Chicago Tribune*, June 5, 1903.
28. *Chicago Tribune*, June 21, 1903.
29. *Chicago Tribune*, August 27, 1903.
30. *Chicago Tribune*, August 14, 1910.
31. Loraine Diehl and Marianne Hardart, *The Automat* (New York: Clarkson and Potter, 2002), 28.
32. Ibid., 19.
33. "Two Country Boys Who Serve 45 Million Meals a Year," *American Magazine* (November 1921). Childs wasn't the first American restaurant chain to spread from neighborhood to neighborhood, city to city, region to region. A chain called the Waldorf System (the name supposedly came from an early customer who'd joked about the service being almost as good as New York's Waldorf-Astoria Hotel), based in Springfield, Massachusetts, had grown by absorbing other local and regional chains, with more than one hundred outlets in forty U.S. cities. Other chains with as many outlets in as many cities were Baltimore Dairy Lunch (begun in 1880 in Baltimore) and Thompson's (begun in 1893 in Chicago; during the general restaurant strike in Chicago in 1903,

Thompson's was one of the first restaurant companies to reach a wage agreement with its workers). For an account of the Waldorf System and other chains, see Philip Langdon, *Orange Roofs, Golden Arches* (New York: Knopf, 1986); see also Grimes, *Appetite City*, 119–20, 183–84; and Jan Whittaker, "One Arm Joints" in "Restaurant-ing Through History," at http://victualling.wordpress.com.

34. For more about "home made food" as a marketing strategy, see Samantha Barbas, "Just Like Home / 'Home Cooking' and the Domestication of the American Restaurant," *Gastronomica* 2, no. 4 (Berkeley: University of California Press, 2002): 48–49.

35. A 1901 cookbook titled *The Picayune's Creole Handbook* described "Creole Cream Cheese" in this way: "Cream cheese is always made from clabbered milk. The 'Cream Cheese Woman' is [a] common sight on our New Orleans streets . . . She carries a covered basket in which are a number of small, perforated tins in which the Cheese are. In her other hand she carries a can of Fresh Cream . . . when once a good, careful, clean woman gets a [regular] 'customer,' she keeps her during her period of business, coming every fast day and Friday with her Cheese and Cream, for this is a great fast-day breakfast and luncheon dish." See http://neworleanscuisine. blogspot.com/2005/04.

36. The fact that griddlecakes (pancakes) were even on the Childs menus is the result of the brothers' earliest restaurant experience. Before William and Samuel opened their first restaurant they worked for a chain called Dennett's that had outlets in Baltimore, Philadelphia, Boston, Manhattan and Brooklyn, Chicago, and San Francisco. Dennett's advertised its "Surpassing Coffee," but its trademark was a griddle chef, dressed in white, stationed in every outlet's front window, pouring and flipping pancakes. The aroma drew people in from the street.

Mr. Dennett himself was a Christian businessman who posted Bible verses on the walls of his restaurants and required his employees to study a Bible verse and pray before they opened for business each day. Dennett dressed his waitresses in black and fined them if they appeared inattentive during morning prayers.

The Childses hoped Mr. Dennett would train them to become managers. He fired them after six months. They took his griddle chef idea with them. By 1910 Childs had forty outlets in Manhattan. Dennett's had only seven. By then Mr. Dennett was dead. As he opened more outlets in more cities, his behavior became steadily more erratic, until he was committed to a mental hospital. He died in 1908 after being released from an asylum in California. (Grimes, *Appetite City*, 120; see also *Trow Business Directory of New York*, Trow Directory Company, New York, 1910.)

37. "Two Country Boys Who Serve 45 Million Meals a Year."

38. Lewis Mumford, "Machinery and the Modern Style," *New Republic* (August 3, 1921): 261.

39. Diehl and Hardart, *Automat*, p.18.

40. Whittaker, "Quick Lunch."

41. Richard Papernik, "Joseph V. Horn and Frank Hardart," *National Restaurant News* (February 1996).

42. Lobster Newburg (originally named "Lobster Wenberg" in honor of a patron who later got into some sort of an argument with Delmonico's restaurant) was first prepared in 1876 by Delmonico's chef Charles Ranhofer. A recipe for the dish appeared for the first time, in print, in Ranhofer's culinary masterpiece, *The Epicurean*, in 1896.

43. See Whittaker, "The Automat, an East Coast Oasis," in "Restaurant-ing Through History," March 25, 2009.

44. *Evening Bulletin*, June 7, 1902, as quoted in Langdon, *Orange Roofs, Golden Arches*, 16.

45. Carolyn Crowley, "Meet Me at the Automat," *Smithsonian* (August 2001).

46. Daniel Cohen, "For Food Both Hot and Cold, Put Your Nickels in the Slot," *Smithsonian* (January 1986).

47. Langdon, *Orange Roofs, Golden Arches*, 16–17.

CHAPTER 3: HER FOOD

1. "Chicago Woman Lives Five Weeks on Less than Seven Dollars," *Chicago Tribune*, August 2, 1903.

2. The one thing that no one who could avoid it would consider was domestic service. A generation earlier, immigrant girls and the uneducated poor might have taken positions in wealthy households, but by 1900 the lack of privacy and the expectation that a household servant would be at the employer's beck and call at all times deterred anyone who had a choice—and some who didn't. Newspapers devoted frequent columns to "the servant problem." As white women avoided service, their positions began to be filled by African-American women, who were excluded from many other workplaces. The disappearance of domestic help fed the demand for restaurants among middle- and upper-middle-class families. Alice Kessler-Harris, *Out to Work: A History of Wage-Earning Women in the United States* (New York: Oxford University Press, 1982), 128.

3. "A Young Woman's Chances of Getting Work in Five American Cities," *New York Times*, August 12, 1906.

4. Sue Ainslie Clark and Edith Wyatt, "Working Girls' Budgets," *McClure's* 35, no. 6 (October 1910): 595–605.

5. "The Story of Rose Fortune," *Frank Leslie's Illustrated Monthly* 57, no. 2 (December 1903): 7.

6. The incident with the questionable roommate and the subsequent night of homelessness appeared in the book version of the story, *The Long Day* (subtitled *The Story of a New York Working Girl*), with an introduction by Cindy Sondik Aron (Charlottesville: University Press of Virginia, 1990 [originally published in 1905]) but was omitted from the serialized version.

7. "Making Flowers on Broadway," *Frank Leslie's Illustrated Monthly* 57, no. 4 (February 1904): 34.

8. Sue Ainslie Clark and Edith Wyatt, "Women Laundry Workers in New York," *McClure's* (February 1911): 401.

9. Richardson, *The Long Day*, 245–59.

10. Laura A. Smith, "The Girl in the Small Town: How She Can Best Succeed in the City," *Ladies' Home Journal* 23, no. 11 (October 1906): 24.

11. Richardson, *The Long Day*, 253–61.

12. George Kibbe Turner, "The Daughters of the Poor," *McClure's* (November 1909): 45.

13. "Five White Slave Trade Investigations," *McClure's* (July 1910): 346.

14. Theodore Dreiser, *Sister Carrie* (New York: Barnes & Noble Classics, 2005 [1900]), 57.

15. Kathy Peiss, *Cheap Amusements: Working Women and Leisure in Turn of the Century New York* (Philadelphia: Temple University Press, 1986), 54.

16. Christine Terhune Herrick, "Office Girls' Lunch," *Los Angeles Times*, September 25, 1902. In a November 17, 1907, article in the *Chicago Tribune*, reporter Hollis Field estimated that 45 percent of workers in the Loop were women, nicknaming the area "Petticoat Lane." A May 22, 1904, *Boston Globe* article announced "Woman's Invasion of State Street."

17. Margery Davies, *Woman's Place Is at the Typewriter: Office Work and Office Workers, 1870–1930* (Philadelphia: Temple University Press, 1982), 39, 52–55.

18. Ibid., 57.

19. Individual employers could and did apply the "marriage bar" with their female staff, and many women assumed they'd stop working at marriage in order to keep house, but first-person accounts of office workers in newspapers and magazines include references to married women supervisors and colleagues. In teaching, the marriage bar seems to have been enforced more consistently.

20. For accounts of department store clerks and the hours of standing, see Clark and Wyatt, *McClure's* 35, no. 6

(October 1910): 600–605. For working conditions of waitresses, see "The Story of the Waitress," *Independent* 64:3107 (June 18, 1908): 1379.

21. Laura Shapiro, *Perfection Salad: Women and Cooking at the Turn of the Century* (Berkeley: University of California Press, 2009), 91.

22. "Women in Restaurants," *Washington Post*, April 26, 1903.

23. Maud Younger, "The Diary of an Amateur Waitress," *McClure's* 28, no. 6 (April 1907): 665.

24. D. W. Frederick, "Ten Cent Lunch Business Offers Way to Riches," *Chicago Daily Tribune*, August 20, 1905.

25. "Basket Dinners," *New York Sun*, October 25, 1903.

26. "How the Pretty Business Girl Takes Her Luncheon at the Candy Store on a Chocolate Soda and a Cracker," *Chicago Tribune*, May 10, 1908.

27. John A. Jakle and Keith A. Sculle, *Fast Food: Roadside Restaurants in the Automobile Age* (Baltimore: Johns Hopkins University Press, 1999), 29.

28. "'Hello' Girls Are Happy," *Chicago Daily Tribune*, June 18, 1901.

29. "How Big Department Stores Cater to Employes' Comfort," *New York Times*, May 17, 1903.

30. "How Women of Chicago Protect Girl Strangers," *Chicago Daily Tribune*, October 14, 1906.

31. "The Millionaire Has His Noonday Rest," *Chicago Daily Tribune*, September 1, 1907.

32. *Chicago Daily Tribune*, July 11, 1899.

33. "Terry Visits Noonday Rest," *Chicago Daily Tribune*, December 21, 1901.

34. "The Feeding of New York's Down Town Office Workers—A New Social Phenomenon," *New York Times*, October 15, 1905.

35. "Firetrap Restaurants," *Chicago Daily Tribune*, May 3, 1907.

36. "One Window for Escape," *Boston Daily Globe*, May 2, 1907.

37. "Firetrap Restaurants."

38. "Bonney Royal at the Cafeteria," *Chicago Daily Tribune*, May 2, 1909.

39. "Lunch Room to Suit Women Offers Woman Good Field," *Chicago Daily Tribune*, April 29, 1906.

40. Jan Whittaker, *Tea at the Blue Lantern Inn* (New York: St. Martin's Press, 2002), 163–67.

41. Tearooms also had roots in the Women's Exchange movement. The exchanges were founded by society women to aid sisters who'd fallen on hard times and needed to earn a living while keeping up appearances. The first, the Ladies' Depository Association, opened in Philadelphia in 1833, with the goal of "arousing in the community an interest in the hard and often bitter struggle to which educated, refined women are so frequently exposed when financial reversals compel them to rely upon their own exertions for support." Exchanges sold handcrafted linens and baby clothes, jams, pickles, and homemade breads and cakes—made by members and sold under the cloak of anonymity. Some began offering tea and light luncheons to passersby. Women's exchanges in some southern cities such as Charleston and Savannah became known as places where groups of women could obtain an affordable luncheon or afternoon tea. Marion Harland, "School for Housewives," *Los Angeles Times*, September 25, 1910; "Charm of the Colonial Tea Room," *New York Times*, January 26, 1908.

42. "Gentlewomen in Business," *Town and Country* (January 27, 1906): 16.

43. "Society's Latest Fad—Tearooms," *New York Times*, April 25, 1909.

44. Whittaker, *Tea*, 24.

45. Grace Alexander Fowler, "The Development of the Tea Room," *Harper's Bazaar* 42, no. 3 (March 1908): 259.

46. "Men Invade Women's Cafes: 'Big Checks' Remove Barriers," *Chicago Daily Tribune*, July 25, 1909.

47. "Crowd Women Out," *Chicago Daily Tribune*, March 27, 1904.

48. Fowler, "Development of the Tea Room," 260.

49. Kessler-Harris, *Out to Work*, 112–14.

50. Ibid., 113–14.

51. "Large Profits in Tea Rooms," *Washington Post*, June 27, 1909.

52. Ibid.

53. "'Boiling Sisters' Doing Bubbling Business," *Los Angeles Times*, December 24, 1908. Still other college women set up tearooms in popular tourist destinations, a trend that peaked once automobile travel made daytrips and motor touring commonplace in the 1910s and 1920s, as described in Whittaker's *Tea at the Blue Lantern Inn*.

54. Fowler, "Development of the Tea Room," 259.

55. "Jostled Count and Duke," *Washington Post*, January 12, 1908.

56. "Bow-Wows Checked for Hotel Guests," *New York Times*, December 16, 1907.

57. "The Feeding of New York's Down Town Office Workers—A New Social Phenomenon."

58. "Mrs. Blatch to Sue the Hoffman House," *New York Times*, August 6, 1907.

59. "Custom Prescribes Good Form," *Chicago Sunday Tribune*, December 12, 1909.

60. *New York Times*, May 17, 1903.

61. Phillis Alvic, *Weavers of the Southern Highlands* (Lexington: University Press of Kentucky, 2003), 39.

62. *New York Times*, August 6, 1907.

63. *New York Times*, October 5, 1907.

64. *Independent* 63:3063 (August 15, 1907): 410.

65. "To Let Women Dine Alone," *New York Times*, February 7, 1908.

66. *Washington Post*, February 12, 1908.

67. "Any Woman's a Lady Who Behaves That Way," *New York Times*, January 12, 1907.

68. In *Turning the Tables: Restaurants and the Rise of the American Middle Class, 1880–1920* (Chapel Hill: University of North Carolina Press, 2011), Andrew P. Haley suggests that women like Blatch and Graham were turned away because they were middle-class challengers to the elite, old-money aristocracy that frequented places such as the Hoffman House. But the life experiences of these women were far from typical of middle-class people of the era: Harriot Stanton Blatch was a national leader in the suffrage movement. Her daughter Nora was the first woman admitted to the American Society of Civil Engineers. She was profiled as the "girl engineer" in several major newspapers. Nora Blatch's 1907 engagement to the inventor Lee DeForest made the society pages in New York, Chicago, Boston, and Washington. Fairer, perhaps, to understand the Blatches and Graham as prominent members of an emerging class of elite, highly educated women, who were increasingly able to navigate the business world and the professions alongside men. (See pp. 146–47.)

69. *New York Times*, August 26, 1907.

70. Haley, *Turning the Tables*, 161.

CHAPTER 4: OTHER PEOPLE'S FOOD

1. "In the Waldorf kitchen . . . the soup was made in a receptacle about the size of a hogshead and stirred 'round and 'round by a huge German with an implement as big as a snow shovel. There was a line of men, twenty strong, preparing sweetbreads, slapping them into tiny cups by the hundred" (*New York Times*, February 14, 1905).

2. Ibid.

3. "New York City is the third largest Hungarian city in the world. It has been estimated that 60,000 Hungarians live between Houston and 12th Street and Second Avenue. They are equally divided between Slav Hungarians and Magyar Hungarians. Most of the so-called Hungarians in this neighborhood are Hungarian Jews" (*New York Times*, April 3, 1910).

4. *New York Times*, February 15, 1905. The congressman was correct. George Washington had bought drinks and said farewell to his officers at Fraunces Tavern on Pearl Street in 1783, but it would be another six years before he became president.

5. Many white workingmen, East and West, thought Chinese immigrants routinely ate rats as well as cats and dogs. Ignatius Donnelly, in his novel of the future *Caesar's Column*, published in Chicago in 1890, predicted that "cheap coolie labor" would force American workers to eat rats too. See Ivan Light, "From Vice District to Tourist Attraction," *Pacific Historical Review* 43, no. 3 (Berkeley: University of California Press, August 1974): 378.

6. Donna Gabaccia, *We Are What We Eat* (Cambridge, MA: Harvard University Press, 1998), 123–24. See also Bertha Woods, *Foods of the Foreign Born* (Boston: Whitcomb and Barrows, 1922).

7. *New York Times,* February 15, 1905.

8. Of the four hundred Rough Riders—men and officers—who'd charged up the Kettle and San Juan hills, 86 had been killed or wounded, 40 had collapsed from heatstroke, and 5 had gone missing. Thirty percent of Rough Riders were either killed, wounded, or disabled by disease or malnutrition during their time of service. The Rough Riders' casualty rate was the highest of any unit during the Spanish-American War. See Nathan Miller, *Theodore Roosevelt* (New York: William Morrow, 1992), 278, 305.

9. Edwin Burrows and Mike Wallace, *Gotham* (New York: Oxford University Press, 1999), 745; see also William Grimes, *Appetite City* (New York: North Point Press, 2009), 86.

10. In 1907, when Klein's, the oldest German wine bar in New York, closed, five hundred people came to drink a final toast to a place that had been serving *Weiser mit* (white wine with seltzer) for more than forty years. Ed Klein had inherited the place from his father, Karl, who opened his wine *Stube*, at 31 Avenue A, in 1863. Ed Klein's mother, wife, and his two youngest children had drowned, along with more than a thousand other women and children from Kleindeutschland, when the ferry *General Slocum* burned and sank on its way to a church picnic on Long Island in June 1904. Soon after that, Klein's twenty-one-year-old son also died—by drowning. The deaths broke Klein's spirit and tore the heart out of Kleindeutschland. Klein's closing signaled a larger change: New York's German community had begun a collective move to a new neighborhood, north of Seventy-ninth Street, south of Ninety-sixth, between Third Avenue and the East River, an area once occupied by the village of Yorkville. (*New York Times*, April 27, 1907.)

11. "By the 1890's, there were 60 delicatessens in New York, 80 percent on the east side, all but a dozen or

so owned by Germans . . . They roasted meats for their customers and kept pates, roast pork, and pigs feet on hand for takeout. The list of takeout food was astounding: game pies cooked to order, baked beans, smoked beef shoulder, smoked jowls, fresh ham, meat jelly, blood pudding, liver pudding . . . Salads galore were sold from stone crocks: potato salad, beet salad, parsnip salad, and herring salad" (Grimes, *Appetite City*, 89).

12. Examples from the Buttolph Menu Collection of the New York Public Library include the cold meats that Blanco's Restaurant in San Francisco served in 1907; the roasts, schnitzels, and wursts served by New York's Flatiron Restaurant and Café in 1905; the sauerbraten served by Hick's Restaurant in Savannah in 1906; and the German fried potatoes, German small steak, and wiener schnitzel offered by Lippe's Restaurant in St. Louis in 1907. The Schulz Restaurant's bill of fare, described earlier, can also be found in the Buttolph Menu Collection.

13. *New York Times*, April 3, 1910.

14. Clarence Edwards, *Bohemian San Francisco* (San Francisco: Paul Elder & Co., 1914), 4–5.

15. *Chicago Tribune*, January 12, 1908.

16. *Chicago Tribune*, August 29, 1909.

17. Before considering the American pursuit of *Gemütlichkeit*, it may be useful to know a few things about lager itself. Unlike English ales whose high-temperature, fast-acting yeasts floated to the top of the brew (called the *wort* before hops have been added; called the *hopped wort* after they've been added) after fermentation (a process that might take just a few days or a few weeks depending on the temperature), lager yeasts thrived at lower temperatures and settled to the bottom of the wort (to which lesser amounts of hops were added, compared to ales) after a month or two. Ales, after they fermented, were ready to be served; lagers, instead of being served, were stored, sometimes for as long as six months, in cellars and caves, where they went through a second fermentation. The result was a beer that was clearer, milder tasting, mellower, and easier to drink than the sharp (or sweet and fruity) English ales. At 5 percent alcohol (alcohol per volume, or APV), lagers were also stronger.

18. *Chicago Tribune*, March 6, 1903.

19. The bar of the St. Louis Hotel in New Orleans may have been the first place in the United States to serve a free lunch to its customers. The year was 1843. John Mariani, *The Dictionary of American Food and Drink* (New York: Hearst Books, 1994), 128. An article in the December 1860 (vol. 3, no. 1) *Harper's*

magazine refers to "free lunch establishments" in San Francisco. Sir William Craige and John Hulbert, eds., *A Dictionary of American English* (Chicago: University of Chicago Press, 1966), 1062.

20. Perry Duis, *The Saloon: Public Drinking in Boston and Chicago, 1880–1900* (Champaign: University of Illinois Press, 1983), 154.

21. Published in 1866 by J. C. Haney and Company.

22. Junius Brown, *The Great Metropolis* (Hartford, CT: American Publishing Company, 1869), 165–66.

23. *New York Times*, May 30, 1908.

24. Over the course of many decades, and many state, local, and municipal elections, voters in Boston and New York passed laws to curtail the Sunday sale of alcohol. The Raines law, passed by the New York State Legislature in 1896, permitted only hotels (defined as places that had at least ten beds) to sell drinks — but only if they served sandwiches with them. Saloons obeyed the letter of the law by (1) offering free sandwiches, made of bricks; (2) adding the word "hotel" to their names; and (3) installing beds in rooms above their bars. (Prostitutes and their clients welcomed the new beds.) See *New York Times*, April 6, 1896, and Jacob Riis, *The Battle with the Slum* (New York: Macmillan, 1902), 224.

State legislators responded. No hotel/saloon could sell drinks on Sunday unless it *seated* its customers at tables. New York City added refinements and adjustments. Saloons didn't have to install beds or change their names, but they couldn't open before noon. Saloons also had to keep their front doors open so that passing patrolmen could see that no one was *standing* at their bars. Saloons met this new challenge by putting tables and chairs in their back rooms, unlocking their side doors (which they called "Family Entrances" or "Ladies Entrances"), and by seating their customers at these new tables, now decorated with the brick sandwiches that had once adorned their bars.

German taverns and wine bars continued to serve and entertain their *Stammgasten* as they always had.

25. "Treating" referred to the American custom of buying rounds of drinks, one patron matching the other. "Drink up, boys! The next round's on me!" was believed to increase the rate of drinking. Critics believed that rapid intoxication led to disorderly conduct and habitual alcoholism.

26. *New York Times*, September 13, 1909.

27. In 1913 the Woman's Christian Temperance Union's world convention passed a resolution asking the "Protestant Episcopal Church" in America and England to replace communion wine with grape

juice. The Reverend Dr. Henry Antice, secretary of the church's House of Deputies, was appalled. "This is not a grape juice church," he said (*New York Times*, October 26, 1913).

28. Ray Oldenberg, *The Great Good Place* (Cambridge, MA: Da Capo Press, 1999), 98–99.

29. Many families brought their own food and enjoyed elaborate picnics. In a scene from Frank Norris's novel *McTeague*, set in San Francisco in 1899, the novel's principal character is invited to a picnic by the family of the young woman he hopes to marry. The young woman's name is Trina; her parents, the Sieppes, are German émigrés. *"The lunch was delicious. Trina and her mother made a clam chowder that melted in one's mouth . . . The party was fully two hours eating. There were huge loaves of rye bread full of grains of chickweed. There were wienerwurst and frankfurter sausages. There was unsalted butter. There were pretzels. There was cold, underdone chicken, which one ate in slices, plastered with a kind of mustard that did not sting. There were dried apples . . . There were a dozen bottles of beer, and last of all, a crowning achievement, a marvelous Gotha truffle. After lunch came tobacco . . . In the afternoon, Mr. Sieppe disappeared. They heard the report of his rifle on the range. The others swarmed over the park, now around the swings, now in the Casino, now in the museum, now invading the merry-go-round."* Frank Norris, *Novels and Essays* (New York: The Library of America, Viking Press, 1986), 316.

30. *Chicago Tribune*, July 12, 1903.

31. James L. Ford, *Bohemia Invaded and Other Stories* (New York: Frederick A. Stokes, 1895), 3–4.

32. Henri Murger's 1851 novel *Scènes de la Vie de Bohème* was an early indication of the vicarous pleasure members of the middle class derived from the improprieties of this caste of artist-gypsies. By the end of the nineteenth century, bohemians appeared as principal characters/protagonists in George du Maurier's best-selling novel *Trilby* (1895) and Giacomo Puccini's opera *La Bohème* (1896). The more regulated, constrained, and constricted became the lives of the middle class, the greater the pleasure the bourgeoisie took from the antic transgressiveness of the group of "others" who called themselves "bohemians."

33. The place was originally owned and operated by a French woman when the neighborhood was still French. See Grimes, *Appetite City*, 128.

34. Maria Sermolino, *Papa's Table d'Hôte* (Philadelphia: Lippincott, 1952), 15, 40–41.

35. The table d'hôte consisted of a pint of California red wine, an antipasto plate, a bowl of minestrone, a dish of spaghetti, a choice of roast beef, chicken, or fish, a green salad, a choice of spinach or brussels sprouts, a dessert, and a cup of espresso — all for the equivalent of twelve dollars.

36. Sermolino, *Papa's Table d'Hôte*, 15–16.

37. Ibid.

38. That "something darker" was based more often than not on xenophobic stereotypes. For example, one of Gonfarone's predecessors was a restaurant in the financial district called Caffe Moretti. The owner of the place, Stefan Moretti, was a cultured man, a freethinker who had once studied for the priesthood. In 1880 a reporter for the *New York Tribune* was sent to interview him. Moretti was known to have a very dry wit and a cultivated love of opera, but because stereotypically Italian men were unkempt, uncouth, hot tempered, and swarthy, the reporter turned Moretti into a caricature: "a burly, brigandish Italian who is never known to wear a cravat, or, for that matter, clean linen." (See Grimes, *Appetite City*, 96).

39. The man who was killed and then stuffed into a barrel knew too much about an international counterfeiting ring based in Sicily. Counterfeiters in Palermo produced $2 and $5 bills that they smuggled into the United States in crates of olives, wine, cheese, pasta, and olive oil. Some of the crates went to wholesalers in New Orleans; many more went to an importer in New York named Ignazio Lupo — a merchant prince whose fine houses, handsome delivery wagons, and splendid store on Mott Street had made him a celebrity in Little Italy.

40. Eighteen men were charged. Fourteen were arrested. The other four had been murdered by fellow conspirators during the six-year investigation. The body of one of the dead, a man nicknamed "Petto the Ox," had been found in Wilkes Barre, Pennsylvania. He'd been stabbed sixty-two times (*New York Times*, July 29, 1909).

41. *New York Times*, December 19, 1909.

42. "The Syrian Colony in Manhattan runs from Albany Street to the Battery and is boundedon the eat by Greenwich Street," *New York Times*, May 25, 1902.

43. *New York Times*, March 29, 1903.

44. According to the political geography of the time, these immigrants came from the Mount Lebanon region of Syria. Syria itself was a province of the Ottoman empire.

45. Casey McWilliams, "Cathay in Southern California," *Common Ground* (Autumn 1945): 34–35.

46. Joel Denker, *The World on a Plate* (Boulder, CO: Westview Press, 2003), 90–92; Andrew Coe, *Chop Suey* (New York: Oxford University Press, 2009), 119, 134–35.

47. Charles Nordhoff, *California for Health, Pleasure, and Residence* (New York: Harper, 1873), 190, cited in Coe, *Chop Suey*, 138–39.

48. Coe, *Chop Suey*, 79.

49. In that year, Congress passed the Exclusion Act. The act not only ended the legal immigration of Chinese workingmen to the United States but severely restricted the entry of Chinese women as well. Merchants, scholars, their wives, children, and servants were exempt.

50. The 1890 U.S. Census counted 103,620 Chinese in the United States. The 1900 Census counted 85,341. It's impossible to know how accurate these totals were. What is correct is that emigration and mortality did account for the 1900 decrease.

51. Though opium smoking was considerably less addictive than the nineteenth- and early-twentieth-century, middle-class American habit of injecting morphine, smoking opium daily for more than fourteen days usually resulted in addiction. See Richard Davenport-Hines, *The Pursuit of Oblivion* (New York: W. W. Norton, 2002), 125.

52. H. H. Kane, M.D., *Opium Smoking in America and China* (New York: Putnam's, 1882), cited by Davenport-Hines, *Pursuit of Oblivion*, 125, and David T. Courtwright, *Dark Paradise: A History of Opiate Addiction in America* (Cambridge, MA: Harvard University Press, 2001), 68.

53. This 1900 estimate was made by two separate Methodist missionaries living in San Francisco. Contemporaries considered both missionaries to be experienced observers and cautious in their estimates. Cited by Courtwright, *Dark Paradise*, 68.

54. Kane, *Opium Smoking*, 72; Davenport-Hines, *Pursuit of Oblivion*, 127.

55. Light, "From Vice District to Tourist Attraction," 378.

56. European bohemians preferred hashish.

57. Coe, *Chop Suey*, 156–59; "The Quest for Bohemia," *Washington Post*, October 23, 1898.

58. *Chicago Tribune*, January 26, 1906.

59. *Los Angeles Times*, November 4, 1901.

60. "Quest for Bohemia."

61. Between 1877 and 1900, ten western states—including California—outlawed opium smoking. In 1909 the United States banned "the importation and use of opium for other than medicinal purposes." Courtwright, *Dark Paradise*, 81; Light, "From Vice District to Tourist Attraction," 368.

62. *Los Angeles Times*, September 18, 1904.

63. *New York Times*, February 16, 1902.

64. For example, the menu of a medium-priced restaurant on Pell Street offered a choice of roast pork or roast duck; chicken with pineapple; chicken with dumplings; chop suey with white mushrooms; white rice plain or with maple syrup.

65. Light, "From Vice District to Tourist Attraction," 389–90; *New York Times*, May 14, 1913. Connors's San Francisco counterparts also hired blind beggars and singing children as well as opium den workers, smokers, and gamblers as cast members. See *New York Times*, July 23, 1909.

66. The phenomenon seems to have begun in London in the late 1860s when Charles Dickens, and later the prince of Wales, visited opium shops in New Court off Victoria Street. In 1872 Gustave Doré, along with a member of Napoleon III's household, were escorted through the slums of Bluegate Fields in East London by a Scotland Yard detective. See Davenport-Hines, *Pursuit of Oblivion*, 123–24. In the United States the phenomenon seems to have started in the 1880s. By the 1920s white sophisticates from New York and Connecticut visited Harlem the way some of their parents or grandparents had visited Chinatown.

67. *New York Times*, October 17 and November 26, 1904.

68. *New York Times*, August 8, 1905, and *New York Times*, April 17, 1910.

69. Luc Sante, *Low Life* (New York: Farrar, Straus and Giroux, 1991), 227–29.

70. According to the 1900 U.S. Census, 25 percent of Chinese workers were laundry men; another 20 percent were cooks, waiters, and household servants. In 1903 an esteemed social and political reformer from China, while on a visit to the United States, estimated that 90 percent of Chinese workers in the eastern part of the country were laundry men. Cited by Joan S. Wang, "Race, Gender, and Laundry Work," *Journal of American Ethnic History* 24, no. 1 (Champaign: University of Illinois Press, 2004).

71. *Chicago Tribune*, July 19, 1903. The article included a sixteen-item bill of fare, served by an unidentified, local restaurant. Two "chop suey and rice" dishes were offered, one for the equivalent of $6, one for the equivalent of $10. Chow mein sold for either $20 or $26. A dish of "steak and green peppers and rice" cost $8.

72. *New York Times*, November 5, 1903.

73. *Chicago Tribune*, January 26, 1902.

74. *Chicago Tribune*, July 31, 1908. The restaurant was managed by a German-American named Shuck. During its opening week, the restaurant featured a soloist named "Edgar Don Sang, the only Chinaman in the world who has mastered the Italian method. [He] will sing a number of songs in English, wearing native costume."

75. *Los Angeles Times*, January 28, 1907; *Chicago Tribune*, July 20, 1908; Haiming Lu, "Chop Suey as Imagined, Authentic, Chinese Food," *Journal of Transnational American Studies* 1, no. 1 (Berkeley: University of California Press, 2009): 12.

76. A vice district known at the time as "Satan's Circus."

77. *New York Times*, November 5, 1903.

78. Edwards, *Bohemian San Francisco.*

79. *New York Times*, August 29, 1904.

80. Fremont Rider, *Rider's Guide to New York City* (New York: Henry Holt, 1916), 171.

81. Ibid.

82. Ibid. Other luxury hotels in other cities copied the Astor by building rathskellars of their own. In 1907 Chicago developers announced plans for a twenty-two-story, 1,200-room hotel—"the tallest hotel in the world"; "the finest hotel in the West," they called it, to be built on the corner of La Salle and Madison Streets. Two stories beneath a lobby with a twenty-foot ceiling, crowned with a dome of stained glass and mosaics, the builders planned a rathskellar where, they said, "distinctively German cooking will be provided" (*Chicago Tribune*, June 2, 1907). In that same year, in Louisville, that city's newly rebuilt Seelbach Hotel installed a finely detailed, medieval rathskellar modeled on that of a castle on the Rhine.

CHAPTER 5: SPLENDID FOOD

1. "Art: Tales of the Hoffman House," *Time*, January 25, 1943.

2. Karl Schriftgiesser, *Oscar of the Waldorf* (Philadelphia: Blakiston Company, 1943), 27–30.

3. Stokes, the heir to an oil fortune, was both admired and notorious. He'd shot a romantic rival, Jim Fisk, after Fisk attempted to steal the affections of Stokes's girlfriend the showgirl Josie Mansfield. For that, Stokes had served a four-year term at Sing Sing. Once he was back in the city, Stokes lived as large as his wealthy patrons. Ibid., 26–33.

4. Ibid., 33.

5. Lately Thomas, *Delmonico's: A Century of Splendor* (Boston: Houghton Mifflin, 1967), 214.

6. Schriftgiesser, *Oscar of the Waldorf*, 34.

7. Walter Germain Robinson, "Famous New York Restaurants," *Town and Country* (March 26, 1904): 21.

8. Elliott Shore, "Dining Out: The Development of the Restaurant," in Paul Freedman, ed., *Food: The History of Taste* (Berkeley: University of California Press, 2007), 305–6.

9. Thomas, *Delmonico's*, 132.

10. Robinson, "Famous New York Restaurants," 19.

11. "A Famous Chef," *Current Literature* 26, no. 6 (December 1899): 519.

12. Alain Drouard, "Chefs, Gourmets, and Gourmands: French Cuisine in the 19th and 20th Centuries," in Freedman, *Food: The History of Taste*, 263–64.

13. Roy Strong, *Feast: A History of Grand Eating Food* (New York: Harcourt, 2002), 282–84.

14. At that time, restaurants serving food that was European in style and caliber were few, clustered mostly in the major cities of the Northeast and mid-Atlantic and in New Orleans, where high-end restaurants served the region's distinctive Creole cuisine.

15. Thomas, *Delmonico's*, 88.

16. "Takes Two Hours for Formal Dinner," *Chicago Daily Tribune*, November 9, 1902.

17. Thomas, *Delmonico's*, 260. The avocados were a gift to Charles Delmonico from the dashing war correspondent Richard Harding Davis. Ranhofer knew about avocados when Davis brought them in—they appeared in *The Epicurean* in 1894—but 1895 seems to mark the year that East Coast restaurants, starting with Delmonico's, began to order and serve them. The avocado gradually spread into the interior of the country.

18. *New York Times*, March 17, 1893, and January 8, 1895. The "assemblies" of the Patriarchs ended in the mid-1890s. The last Matriarchs' ball was given in 1903; a brief item in the March 18, 1903, issue of the *Times* noted that society had become too large to sustain the events, which were intended to be highly exclusive.

19. "Arrested the Cab Criers," *New York Times*, February 8, 1894.

20. M. H. Dunlop, *Gilded City: Scandal and Sensation in Turn of the Century New York* (New York: William Morrow, 2000), 170–73. Dunlop's book provides a detailed account of the Seeley affair and its coverage in the press.

21. Roger Butterfield, *The American Past* (New York: Simon and Schuster, 1957), 261.

22. Little Egypt disappeared, only to surface the following year as the star of an Oscar Hammerstein musical parody, *Silly's Dinner*. Hammerstein's revue was a big hit, until Hammerstein was himself indicted for "maintaining a public nuisance." "Oscar Hammerstein Indicted," *Washington Post*, January 23, 1897.

23. The Brunswick Hotel agreed to hold a dinner for Billy McGlory, a notorious saloonkeeper who had come to the hotel to arrange the dinner posing as a respectable gentleman. McGlory paid in advance, and when he

arrived with fifty underworld guests in tow (including three transvestite "dancing girls") the Brunswick had no choice but to let the all-night bacchanal go forward. The hotel never recovered from the very public blow to its reputation. See Michael Batterberry and Ariane Batterberry, *On the Town in New York* (New York: Routledge, 1999), 155–57.

24. Thomas, *Delmonico's*, 236.
25. Ranhofer died of Bright's disease (kidney failure) in New York in October 1899.
26. Charles Ranhofer, *The Epicurean* (1894), 620.
27. Thomas, *Delmonico's*, 279.
28. A 1909 edition of *A Selection of Dishes and the Chef's Reminder* includes a listing of Hotel Monthly Press titles. *The Epicurean*, "the king of cookbooks," sold for $7; pocket guides such as the *Chef's Reminder* and *Vest Pocket Pastry Book* cost $1 each.
29. John Tellman, *The Practical Hotel Steward*, 4th ed. (Chicago: Chicago Hotel Monthly Press, 1913).
30. An English translation of Escoffier's *Le Guide Culinaire* was published in the United States in 1907.
31. Ostensibly Henry, an avid sailor, was visiting the United States to christen his brother the kaiser's new yacht. The prince's visit had another purpose as well: to patch over strained relations between President Roosevelt and Kaiser Wilhelm. By early 1902 Venezuela was about to default on its debt. In response, Germany and Great Britain planned a naval blockade of the country, to be followed by a possible occupation. Roosevelt believed all of Latin America to be within the sphere of influence of the United States. He saw the imperially minded Wilhelm as a threat. Roosevelt was prepared to send Admiral George Dewey to break up any potential blockade. Prince Henry's trip in 1902 was a mission of "friendship" designed to defuse tensions as the kaiser weighed his options.
32. *Chicago Daily Tribune*, February 24, 1902, and *Chicago Daily News*, March 3, 1902.
33. "Select Dinner to Henry," *Chicago Daily News*, February 2, 1902.
34. In 1902, the *Chicago Daily Tribune* reported that "the genuine terrapin of the ordinary size [5½ to 6 inches in length, yielding about four banquet servings when cleaned and cooked] brings $30 a dozen, and the larger ones from $90 to $100." In 2010 dollars, the smaller terrapin would have cost $600 and the larger $1,800 to $2,000, respectively. "The Terrapin Disappearing," *Chicago Daily Tribune*, November 24, 1902.
35. Small patties, or *bouchées*, were puff pastry shells. According to Ranhofer, "à la Reine" referred to patties filled with a mixture of minced cooked

chicken breast, puréed rice, and velouté sauce. The patties were topped with slices of black truffle, in lieu of their usual puff pastry lids.

Although there were fancy dinners where men and women ate together, at public dinners of an official or commemorative sort the common practice was for the guest of honor to dine only with male guests. The guests' wives were sometimes seated in galleries above the main dining room, where they would be served a simpler, lighter meal, or, as in this case, they would stay away until the ball, joining the men for a late-night buffet supper.

36. *Chicago Daily Tribune*, March 4, 1902.
37. *New York Herald*, February 26, 1902.
38. "Prince Henry to the German Society," *New York Times*, March 9, 1902.
39. Bradley and Cornelia Martin, a lawyer and his socially ambitious wife, spent just enough of the year in England to avoid paying U.S. income taxes, then returned to New York for the height of each social season. Mrs. Martin inherited a family fortune in the early 1880s. She spent the decade that followed working her way into the good graces of people such as the Astors and Vanderbilts by throwing and attending a series of lavish dinner parties. The Martins married their daughter off at sixteen to the cash-poor earl of Craven. The marriage allowed Mr. and Mrs. Martin to mingle with the titled and stay at an estate near Loch Ness during their months of tax exile each year. The wedding, an exercise in unbridled spending and a dress rehearsal of sorts for Mrs. Martin's 1897 costume ball, was held at Grace Church in Manhattan in 1893. It ended in chaos when a crowd of bystanders rushed the church, tore apart the flowers and decorations, and scuffled with guests. See Dunlop, *Gilded City*, 4–6.
40. William Grimes, *Appetite City* (New York: North Point Press, 2009), 147–48; and Schriftgiesser, *Oscar of the Waldorf*, 83–84.
41. Schriftgiesser, *Oscar of the Waldorf*, 96.
42. Frederick Townsend Martin, *The Passing of the Idle Rich* (New York: Doubleday, 1911), 30–46.
43. "Hyde Best Known as an Exquisite," *Chicago Daily Tribune*, April 2, 1905.
44. Patricia Beard, *After the Ball: Gilded Age Secrets, Boardroom Betrayals, and the Party that Ignited the Great Wall Street Scandal of 1905* (New York: HarperCollins, 2009), 143–46.
45. *New York Sunday Herald*, February 5 and February 12, 1905.
46. "Alexander in Open War on James H. Hyde," *New York Herald*, February 15, 1905.

47. "James Hazen Hyde Dies at 83," *New York Times*, July 27, 1959.

48. In June 1905 James Hyde sold his shares in the Equitable for $2.5 million, as part of a restructuring deal with a new owner, financier Thomas Fortune Ryan, who brought in entirely new leadership. Hyde spent the summer of 1905 in Newport, then sold off his Long Island estate, his coaches and driving teams, even his beloved saddle horses. By the end of 1905 he'd moved to France. He returned to the United States only in 1941. Beard, *After the Ball*, 255–78.

49. " 'Little Father' Hunger's Victim," *New York Herald*, February 15, 1905.

50. *New York Sun*, November 5, 1905.

51. *New York Times*, August 26, 1910.

52. *Boston Daily Globe*, December 30, 1904; *Los Angeles Times*, January 5, 1905; *New York Times*, March 21, 1905, and September 24, 1909.

53. *New York Times*, May 24, 1908.

54. "Vanderbilt Fête Fills Plaza Rooms," *New York Times*, March 26, 1909.

55. Batterberry and Batterberry, *On the Town in New York*, 137.

56. Mamie Fish was known for her love of the outrageous and the well-timed insult. When a neighbor in Newport revealed that he didn't plan to invite her or her boisterous friend Harry Lehr to a dinner he'd planned, because "you make too much noise," she threatened to tell his invited guests that the host's chef had smallpox — and then host her own rival party. Such behavior did not endear her to everyone, but she was influential. Wayne Craven, *Gilded Age Mansions* (New York: W. W. Norton, 2009), 301–2; and ibid.

57. *New York Times*, March 19, 1908.

58. "Newport Reforms, No More Freak Fetes," *New York Times*, March 15, 1908.

59. *New York Times*, September 15, 1908.

60. *Pictorial Review* 4, no. 7 (April 1903): 37.

61. William Griffith, "The New Yorker and His Dinner," *New York Times*, March 26, 1905. See also Emma Seifrit Weigley, *Sarah Tyson Rorer: The Nation's Instructress in Dietetics and Cookery* (Philadelphia: American Philosophical Society, 1977), 2–3.

62. Andrew F. Smith, *Eating History* (New York: Columbia University Press, 2009), 142–46.

63. *Chicago Daily Tribune*, March 10, 1901.

64. "Variety of Habit in 'Luncheons,' " *New York Times*, September 15, 1901.

65. "What Should Be the Gourmet's Dinner," *Town and Country* (April 14, 1906): LS24.

66. Helen Campbell, "A Million a Day for Dinner," *Health* 57, no. 5 (May 1907): 286.

67. Schriftgiesser, *Oscar of the Waldorf*, 91.

68. Ibid., 126.

69. Julian Street, *Welcome to Our City*, 4th ed. (New York: John Lane Company, 1913), 80.

70. Times Square got its name in 1904, when the *New York Times* moved its headquarters to a newly built skyscraper on Broadway. Before that, it had been know as Longacre Square, after a farm that had once stood on the spot and had hosted George Washington. (Ibid., 62.)

71. The Chicago Rector's appears in Dreiser's novel *Sister Carrie* as a symbol of decadence and excess.

72. "Saturday Night in Chicago," *Chicago Daily Tribune*, January 12, 1908.

73. Street, *Welcome to Our City*, 75.

74. Ibid., 76.

75. Grimes, *Appetite City*, 134.

76. *Chicago Daily Tribune*, January 12, 1908.

77. Street, *Welcome to Our City*, 9.

78. Andrew P. Haley, *Turning the Tables: Restaurants and the Rise of the American Middle Class, 1880–1920* (Chapel Hill: University of North Carolina Press, 2011), 122–26.

79. "What Should Be the Gourmet's Dinner," 34.

80. *New York Times*, December 15, 1910.

81. *New York Times*, June 23, 1901.

82. Street, *Welcome to Our City*, 71.

83. Haley, *Turning the Tables*, 193–200. Haley points out that only a person with an elite education would have been able to decipher a menu written entirely in French, since public schools did not routinely offer French classes. Newspapers outside the largest cities advocated doing away with French on menus entirely, as did the *Practical Hotel Steward*, which argued that using French terms was both unnecessarily pretentious and — at a time of growing national pride — un-American. English gradually seeped into fine-dining menus. Certainly, the trend accommodated middle-class diners. The slow transition led to some odd (and ungrammatical) hybrid names for dishes and may also reflect the fact that many restaurant workers below the level of chef had only "kitchen" French at their disposal.

84. This was a cordial of the Bustanobys' own invention, made from Florida grapefruit, which the brothers promoted as an appetizer, as a salad, and in numerous desserts.

85. "How to Order that Little After-the-Theatre Supper," *New York Times*, November 15, 1908.

86. Café Boulevard was the restaurant that had refused service to Rebecca Israel in 1900.

87. Robinson, "Famous New York Restaurants," 23.

88. *New York Times*, April 4, 1909.
89. "Randolph Street Restaurant Row, Where 27,000 People Eat Daily," *Chicago Daily Tribune*, August 29, 1909.
90. Haley, *Turning the Tables*, 138–39.
91. *New York Sun*, March 3, 1907.
92. In 1973 French restaurant critics Henri Gault and Christian Millau published the "ten commandments" of nouvelle cuisine. They are reproduced in Drouard, "Chefs, Gourmets, and Gourmands," 294.
93. Jeremiah Tower, *California Dish: What I Saw (and Cooked) at the American Culinary Revolution* (New York: Free Press, 2003), 98–111.

Afterword: Dining In at the Dawn of the New American Century

1. Based on the 1900 and 1910 U.S. Censuses, the number of restaurants in the United States increased by 78 percent during the decade.
2. Carolyn Goldstein, *Creating Consumers* (Chapel Hill: University of North Carolina Press, 2012), 2; Laura Shapiro, *Perfection Salad* (Berkeley and Los Angeles: University of California Press, 2009), 70–72.
3. Mrs. S. T. Rorer, "What to Eat to Gain Strength," *Ladies' Home Journal* (June 1906): 38.
4. Shapiro, *Perfection Salad*, 75.
5. Rorer, "What to Eat to Gain Strength," 38.
6. Shapiro, *Perfection Salad*, 91.
7. Eleanor M. Lucas, "A Chapter on Salads," *Table Talk*, (May 1903): 172.
8. *Table Talk Illustrated Cook Book* (Philadelphia: Table Talk Publishing Company, 1906), 81–83.
9. Sarah Tyson Rorer, *Mrs. Rorer's New Cook Book* (Philadelphia: Arnold & Co., 1902), 4. Fannie Farmer was a striking exception to the eat-to-live dictum. Although, like Rorer, she was a semi-invalid whose interest in nutrition as a means to healing and health came from her own experiences, Farmer enjoyed food. Her cookbooks offer varied flavors, her suggested garnishes were often whimsical, and her menus reflected an awareness of which flavors complemented each other. See Shapiro, *Perfection Salad*, 114–15.
10. Shapiro, *Perfection Salad*, 91.
11. Lylie O. Harris, "A Story of Tabasco," *Table Talk* (May 1903): 166.
12. Emma Seifrit Weigley, *Sarah Tyson Rorer: The Nation's Instructress in Dietetics and Cookery* (Philadelphia: American Philosophical Society, 1977), 61.
13. Marion Harland, *Mother's Cook Book* (Indianapolis: Homewood Publishing Company, 1902), 8.
14. Mary H. Frost, "Light Housekeeping in Cities," *Table Talk* (June 1903): 214.
15. "Chicago Housekeepers Waste $200,000,000 Annually," *Chicago Daily Tribune*, November 25, 1906.
16. *Cheese Relishes: MacLaren's Imperial Cheese*, company pamphlet (Toronto, 1904), 4.
17. "Practical Cookery for Men: Short Course in Domestic Arts," *Chicago Daily Tribune*, December 9, 1906.
18. "Conveniences for the College Girl," *New York Times*, September 26, 1909.
19. Welsh rarebit was a cheese sauce made with ale or beer, served poured over toast. Golden buck added a poached egg between the toast and the cheese sauce. Scotch woodcock was a white sauce enriched with chopped hardboiled eggs and anchovies, while "English monkey" thickened the Welsh rarebit sauce with bread crumbs.
20. Armour and Company, *Chafing Dish Suppers* (1905), 11.
21. Mrs. Simon Kander and Mrs. Henry Schoenfeld, *The Settlement Cook Book* (Milwaukee: The Settlement, 1903), 95.
22. Weigley, *Sarah Tyson Rorer*, 69.
23. Ibid., 117.
24. Isabel Bates Winslow, "Favored Foreign Fruits," *Table Talk* 28, no. 4 (April 1903): 123.
25. Now owned by Kraft Foods, Knox gelatine and its history are described on the company website: http://www.kraftbrands.com/knox/knox_history.html.
26. Charles B. Knox, "Why You Should Use Knox's Gelatine," *Ladies' Home Journal* (September 1905): 29.
27. A history of canned pineapple and its promotion can be found on the Dole Company website: http://www.dole.com/Company%20Info/Timeline.
28. "Best Things to Eat Are Made at Home," *Chicago Daily Tribune*, October 27, 1907.
29. Florence Pegg Taylor, "Some Oriental Ideas," *Ladies' Home Journal* (March 1903): 36.
30. *Table Talk Illustrated Cook Book*, 108.
31. *Good Recipes* (Winnetka, IL: Women's Society of Winnetka Congregational Church, 1906), 22.
32. Marion Harris Neil, "Curries as They Should Be Made," *Table Talk* (March 1908): 95.
33. *The Times Cookbook—No. 2* (Los Angeles: Times-Mirror Co., 1906), 12.
34. Adelaide Keen, *With a Saucepan over the Sea* (Boston: Little, Brown and Company, 1910), xv.
35. *Mrs. Rorer's New Cook Book*, 691.
36. Amanda Hesser, *The New York Times New Cookbook* (New York: W. W. Norton, 2011), xx.

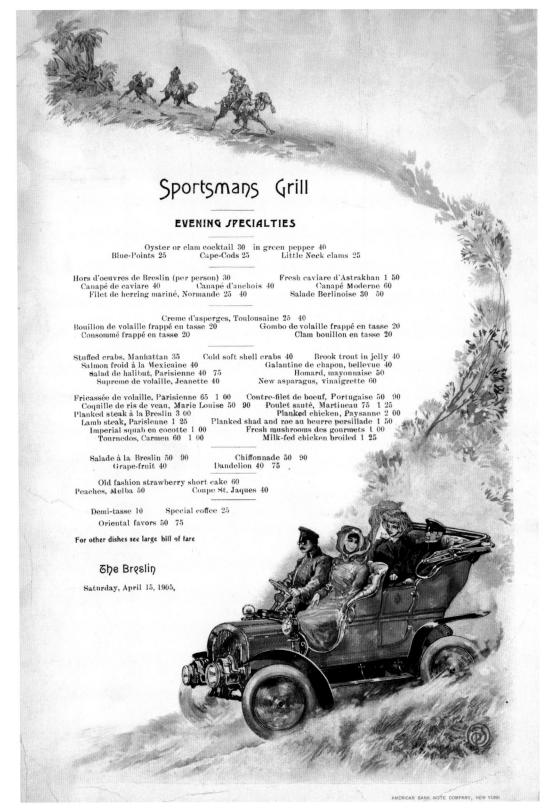

Sportsmans Grill

EVENING SPECIALTIES

Oyster or clam cocktail 30   in green pepper 40

Blue-Points 25   Cape-Cods 25   Little Neck clams 25

Hors d'oeuvres de Breslin (per person) 30   Fresh caviare d'Astrakhan 1 50
Canapé de caviare 40   Canapé d'anchois 40   Canapé Moderne 60
Filet de herring mariné, Normande 25   40   Salade Berlinoise 30   50

Creme d'asperges, Toulousaine 25   40
Bouillon de volaille frappé en tasse 20   Gombo de volaille frappé en tasse 20
Consommé frappé en tasse 20   Clam bouillon en tasse 20

Stuffed crabs, Manhattan 35   Cold soft shell crabs 40   Brook trout in jelly 40
Salmon froid à la Mexicaine 40   Galantine de chapon, bellevue 40
Salad de halibut, Parisienne 40   75   Homard, mayonnaise 50
Supreme de volaille, Jeanette 40   New asparagus, vinaigrette 60

Fricassée de volaille, Parisienne 65   1 00   Contre-filet de boeuf, Portugaise 50   90
Coquille de ris de veau, Marie Louise 50   90   Poulet sauté, Martineau 75   1 25
Planked steak à la Breslin 3 00   Planked chicken, Paysanne 2 00
Lamb steak, Parisienne 1 25   Planked shad and roe au beurre persillade 1 50
Imperial squab en cocotte 1 00   Fresh mushrooms des gourmets 1 00
Tournedos, Carmen 60   1 00   Milk-fed chicken broiled 1 25

Salade à la Breslin 50   90   Chiffonnade 50   90
Grape-fruit 40   Dandelion 40   75

Old fashion strawberry short cake 60
Peaches, Melba 50   Coupe St. Jaques 40

Demi-tasse 10   Special coffee 25
Oriental favors 50   75

For other dishes see large bill of fare

The Breslin

Saturday, April 15, 1905,

Daily menu, dinner specialties, Sportsmans Grill, The Breslin, New York [?], 1905

ACKNOWLEDGMENTS

We are deeply grateful for the support and friendship of our editor, James Mairs, who championed and shepherded *Repast* from its earliest stages. Thanks to his assistant, Austin O'Driscoll, who untangled the permissions that *Repast* required, the copy editor Don Kennison, who endured our many flagrant violations of the *Chicago Manual of Style*, and the designer, Laura Lindgren, who fitted together *Repast*'s jigsaw puzzle of image and text. Thanks also to everyone at W. W. Norton who helped produce and market this book.

The quick and resourceful Allyson Vieira helped with research and word processing. Our agent, Marianne Merola of Brandt & Hochman, offered encouragement and critical advice. Thanks to Carl Brandt for connecting us with Marianne—and for believing in this project from first to last.

Many friends, family members, and colleagues brainstormed with us, pointed the way to people and sources, and read drafts, including Michelle Aldredge, Elizabeth Barker, Ella Christopherson, Renée Fall, Ira Glass, Judy Goldman, John Helde, Elizabeth Kaplan, Roger King, Alex and Nadia Lesy, Greil Marcus, Bruce McClelland, Garth Meader, the late Mary Meader, James Miller, Jeff Sharlet, Steven Weisler, and Joel Wolfe. Hampshire College's Dean of Faculty office provided crucial summer faculty development funding; Hampshire's librarian Jennifer Gunter King offered positive support as the book neared completion. The wonderful staff of the Robert Frost Library at Amherst College, especially Bryn Geffert, Missy Roser, Mike Kelly, and Stephen Heim, provided spot-on research advice and help navigating the interlibrary loan labyrinth. Megan Morey, Mary Ramsay, and Jeanne Weintraub of the Amherst College Advancement Office gave Lisa the flexibility and moral support that made it possible for her to take on this project while working full-time.

Finally, special thanks to Charlene and Bob Moran, for helping in innumerable ways, and to Isabel Masteika, who lived through the creation of this book with grace and good humor.

THE
Cawthon Hot
MOBILE, AL

Happy New Year

1908

New Year's Dinner, Cawthon Hotel, Mobile, Alabama, 1908

INDEX

New Year's dinner, Congress Hotel, Chicago, 1908